When Peter Parker was bitten by a radioac[...] spe[...]
Learning that with great power there must also [...] th[...]
With his wife, Mary Jane, and their daughter, Annie May, the Parker family has beco[...]

**Jul. 2017**

# the AMAZING SPIDER-MAN
## Renew Your Vows

RECENTLY, SPIDER-MAN, MJ AND ANNIE DEFEATED THE VILLAIN REGENT, WHO RULED THE WORLD WITH THE STOLEN POWERS OF EARTH'S SUPER HEROES.

ALTHOUGH RESISTANT TO THE IDEA OF HIS WIFE AND DAUGHTER FOLLOWING IN HIS CRIMEFIGHTING FOOTSTEPS, PETER REALIZES IT'S TWO AGAINST ONE IN THAT ARGUMENT...

# BRAWL IN THE FAMILY

**GERRY CONWAY**
writer

**RYAN STEGMAN** (#1-4) & **NATHAN STOCKMAN** (#5)
artists

**SONIA OBACK** (#1-4) & **JESUS ABURTOV** (#4-5)
colorists

**VC's JOE CARAMAGNA** (#1-4) & **CLAYTON COWLES** (#5)
letterers

## THE EARNEST ADVENTURES OF SPIDER-DAD

**ANTHONY HOLDEN**
story & art

## MAKE IT WORK

**KATE LETH**
writer

**MARGUERITE SAUVAGE**
artist

**VC's JOE CARAMAGNA**
letterer

**RYAN STEGMAN** WITH **DAVID CURIEL** (#1), **SONIA OBACK** (#2-4) & **TAMRA BONVILLAIN** (#5)
cover art

**ALLISON STOCK**
assistant editor

**DARREN SHAN**
editor

**NICK LOWE**
executive editor

SPIDER-MAN created by **STAN LEE** & **STEVE DITKO**

collection editor **JENNIFER GRÜNWALD**
assistant editor **CAITLIN O'CONNELL**
associate managing editor **KATERI WOODY**
editor, special projects **MARK D. BEAZLEY**

svp production & special projects **JEFF YOUNGQUIST**
print, sales & marketing **DAVID GABRIEL**
book designer **ADAM DEL RE**

editor in chief **AXEL ALONSO**
chief creative officer **JOE QUESADA**
president **DAN BUCKLEY**
executive producer **ALAN FINE**

AMAZING SPIDER-MAN: RENEW YOUR VOWS VOL. 1 — BRAWL IN THE FAMILY. Contains material originally published in ma[...] 90580-4. Published by MARVEL WORLDWIDE, INC., a subsidiary of MARVEL ENTERTAINMENT, LLC. OFFICE OF PUBLICATION: 135 [...] characters, persons, and/or institutions in this magazine with those of any living or dead person or institution is intended, and any [...] Entertainment; JOE QUESADA, Chief Creative Officer; TOM BREVOORT, SVP of Publishing; DAVID BOGART, SVP of Business Affair[...] DAVID GABRIEL, SVP of Sales & Marketing, Publishing; JEFF YOUNGQUIST, VP of Production & Special Projects; DAN CARR, Execu[...] Production Manager; STAN LEE, Chairman Emeritus. For information regarding advertising in Marvel Comics or on Marvel.com,[...] inquiries, please call 888-511-5480. **Manufactured between 4/21/2017 and 5/23/2017 by SOLISCO PRINTERS, SCOTT, QC, C[...]

10 9 8 7 6 5 4 3 2 1

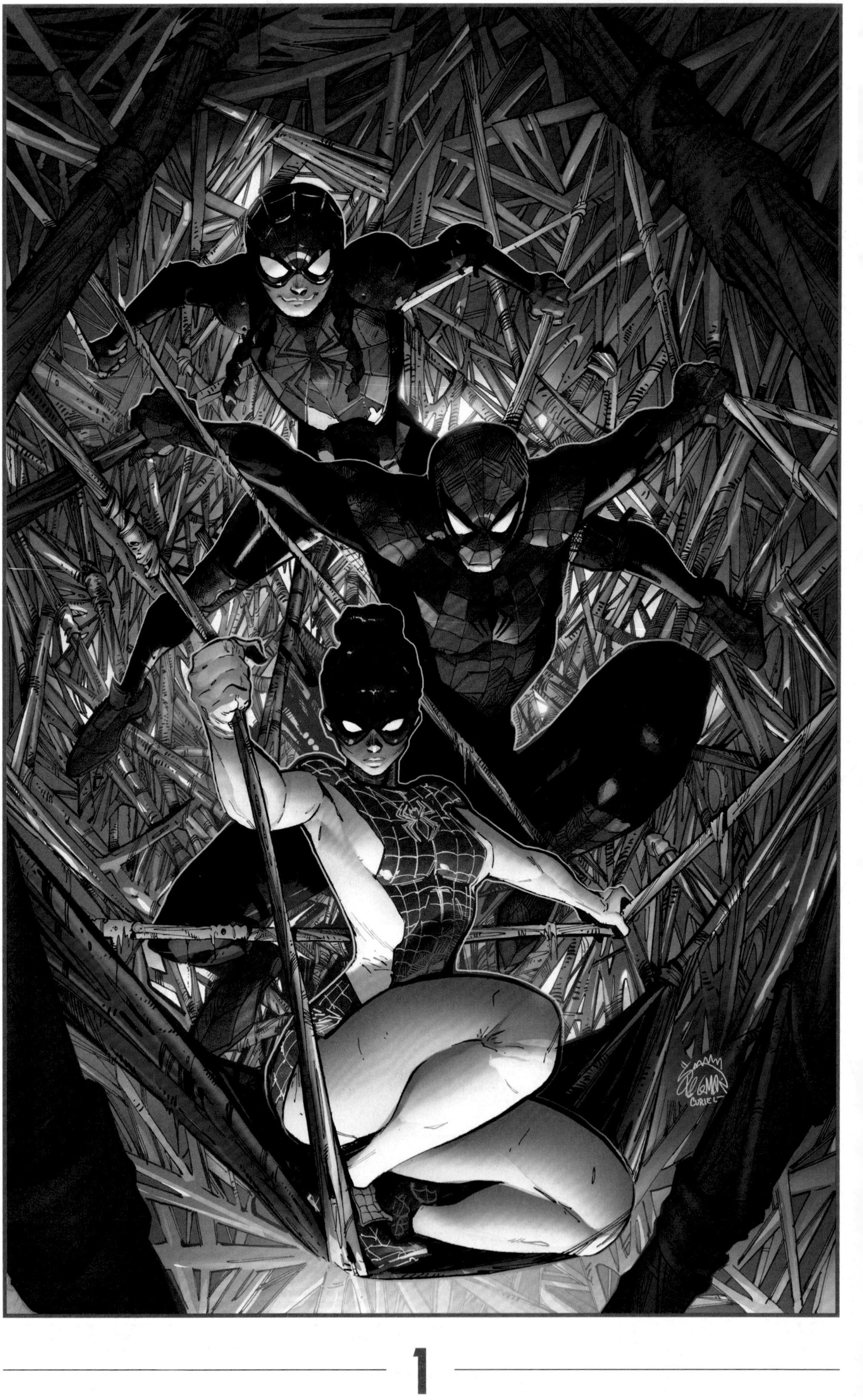
CURIEL

1

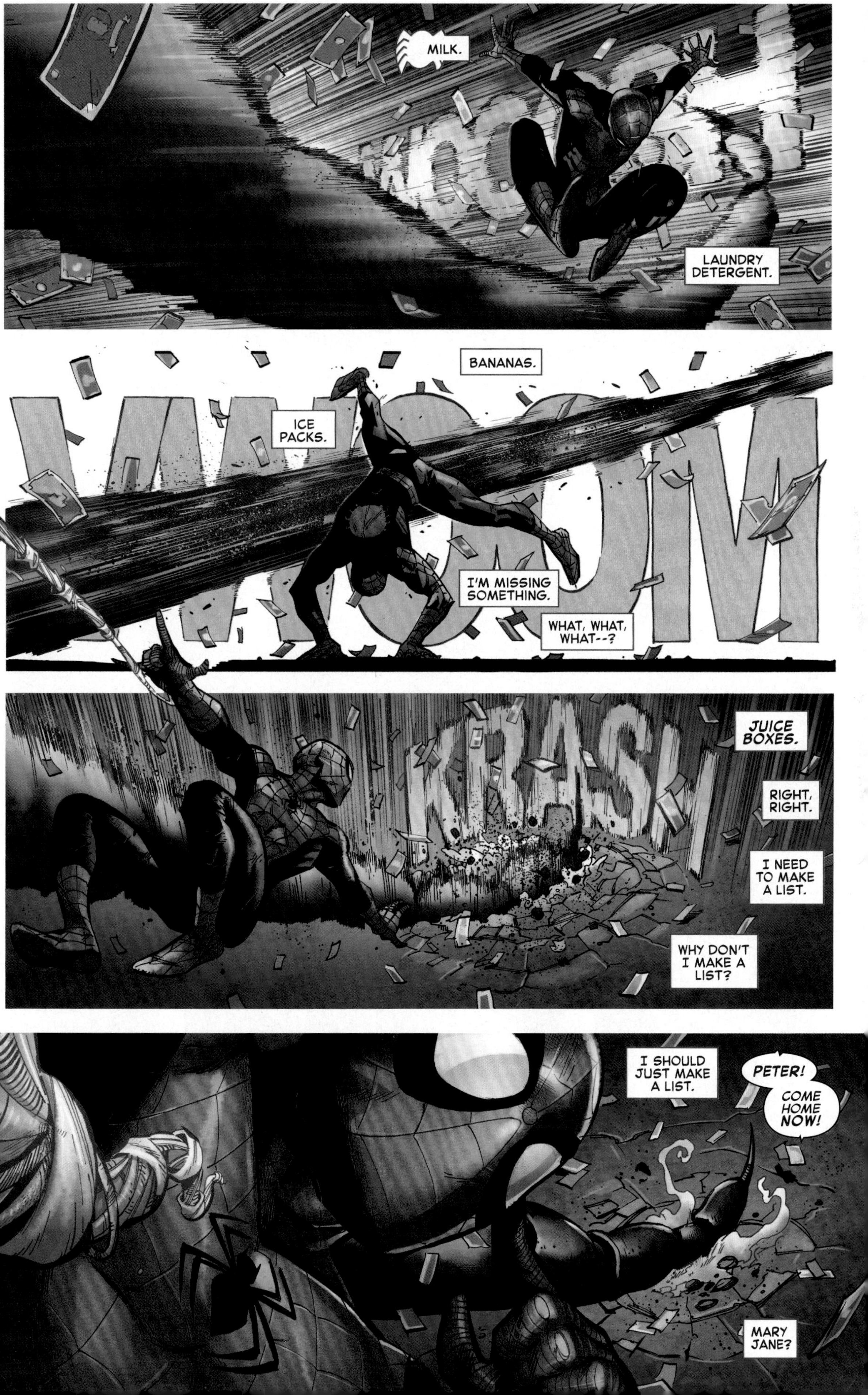
MILK.
LAUNDRY DETERGENT.
BANANAS.
ICE PACKS.
I'M MISSING SOMETHING.
WHAT, WHAT, WHAT--?
JUICE BOXES.
RIGHT, RIGHT.
I NEED TO MAKE A LIST.
WHY DON'T I MAKE A LIST?
I SHOULD JUST MAKE A LIST.
PETER!
COME HOME NOW!
MARY JANE?

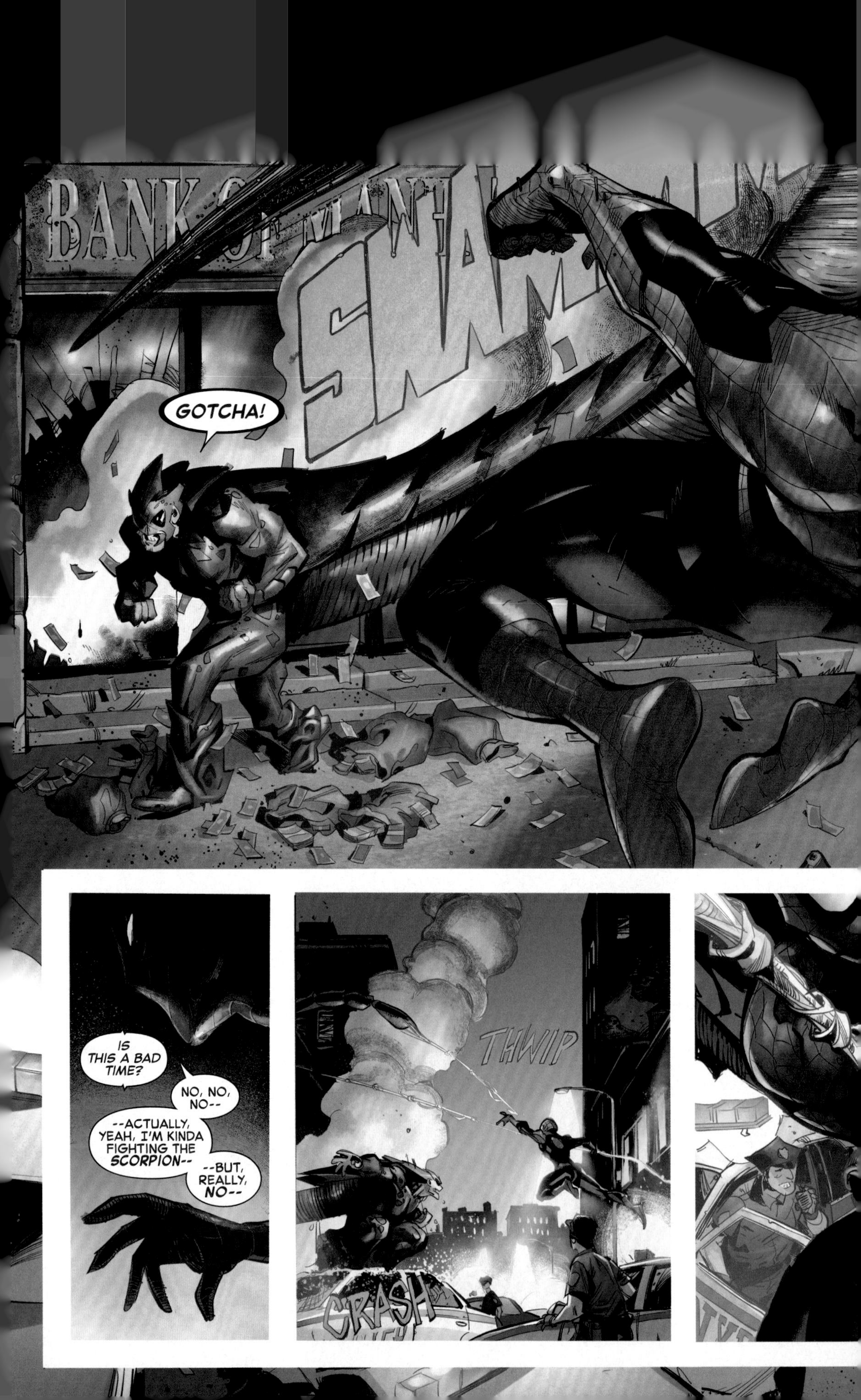
BANK OF MANH
SNAP
GOTCHA!
IS THIS A BAD TIME?
NO, NO, NO--
--ACTUALLY, YEAH, I'M KINDA FIGHTING THE SCORPION--
--BUT, REALLY, NO--
THWIP
CRASH

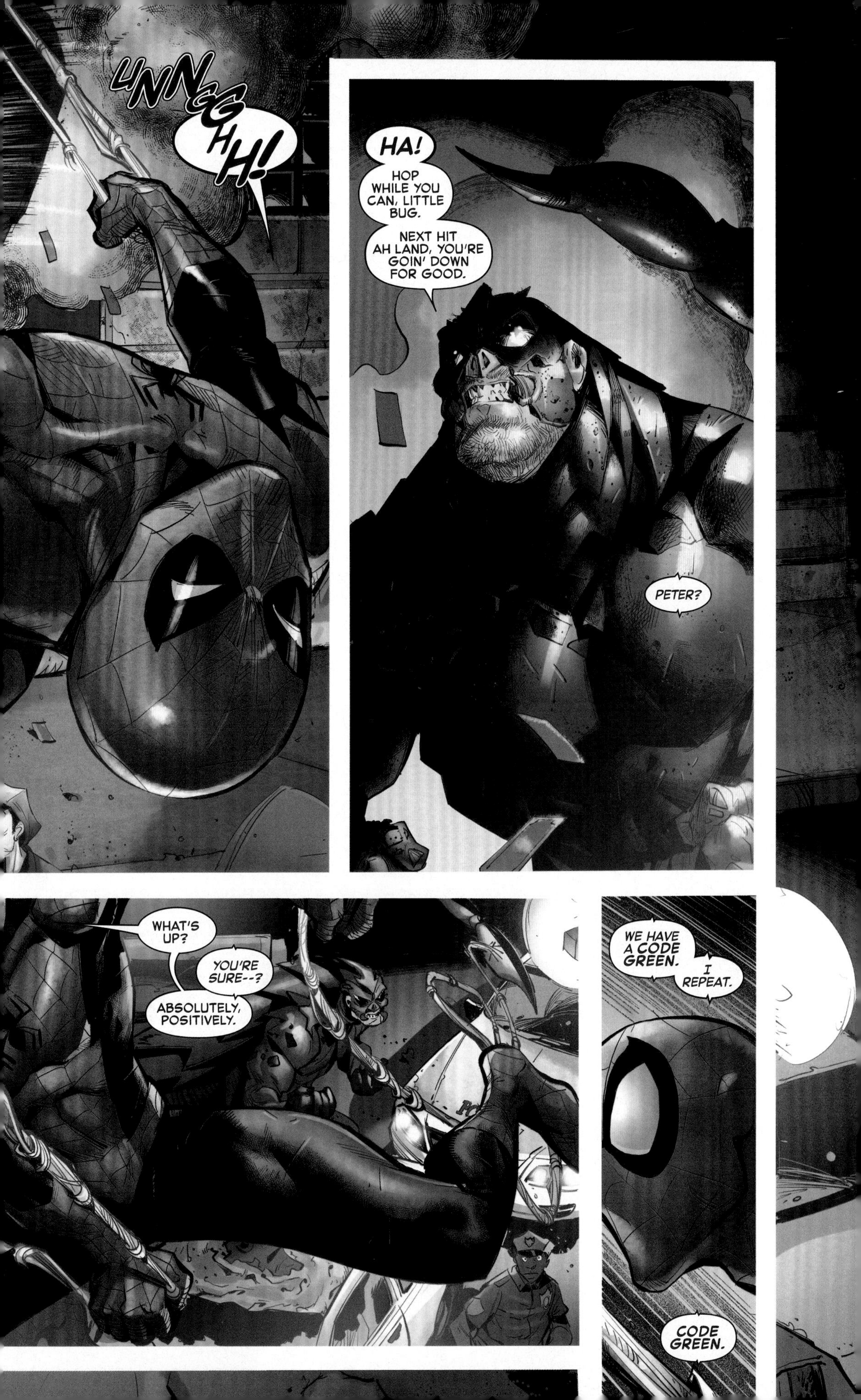
UNNGGHH!
HA!
HOP WHILE YOU CAN, LITTLE BUG.
NEXT HIT AH LAND, YOU'RE GOIN' DOWN FOR GOOD.
PETER?
WHAT'S UP?
YOU'RE SURE--?
ABSOLUTELY, POSITIVELY.
WE HAVE A CODE GREEN.
I REPEAT.
CODE GREEN.

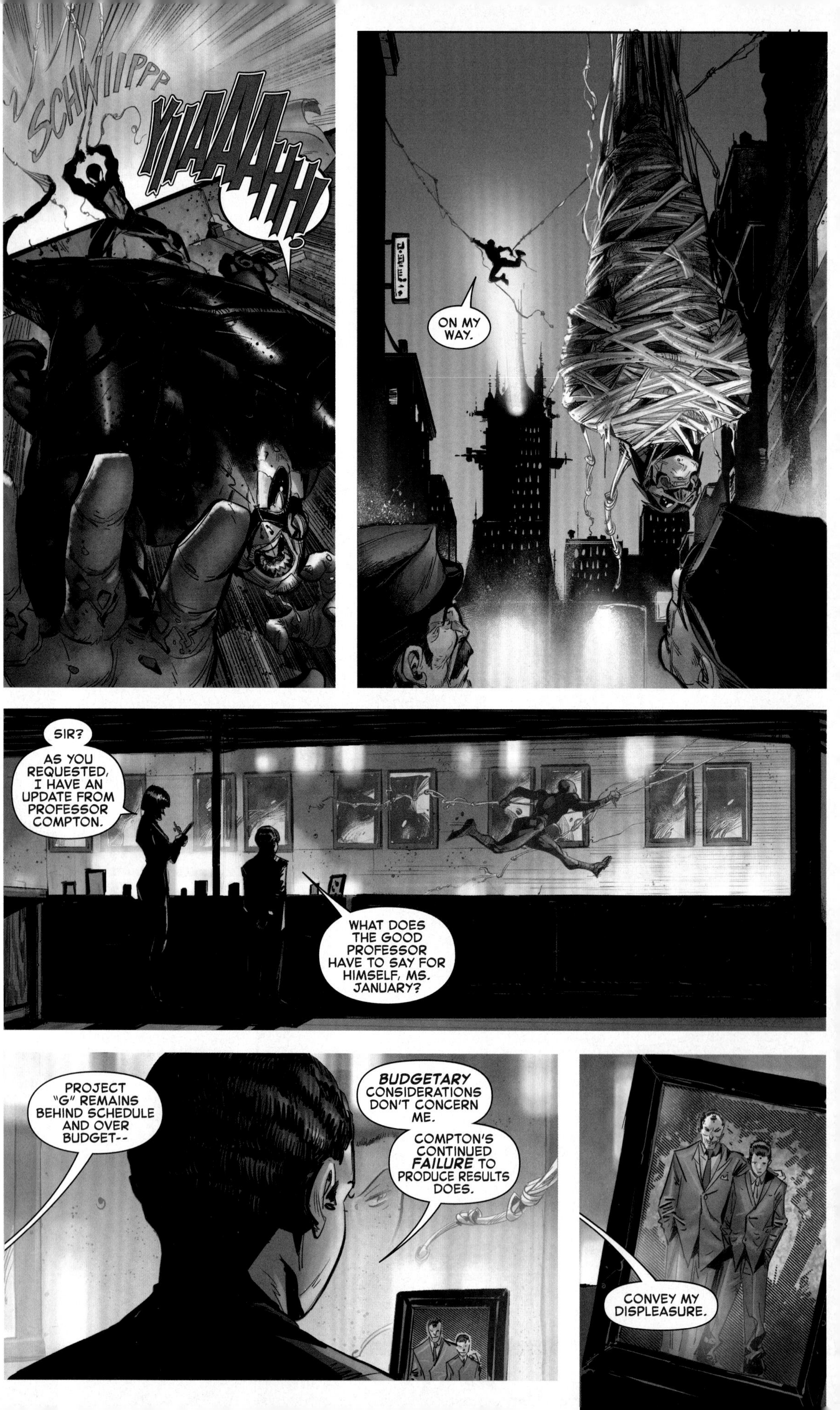
SCHWIIIPPP
YIAAAAHH!
ON MY WAY.
SIR?
AS YOU REQUESTED, I HAVE AN UPDATE FROM PROFESSOR COMPTON.
WHAT DOES THE GOOD PROFESSOR HAVE TO SAY FOR HIMSELF, MS. JANUARY?
PROJECT "G" REMAINS BEHIND SCHEDULE AND OVER BUDGET--
BUDGETARY CONSIDERATIONS DON'T CONCERN ME.
COMPTON'S CONTINUED FAILURE TO PRODUCE RESULTS DOES.
CONVEY MY DISPLEASURE.

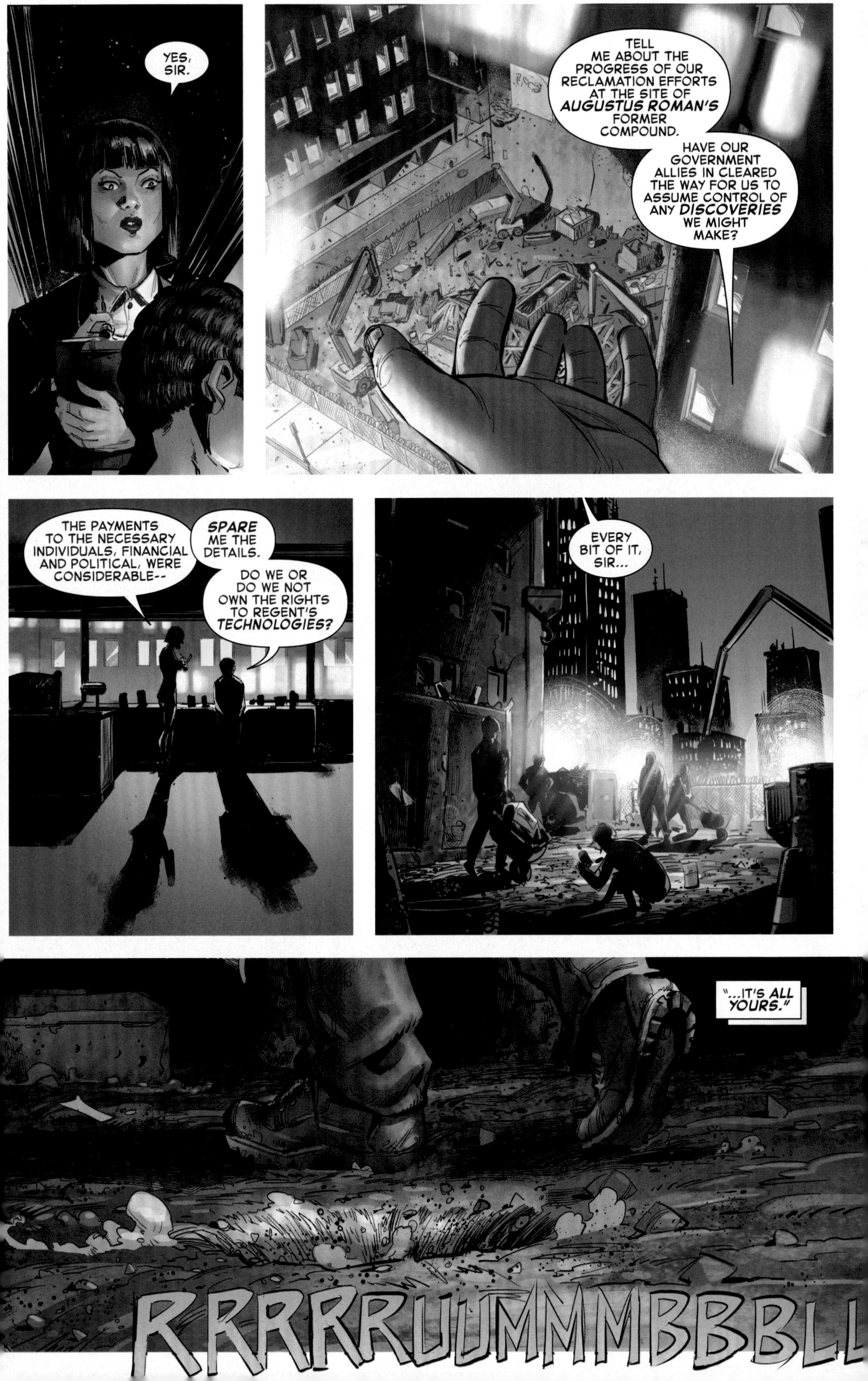
YES, SIR.
TELL ME ABOUT THE PROGRESS OF OUR RECLAMATION EFFORTS AT THE SITE OF AUGUSTUS ROMAN'S FORMER COMPOUND.
HAVE OUR GOVERNMENT ALLIES IN CLEARED THE WAY FOR US TO ASSUME CONTROL OF ANY DISCOVERIES WE MIGHT MAKE?
THE PAYMENTS TO THE NECESSARY INDIVIDUALS, FINANCIAL AND POLITICAL, WERE CONSIDERABLE--
SPARE ME THE DETAILS.
DO WE OR DO WE NOT OWN THE RIGHTS TO REGENT'S TECHNOLOGIES?
EVERY BIT OF IT, SIR...
"...IT'S ALL YOURS."
RRRRRUUMMMBBBLL

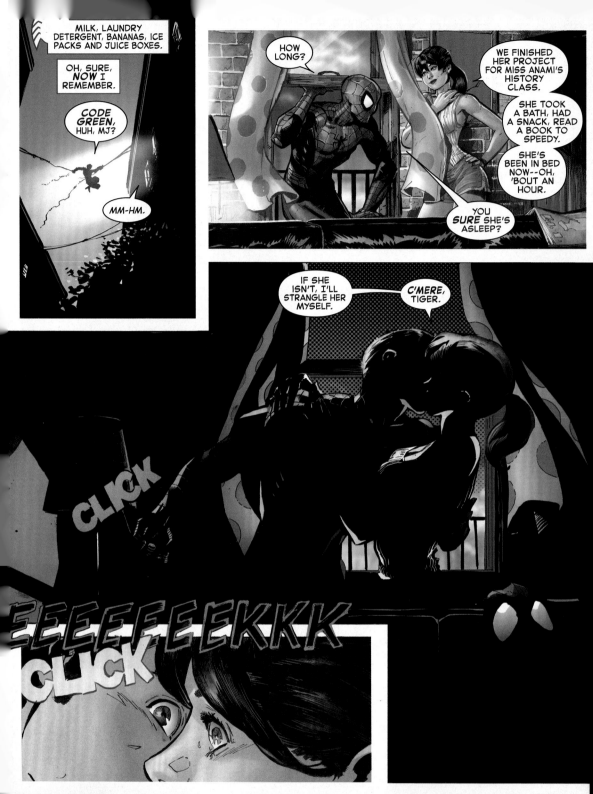

MILK, LAUNDRY DETERGENT, BANANAS, ICE PACKS AND JUICE BOXES.

OH, SURE, *NOW* I REMEMBER.

CODE *GREEN*, HUH, MJ?

MM-HM.

HOW LONG?

WE FINISHED HER PROJECT FOR MISS ANAMI'S HISTORY CLASS.

SHE TOOK A BATH, HAD A SNACK, READ A BOOK TO SPEEDY.

SHE'S BEEN IN BED NOW--OH, 'BOUT AN HOUR.

YOU *SURE* SHE'S ASLEEP?

IF SHE ISN'T, I'LL STRANGLE HER MYSELF.

C'MERE, TIGER.

CLICK

EEEFFEEKKK

CLICK

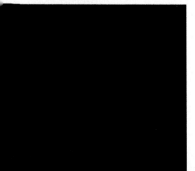

ANNIE!

THWIP THWIP THWIP

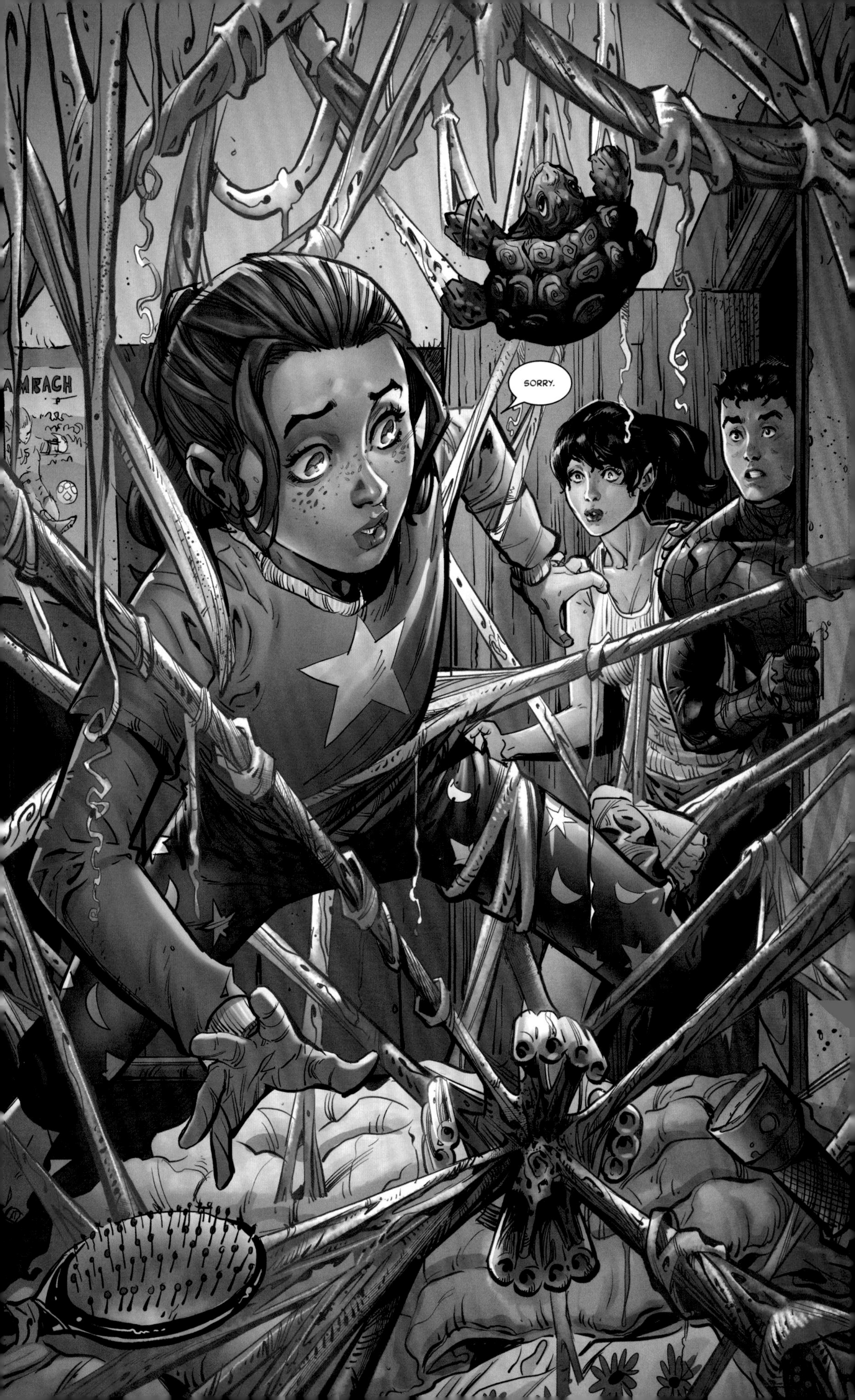
AMBACH
SORRY.

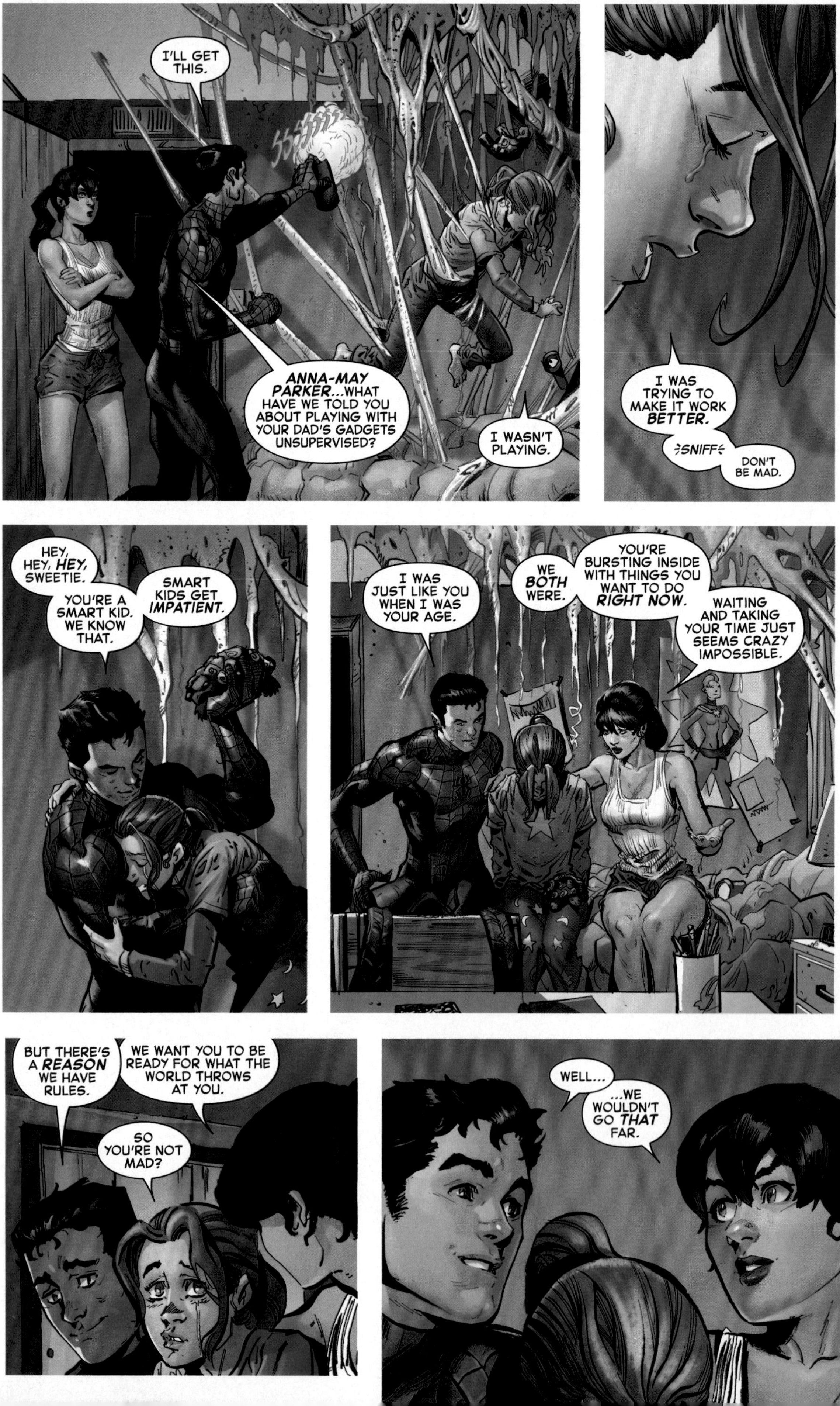

I'LL GET THIS.
SSSSSSSSSS
ANNA-MAY PARKER...WHAT HAVE WE TOLD YOU ABOUT PLAYING WITH YOUR DAD'S GADGETS UNSUPERVISED?
I WASN'T PLAYING.
I WAS TRYING TO MAKE IT WORK BETTER.
SNIFF
DON'T BE MAD.
HEY, HEY, HEY, SWEETIE.
YOU'RE A SMART KID. WE KNOW THAT.
SMART KIDS GET IMPATIENT.
I WAS JUST LIKE YOU WHEN I WAS YOUR AGE.
WE BOTH WERE.
YOU'RE BURSTING INSIDE WITH THINGS YOU WANT TO DO RIGHT NOW.
WAITING AND TAKING YOUR TIME JUST SEEMS CRAZY IMPOSSIBLE.
BUT THERE'S A REASON WE HAVE RULES.
WE WANT YOU TO BE READY FOR WHAT THE WORLD THROWS AT YOU.
SO YOU'RE NOT MAD?
WELL...
...WE WOULDN'T GO THAT FAR.

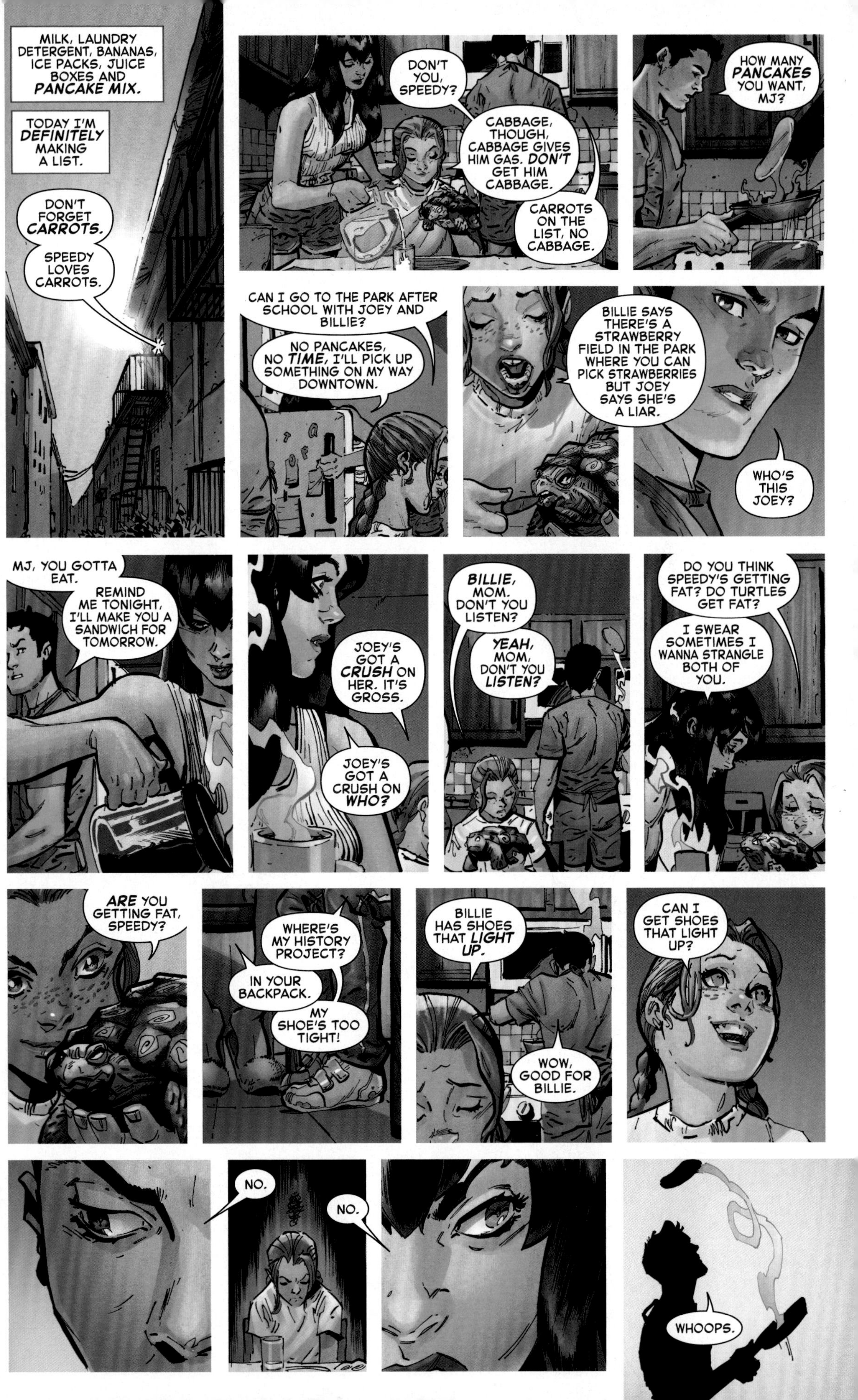

MILK, LAUNDRY DETERGENT, BANANAS, ICE PACKS, JUICE BOXES AND PANCAKE MIX.
TODAY I'M DEFINITELY MAKING A LIST.
DON'T FORGET CARROTS.
SPEEDY LOVES CARROTS.
DON'T YOU, SPEEDY?
CABBAGE, THOUGH, CABBAGE GIVES HIM GAS. DON'T GET HIM CABBAGE.
CARROTS ON THE LIST, NO CABBAGE.
HOW MANY PANCAKES YOU WANT, MJ?
CAN I GO TO THE PARK AFTER SCHOOL WITH JOEY AND BILLIE?
NO PANCAKES, NO TIME, I'LL PICK UP SOMETHING ON MY WAY DOWNTOWN.
BILLIE SAYS THERE'S A STRAWBERRY FIELD IN THE PARK WHERE YOU CAN PICK STRAWBERRIES BUT JOEY SAYS SHE'S A LIAR.
WHO'S THIS JOEY?
MJ, YOU GOTTA EAT.
REMIND ME TONIGHT, I'LL MAKE YOU A SANDWICH FOR TOMORROW.
JOEY'S GOT A CRUSH ON HER. IT'S GROSS.
JOEY'S GOT A CRUSH ON WHO?
BILLIE, MOM. DON'T YOU LISTEN?
YEAH, MOM, DON'T YOU LISTEN?
DO YOU THINK SPEEDY'S GETTING FAT? DO TURTLES GET FAT?
I SWEAR SOMETIMES I WANNA STRANGLE BOTH OF YOU.
ARE YOU GETTING FAT, SPEEDY?
WHERE'S MY HISTORY PROJECT?
IN YOUR BACKPACK.
MY SHOE'S TOO TIGHT!
BILLIE HAS SHOES THAT LIGHT UP.
WOW, GOOD FOR BILLIE.
CAN I GET SHOES THAT LIGHT UP?
NO.
NO.
WHOOPS.

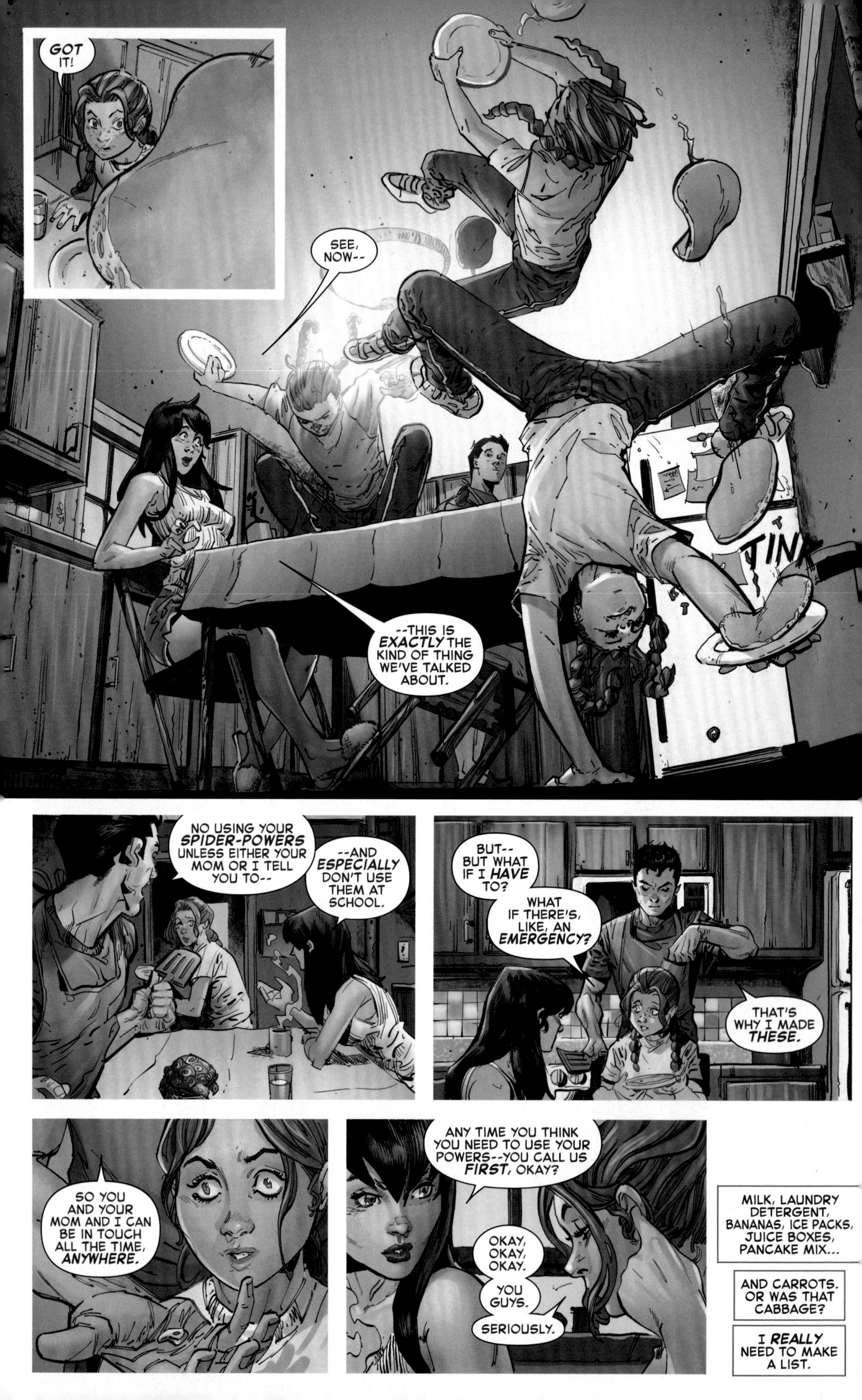
GOT IT!
SEE, NOW--
--THIS IS EXACTLY THE KIND OF THING WE'VE TALKED ABOUT.
TIN
NO USING YOUR SPIDER-POWERS UNLESS EITHER YOUR MOM OR I TELL YOU TO--
--AND ESPECIALLY DON'T USE THEM AT SCHOOL.
BUT-- BUT WHAT IF I HAVE TO?
WHAT IF THERE'S, LIKE, AN EMERGENCY?
THAT'S WHY I MADE THESE.
SO YOU AND YOUR MOM AND I CAN BE IN TOUCH ALL THE TIME, ANYWHERE.
ANY TIME YOU THINK YOU NEED TO USE YOUR POWERS--YOU CALL US FIRST, OKAY?
OKAY, OKAY, OKAY.
YOU GUYS.
SERIOUSLY.
MILK, LAUNDRY DETERGENT, BANANAS, ICE PACKS, JUICE BOXES, PANCAKE MIX...
AND CARROTS. OR WAS THAT CABBAGE?
I REALLY NEED TO MAKE A LIST.

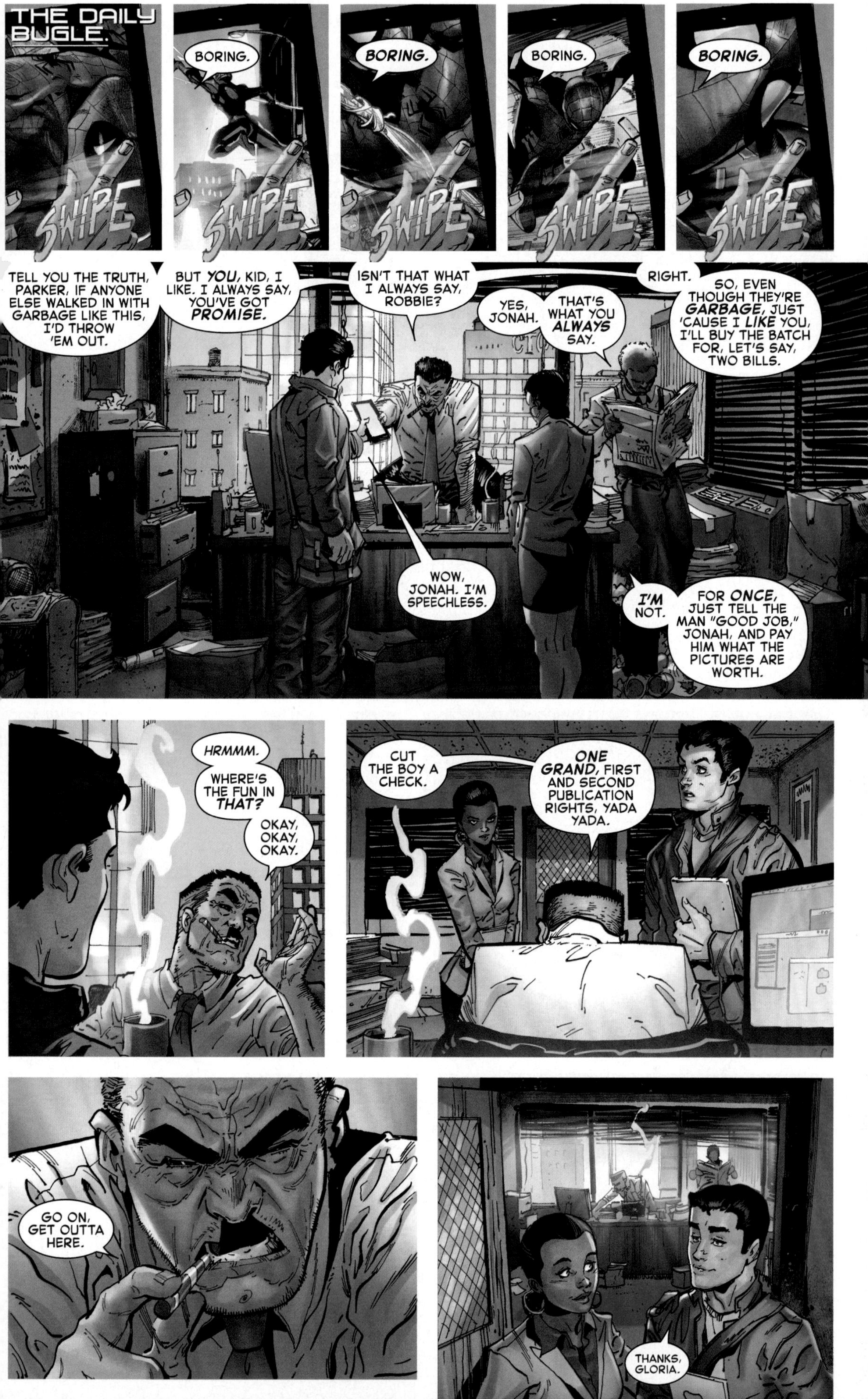
THE DAILY BUGLE.
SWIPE
BORING.
SWIPE
BORING.
SWIPE
BORING.
SWIPE
BORING.
SWIPE
TELL YOU THE TRUTH, PARKER, IF ANYONE ELSE WALKED IN WITH GARBAGE LIKE THIS, I'D THROW 'EM OUT.
BUT YOU, KID, I LIKE. I ALWAYS SAY, YOU'VE GOT PROMISE.
ISN'T THAT WHAT I ALWAYS SAY, ROBBIE?
YES, JONAH.
THAT'S WHAT YOU ALWAYS SAY.
RIGHT.
SO, EVEN THOUGH THEY'RE GARBAGE, JUST 'CAUSE I LIKE YOU, I'LL BUY THE BATCH FOR, LET'S SAY, TWO BILLS.
WOW, JONAH. I'M SPEECHLESS.
I'M NOT.
FOR ONCE, JUST TELL THE MAN "GOOD JOB," JONAH, AND PAY HIM WHAT THE PICTURES ARE WORTH.
HRMMM.
WHERE'S THE FUN IN THAT?
OKAY, OKAY, OKAY.
CUT THE BOY A CHECK.
ONE GRAND, FIRST AND SECOND PUBLICATION RIGHTS, YADA YADA.
GO ON, GET OUTTA HERE.
THANKS, GLORIA.

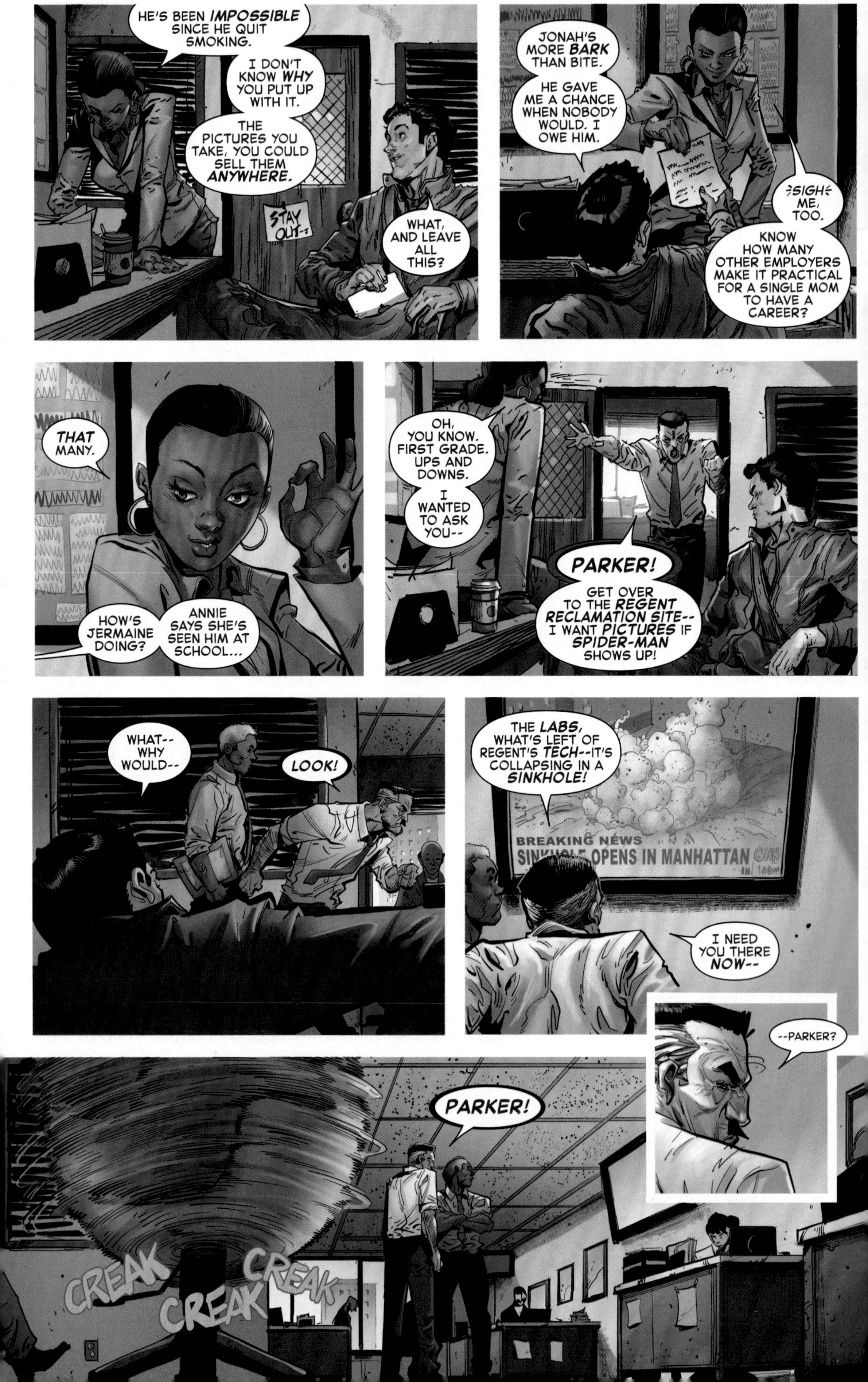

HE'S BEEN IMPOSSIBLE SINCE HE QUIT SMOKING.
I DON'T KNOW WHY YOU PUT UP WITH IT.
THE PICTURES YOU TAKE, YOU COULD SELL THEM ANYWHERE.
STAY OUT-!
WHAT, AND LEAVE ALL THIS?
JONAH'S MORE BARK THAN BITE.
HE GAVE ME A CHANCE WHEN NOBODY WOULD. I OWE HIM.
SIGH ME, TOO.
KNOW HOW MANY OTHER EMPLOYERS MAKE IT PRACTICAL FOR A SINGLE MOM TO HAVE A CAREER?
THAT MANY.
HOW'S JERMAINE DOING?
ANNIE SAYS SHE'S SEEN HIM AT SCHOOL...
OH, YOU KNOW. FIRST GRADE. UPS AND DOWNS.
I WANTED TO ASK YOU--
PARKER!
GET OVER TO THE REGENT RECLAMATION SITE-- I WANT PICTURES IF SPIDER-MAN SHOWS UP!
WHAT-- WHY WOULD--
LOOK!
THE LABS, WHAT'S LEFT OF REGENT'S TECH--IT'S COLLAPSING IN A SINKHOLE!
BREAKING NEWS
SINKHOLE OPENS IN MANHATTAN
I NEED YOU THERE NOW--
--PARKER?
PARKER!
CREAK CREAK CREAK

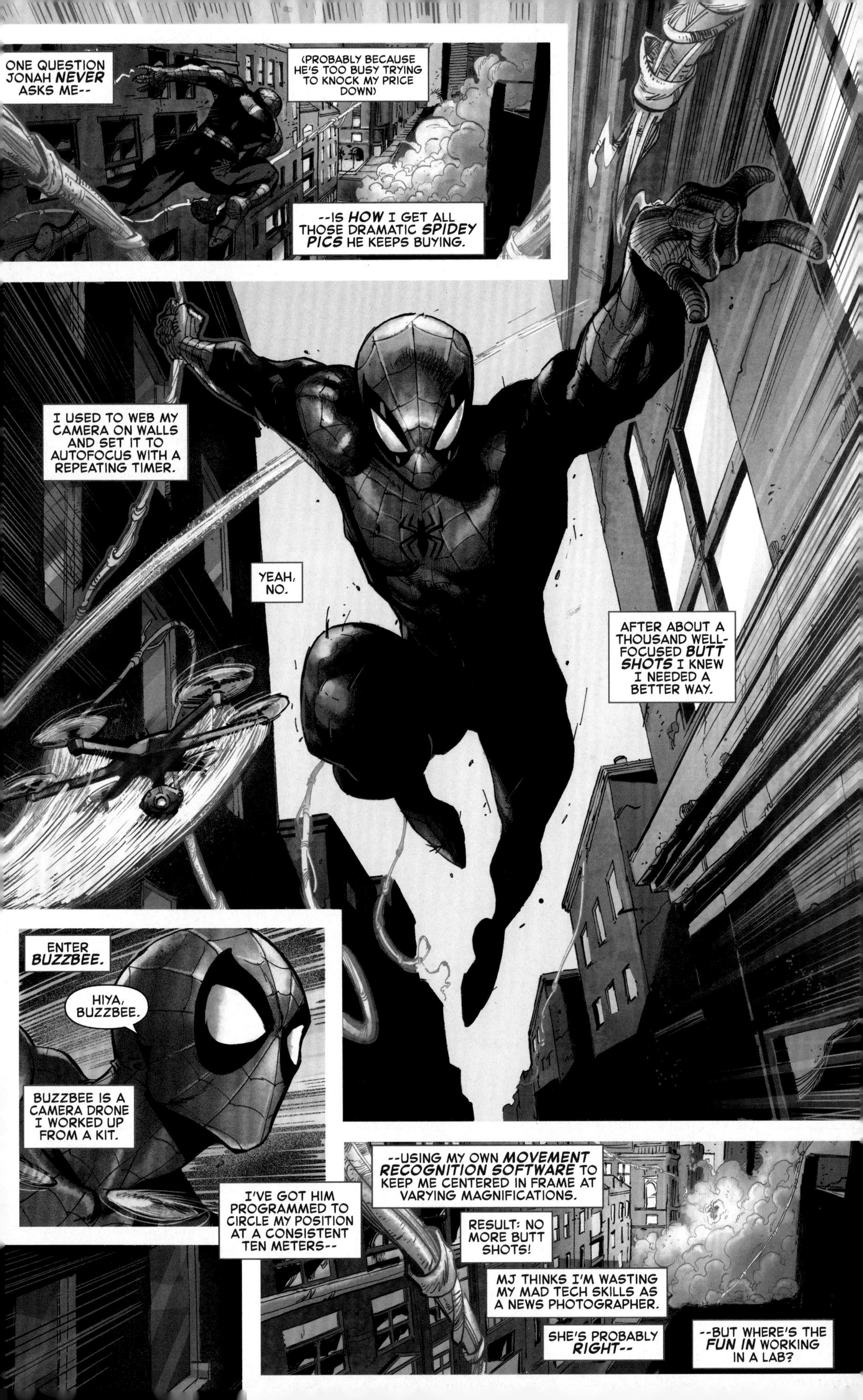
ONE QUESTION JONAH *NEVER* ASKS ME--
(PROBABLY BECAUSE HE'S TOO BUSY TRYING TO KNOCK MY PRICE DOWN)
--IS *HOW* I GET ALL THOSE DRAMATIC *SPIDEY PICS* HE KEEPS BUYING.
I USED TO WEB MY CAMERA ON WALLS AND SET IT TO AUTOFOCUS WITH A REPEATING TIMER.
YEAH, NO.
AFTER ABOUT A THOUSAND WELL-FOCUSED *BUTT SHOTS* I KNEW I NEEDED A BETTER WAY.
ENTER *BUZZBEE.*
HIYA, BUZZBEE.
BUZZBEE IS A CAMERA DRONE I WORKED UP FROM A KIT.
I'VE GOT HIM PROGRAMMED TO CIRCLE MY POSITION AT A CONSISTENT TEN METERS--
--USING MY OWN *MOVEMENT RECOGNITION SOFTWARE* TO KEEP ME CENTERED IN FRAME AT VARYING MAGNIFICATIONS.
RESULT: NO MORE BUTT SHOTS!
MJ THINKS I'M WASTING MY MAD TECH SKILLS AS A NEWS PHOTOGRAPHER.
SHE'S PROBABLY *RIGHT*--
--BUT WHERE'S THE *FUN IN* WORKING IN A LAB?

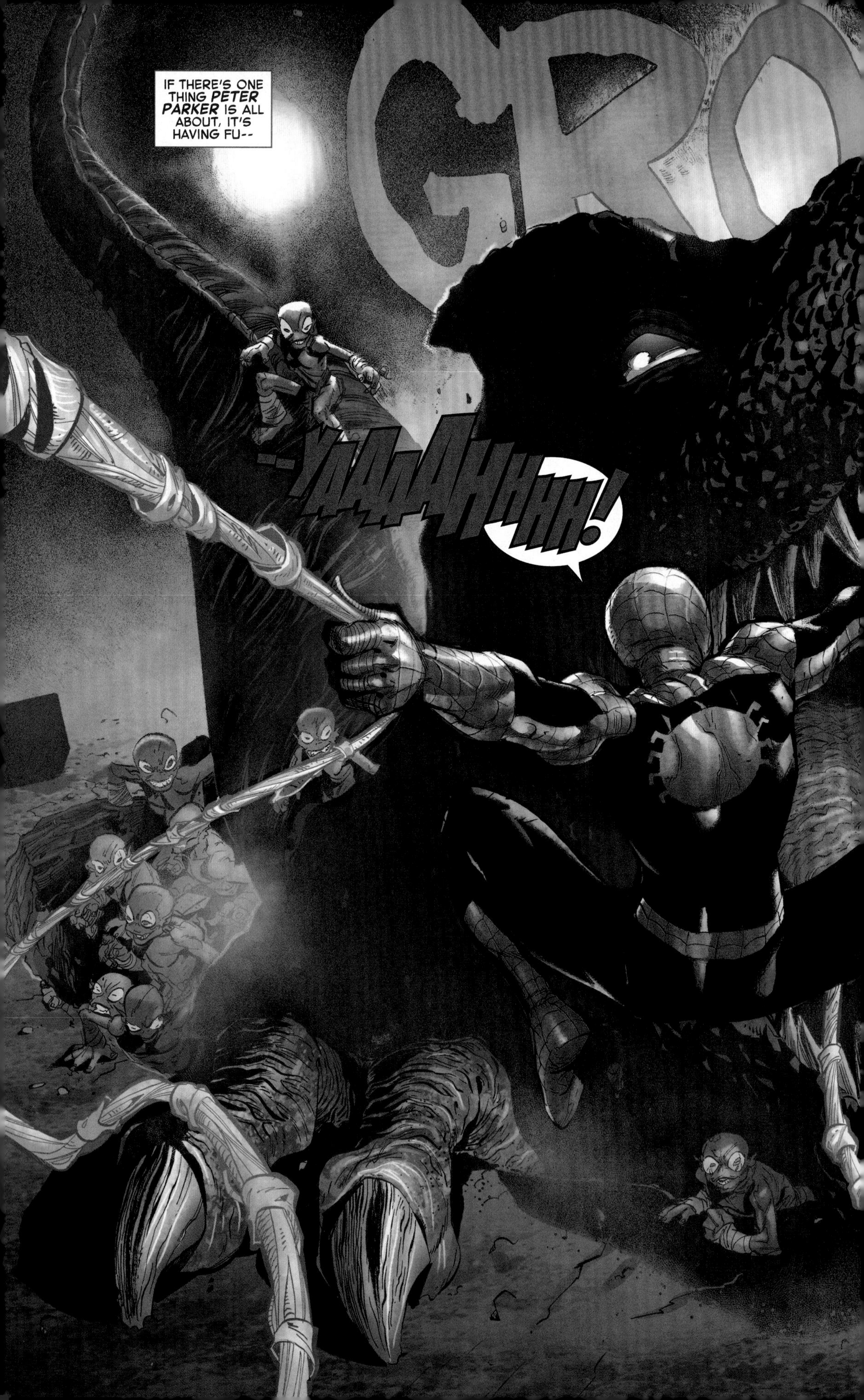
IF THERE'S ONE THING PETER PARKER IS ALL ABOUT, IT'S HAVING FU--
--YAAAAHHHHH!

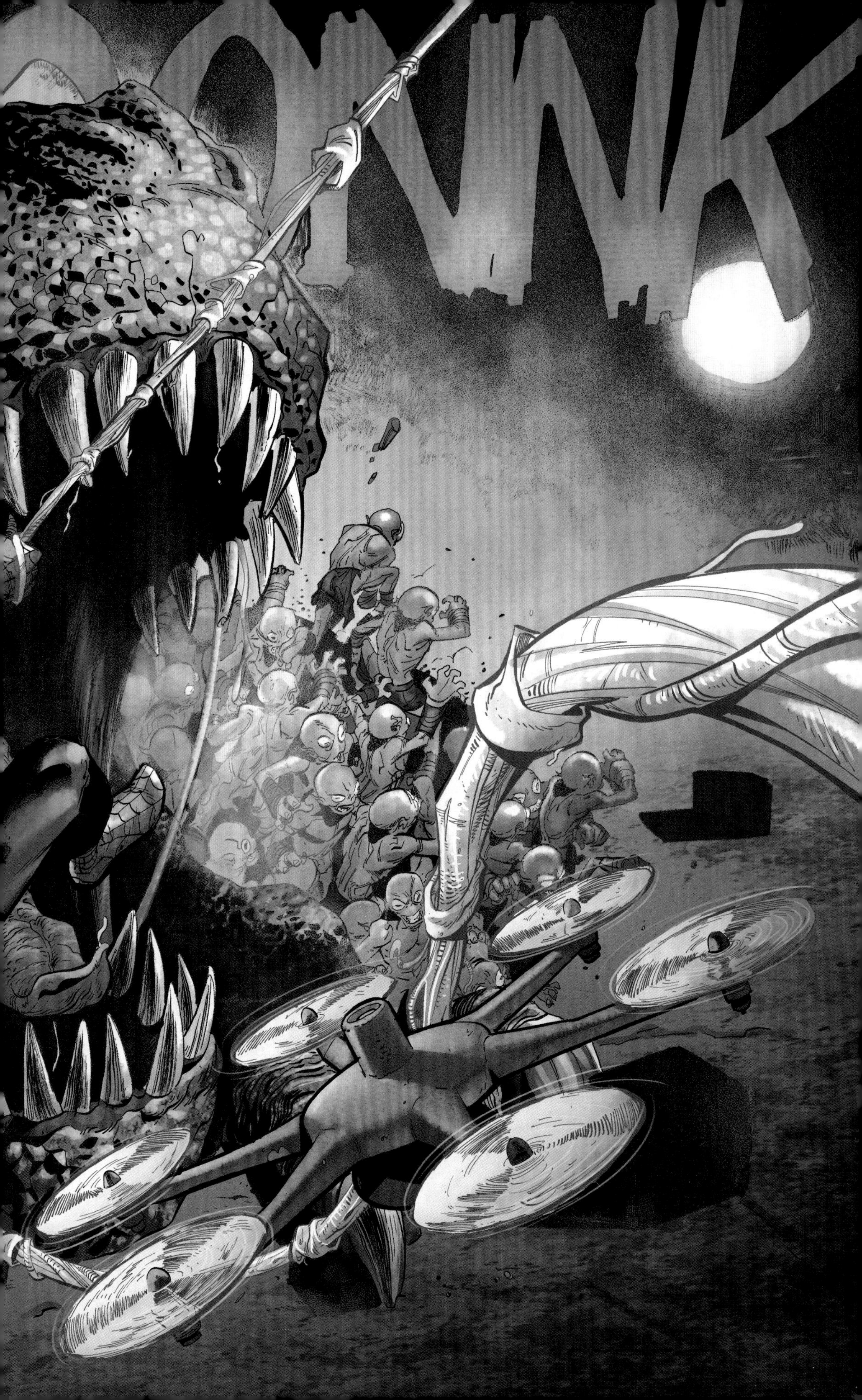

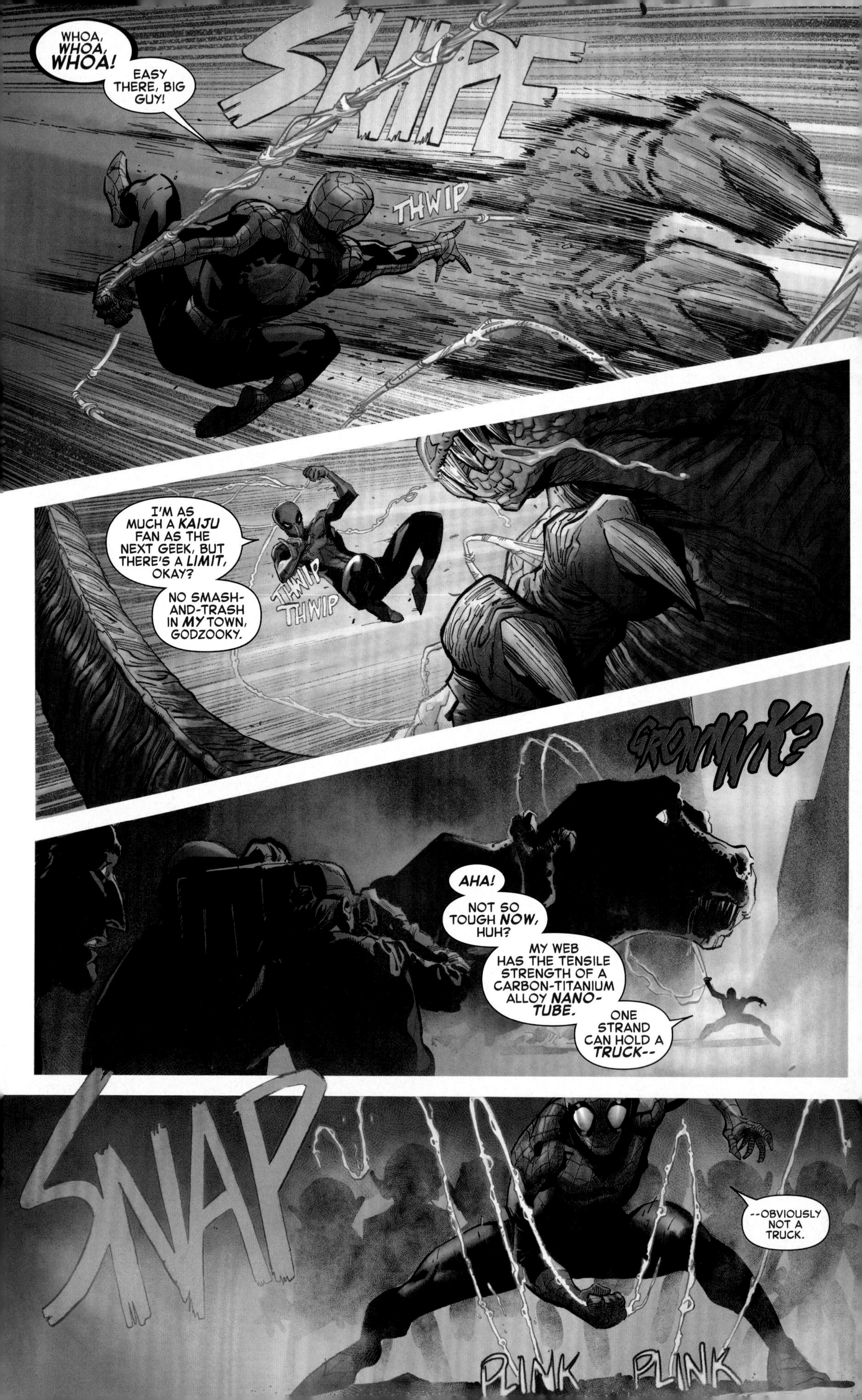
WHOA, WHOA, WHOA!
EASY THERE, BIG GUY!
SWIPE
THWIP
I'M AS MUCH A KAIJU FAN AS THE NEXT GEEK, BUT THERE'S A LIMIT, OKAY?
NO SMASH-AND-TRASH IN MY TOWN, GODZOOKY.
THWIP THWIP
GRONNNK?
AHA!
NOT SO TOUGH NOW, HUH?
MY WEB HAS THE TENSILE STRENGTH OF A CARBON-TITANIUM ALLOY NANO-TUBE.
ONE STRAND CAN HOLD A TRUCK--
SNAP
--OBVIOUSLY NOT A TRUCK.
PLINK PLINK

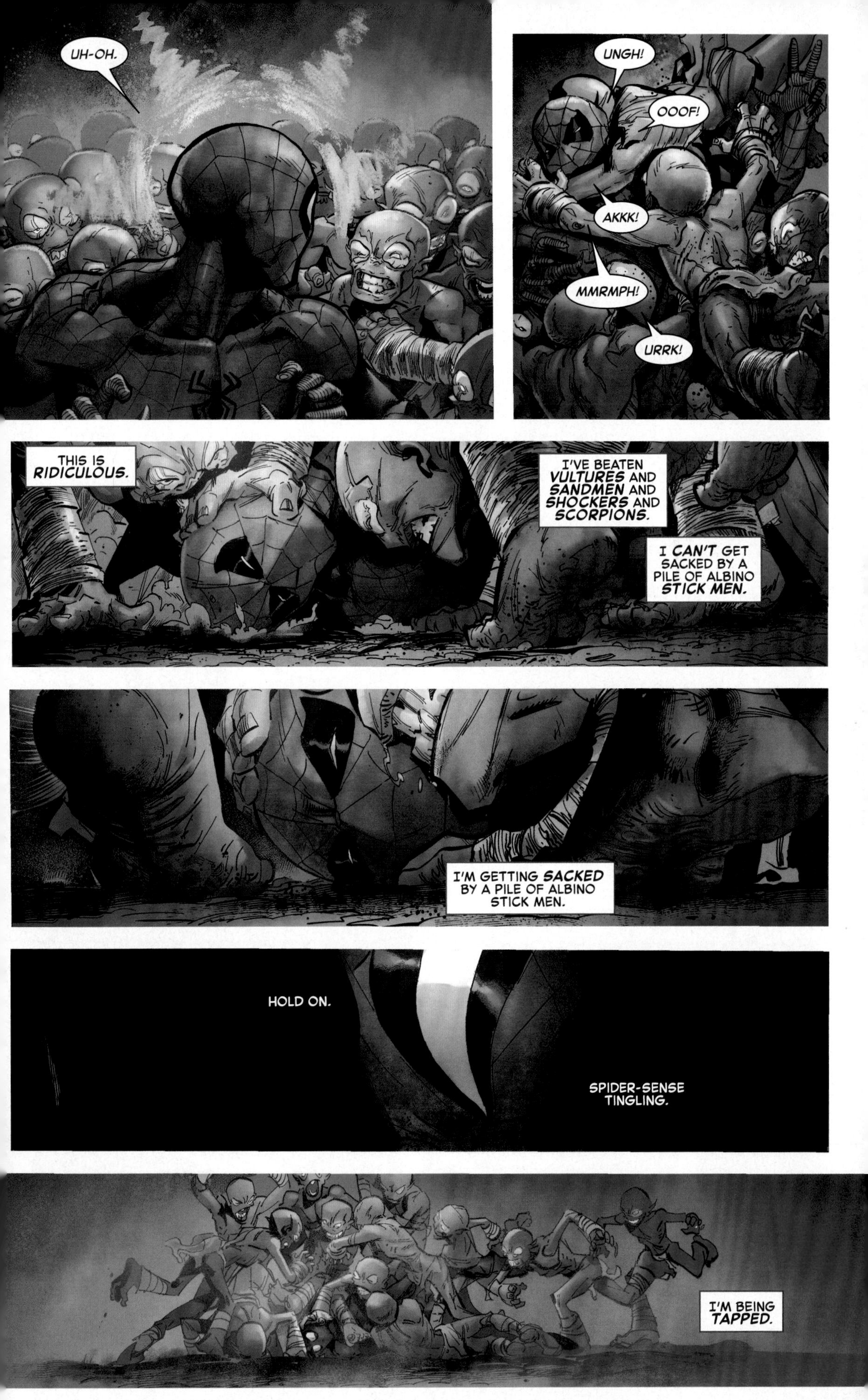
UH-OH.
UNGH!
OOOF!
AKKK!
MMRMPH!
URRK!
THIS IS RIDICULOUS.
I'VE BEATEN VULTURES AND SANDMEN AND SHOCKERS AND SCORPIONS.
I CAN'T GET SACKED BY A PILE OF ALBINO STICK MEN.
I'M GETTING SACKED BY A PILE OF ALBINO STICK MEN.
HOLD ON.
SPIDER-SENSE TINGLING.
I'M BEING TAPPED.

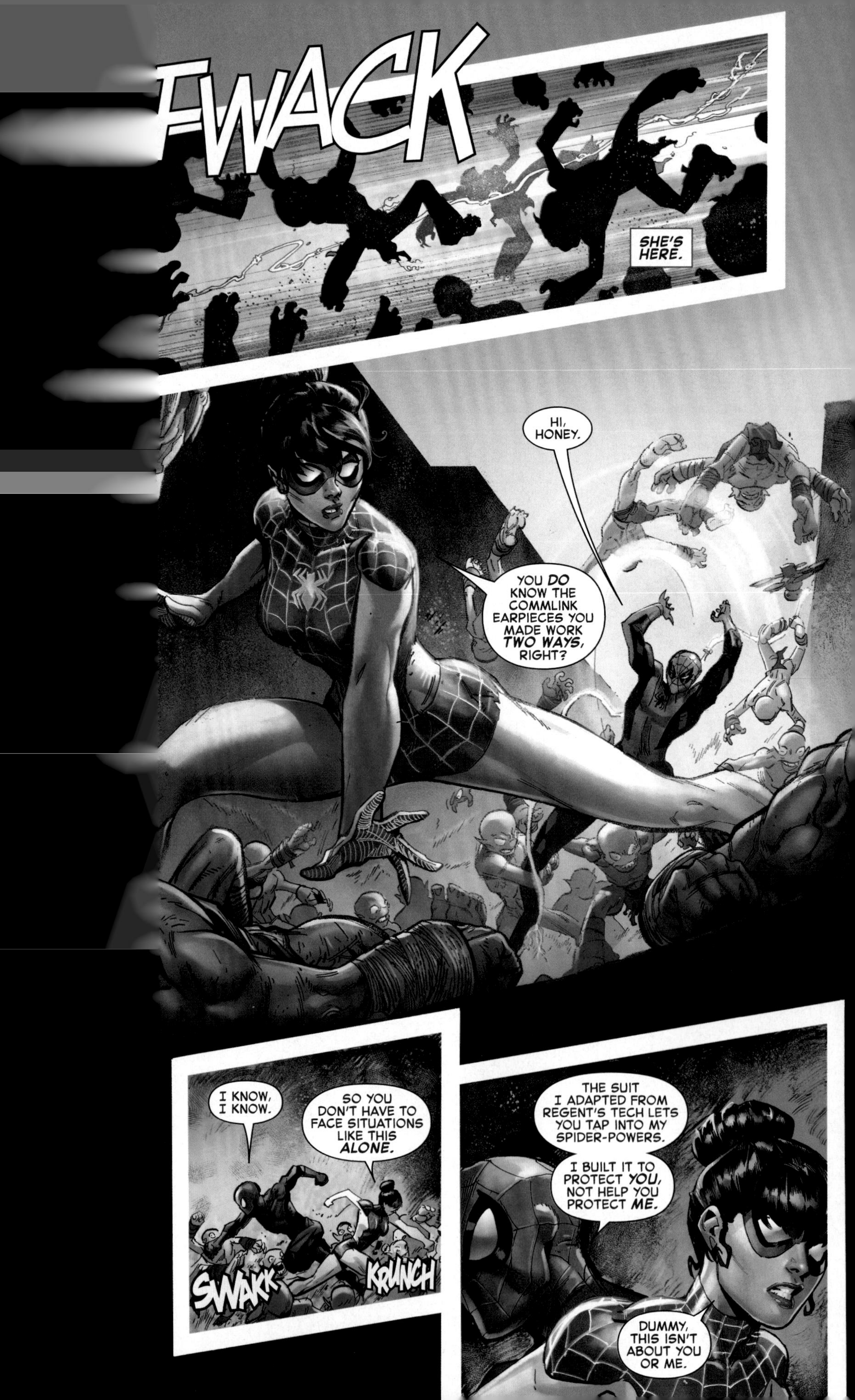
FWACK
SHE'S HERE.
HI, HONEY.
YOU DO KNOW THE COMMLINK EARPIECES YOU MADE WORK TWO WAYS, RIGHT?
I KNOW, I KNOW.
SO YOU DON'T HAVE TO FACE SITUATIONS LIKE THIS ALONE.
SWAKK
KRUNCH
THE SUIT I ADAPTED FROM REGENT'S TECH LETS YOU TAP INTO MY SPIDER-POWERS.
I BUILT IT TO PROTECT YOU, NOT HELP YOU PROTECT ME.
DUMMY, THIS ISN'T ABOUT YOU OR ME.

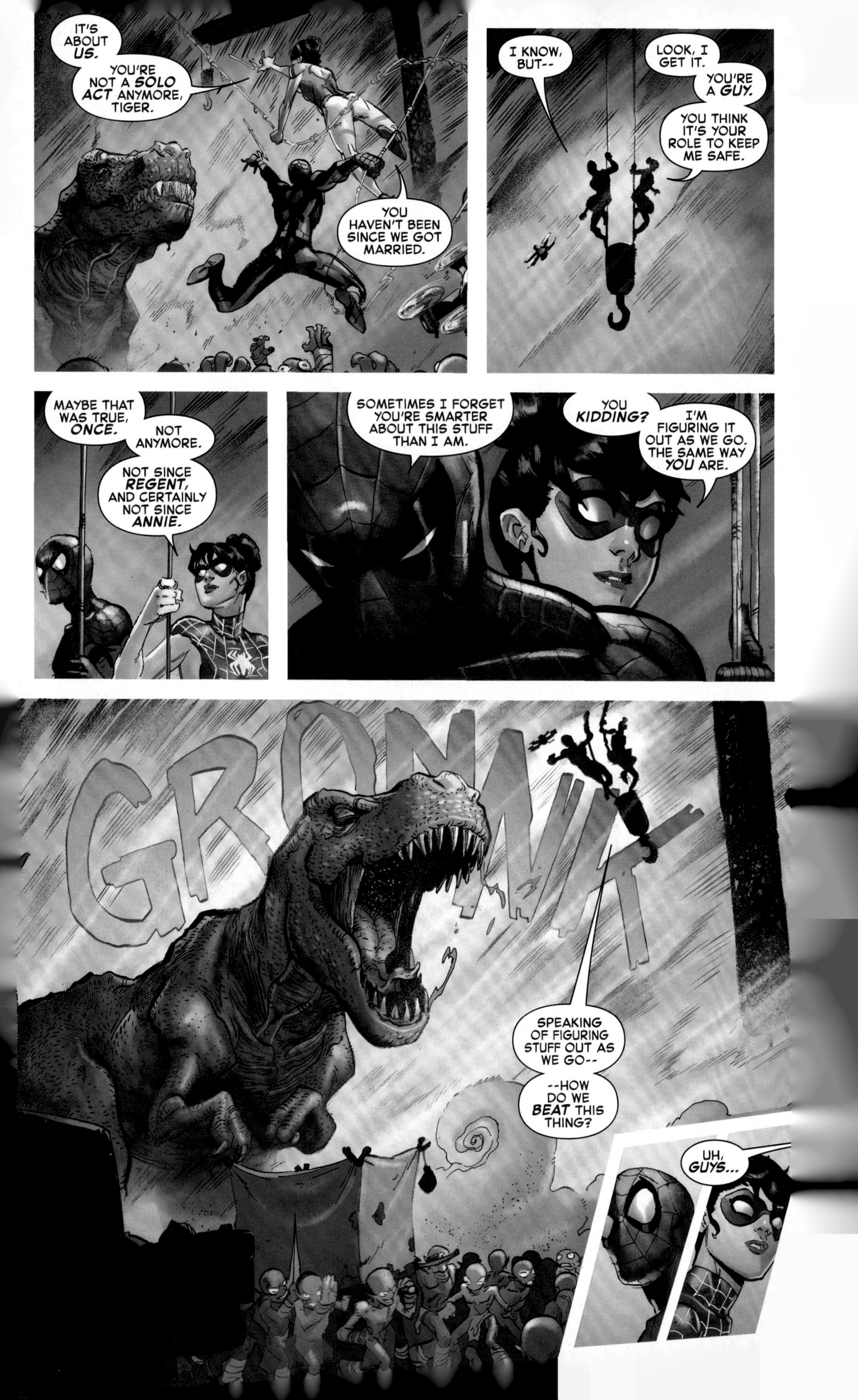
IT'S ABOUT US.
YOU'RE NOT A SOLO ACT ANYMORE, TIGER.
YOU HAVEN'T BEEN SINCE WE GOT MARRIED.
I KNOW, BUT--
LOOK, I GET IT.
YOU'RE A GUY.
YOU THINK IT'S YOUR ROLE TO KEEP ME SAFE.
MAYBE THAT WAS TRUE, ONCE.
NOT ANYMORE.
NOT SINCE REGENT, AND CERTAINLY NOT SINCE ANNIE.
SOMETIMES I FORGET YOU'RE SMARTER ABOUT THIS STUFF THAN I AM.
YOU KIDDING?
I'M FIGURING IT OUT AS WE GO. THE SAME WAY YOU ARE.
GRONNK
SPEAKING OF FIGURING STUFF OUT AS WE GO--
--HOW DO WE BEAT THIS THING?
UH, GUYS...

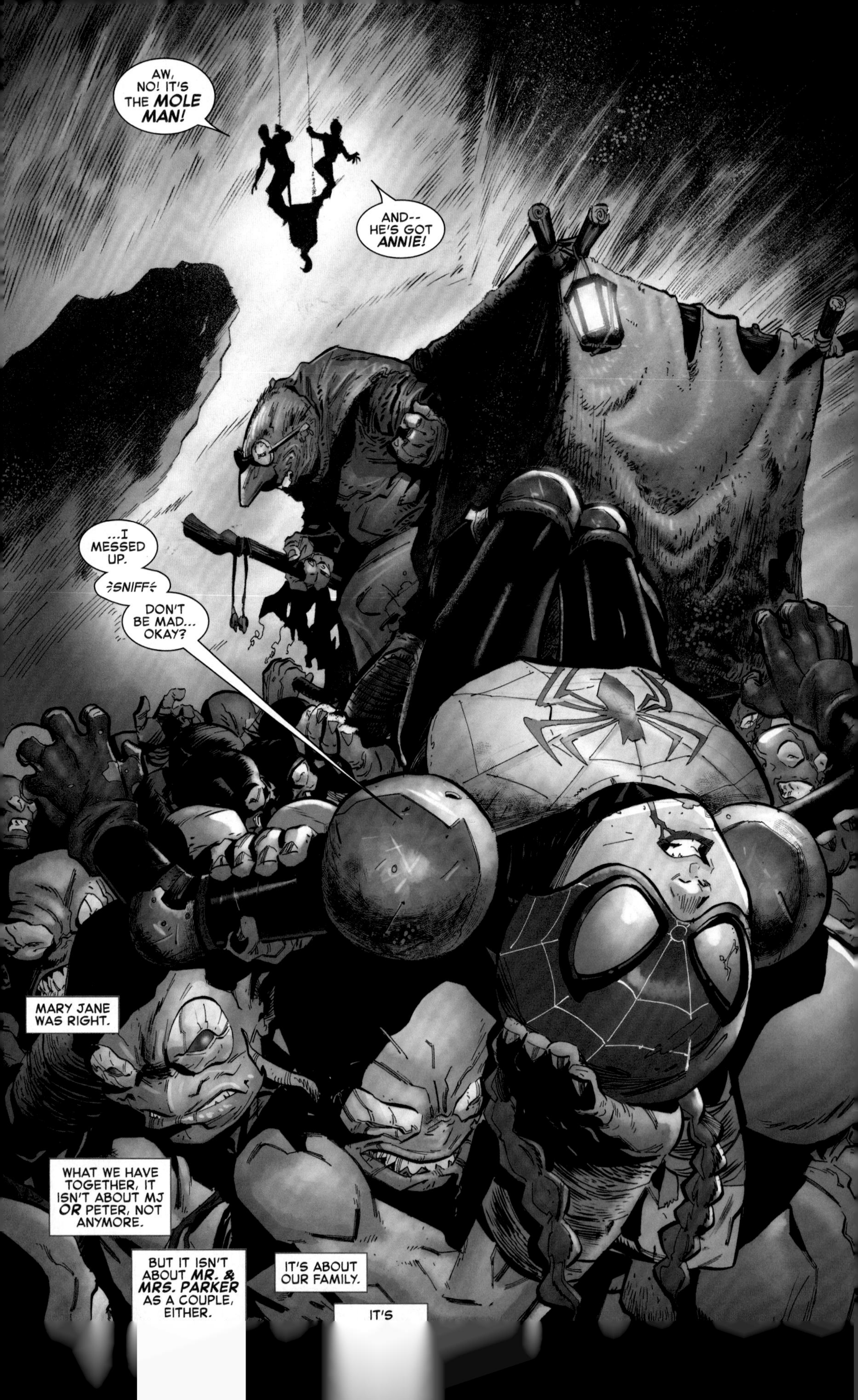
AW, NO! IT'S THE MOLE MAN!
AND-- HE'S GOT ANNIE!
...I MESSED UP.
SNIFF
DON'T BE MAD... OKAY?
MARY JANE WAS RIGHT.
WHAT WE HAVE TOGETHER, IT ISN'T ABOUT MJ OR PETER, NOT ANYMORE.
BUT IT ISN'T ABOUT MR. & MRS. PARKER AS A COUPLE, EITHER.
IT'S ABOUT OUR FAMILY.
IT'S

# THE Earnest ADVENTURES of SPIDER-DAD

by ANTHONY HOLDEN (regular dad)

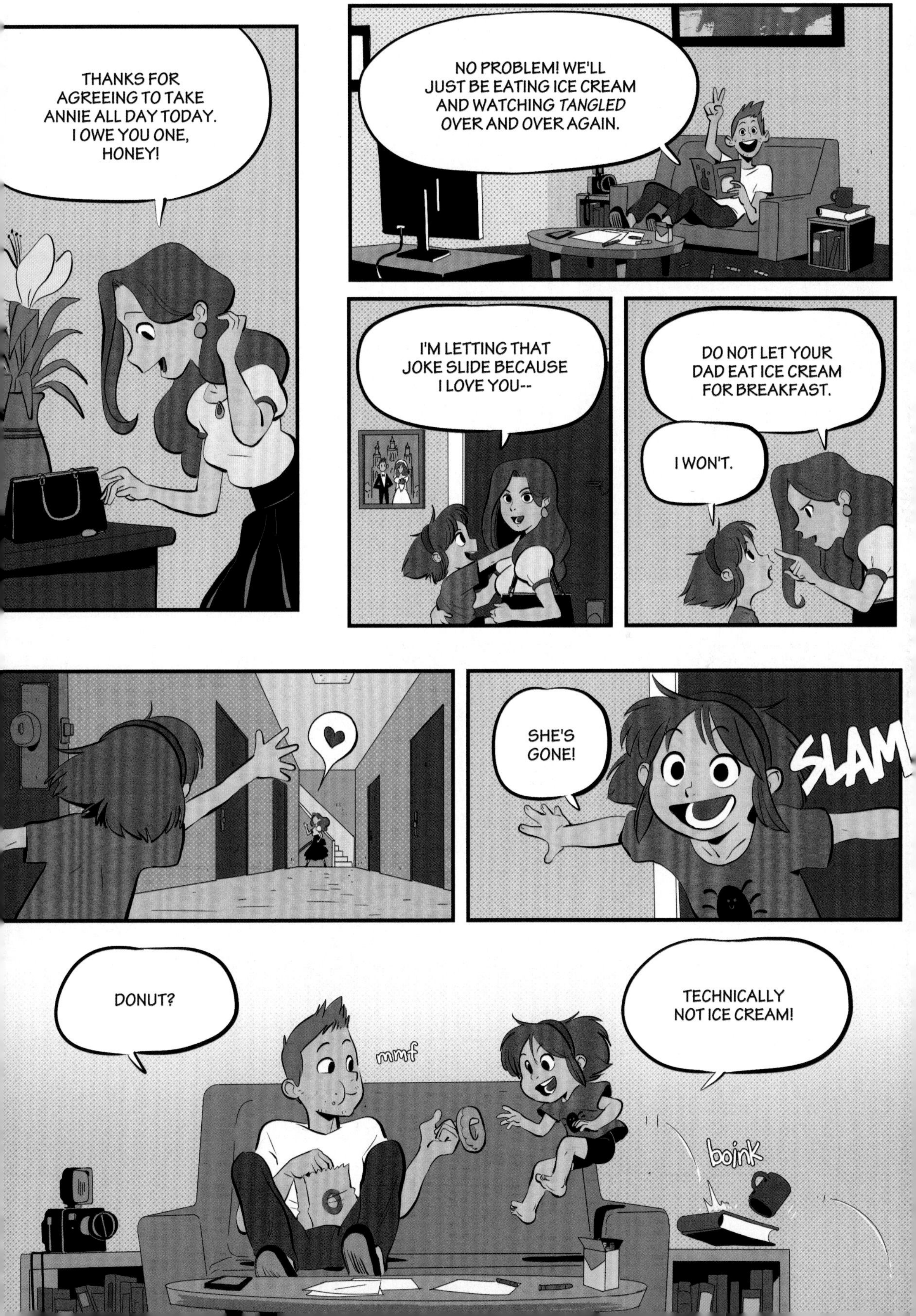
THANKS FOR AGREEING TO TAKE ANNIE ALL DAY TODAY. I OWE YOU ONE, HONEY!
NO PROBLEM! WE'LL JUST BE EATING ICE CREAM AND WATCHING *TANGLED* OVER AND OVER AGAIN.
I'M LETTING THAT JOKE SLIDE BECAUSE I LOVE YOU--
DO NOT LET YOUR DAD EAT ICE CREAM FOR BREAKFAST.
I WON'T.
SHE'S GONE!
SLAM
DONUT?
mmf
TECHNICALLY NOT ICE CREAM!
boink

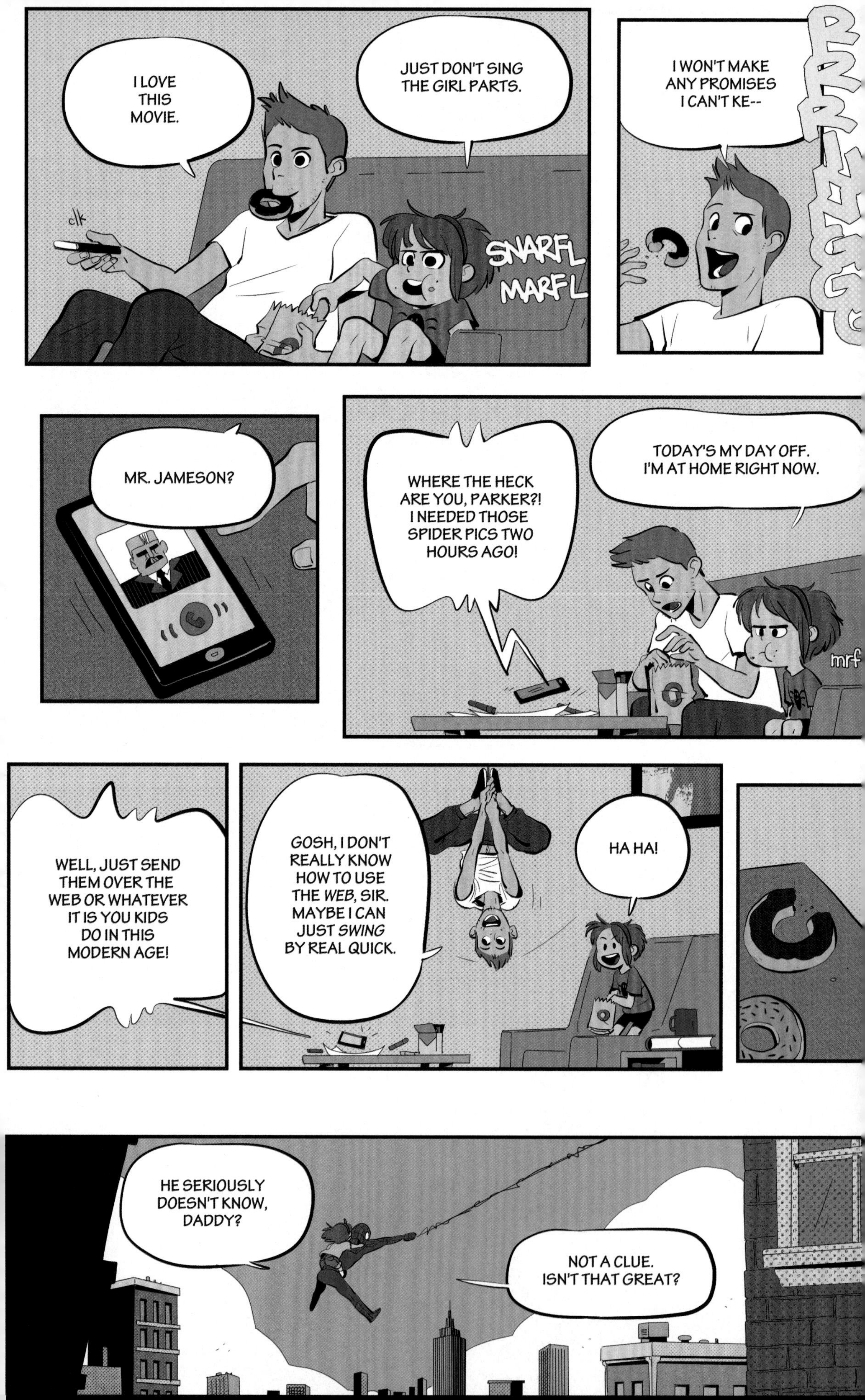

I LOVE THIS MOVIE.
JUST DON'T SING THE GIRL PARTS.
clk
SNARFL MARFL
I WON'T MAKE ANY PROMISES I CAN'T KE--
BRRRUUGG
MR. JAMESON?
WHERE THE HECK ARE YOU, PARKER?! I NEEDED THOSE SPIDER PICS TWO HOURS AGO!
TODAY'S MY DAY OFF. I'M AT HOME RIGHT NOW.
mrf
WELL, JUST SEND THEM OVER THE WEB OR WHATEVER IT IS YOU KIDS DO IN THIS MODERN AGE!
GOSH, I DON'T REALLY KNOW HOW TO USE THE *WEB*, SIR. MAYBE I CAN JUST *SWING* BY REAL QUICK.
HA HA!
HE SERIOUSLY DOESN'T KNOW, DADDY?
NOT A CLUE. ISN'T THAT GREAT?

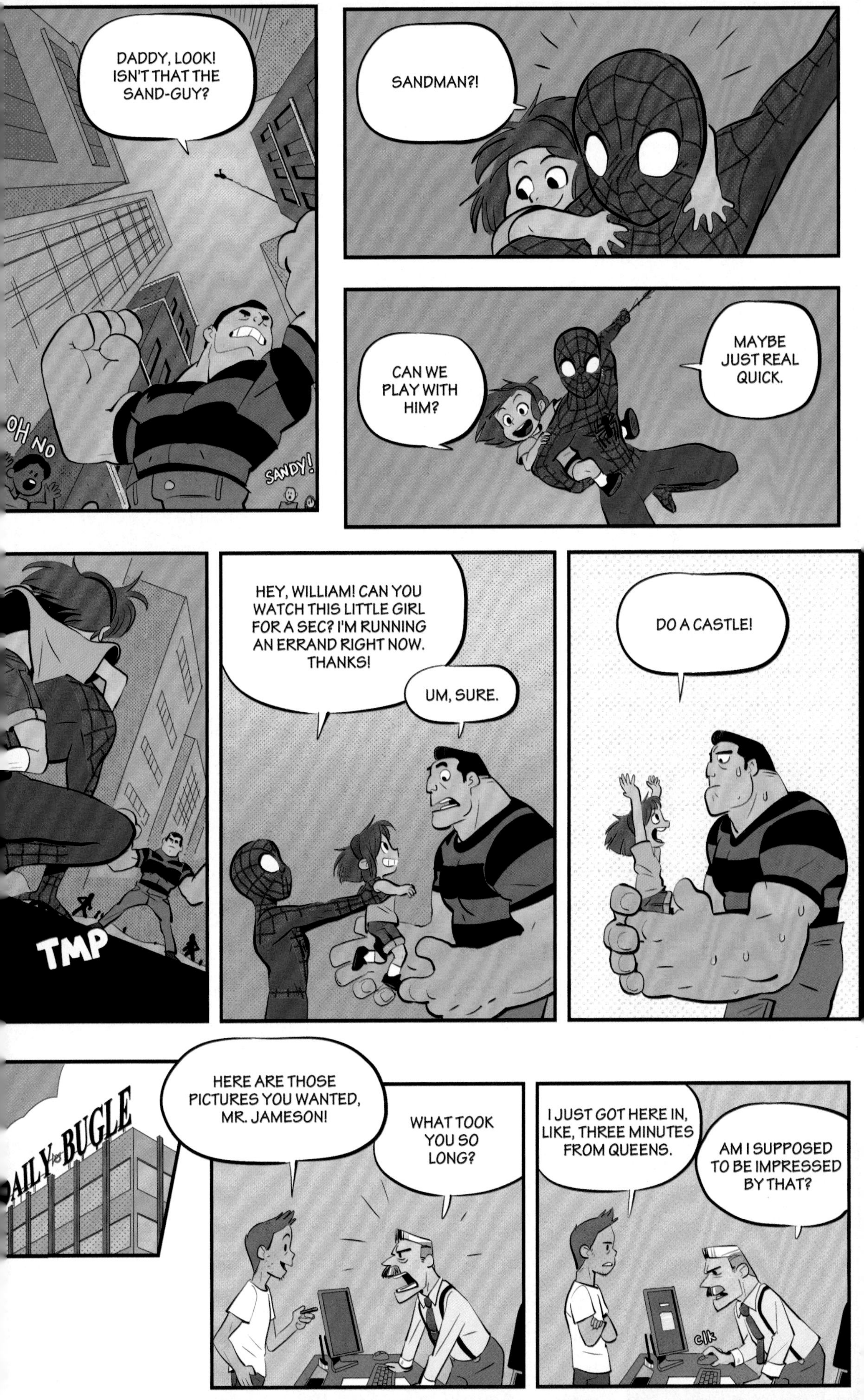
DADDY, LOOK! ISN'T THAT THE SAND-GUY?
OH NO
SANDY!
SANDMAN?!
CAN WE PLAY WITH HIM?
MAYBE JUST REAL QUICK.
TMP
HEY, WILLIAM! CAN YOU WATCH THIS LITTLE GIRL FOR A SEC? I'M RUNNING AN ERRAND RIGHT NOW. THANKS!
UM, SURE.
DO A CASTLE!
DAILY BUGLE
HERE ARE THOSE PICTURES YOU WANTED, MR. JAMESON!
WHAT TOOK YOU SO LONG?
I JUST GOT HERE IN, LIKE, THREE MINUTES FROM QUEENS.
AM I SUPPOSED TO BE IMPRESSED BY THAT?
clk

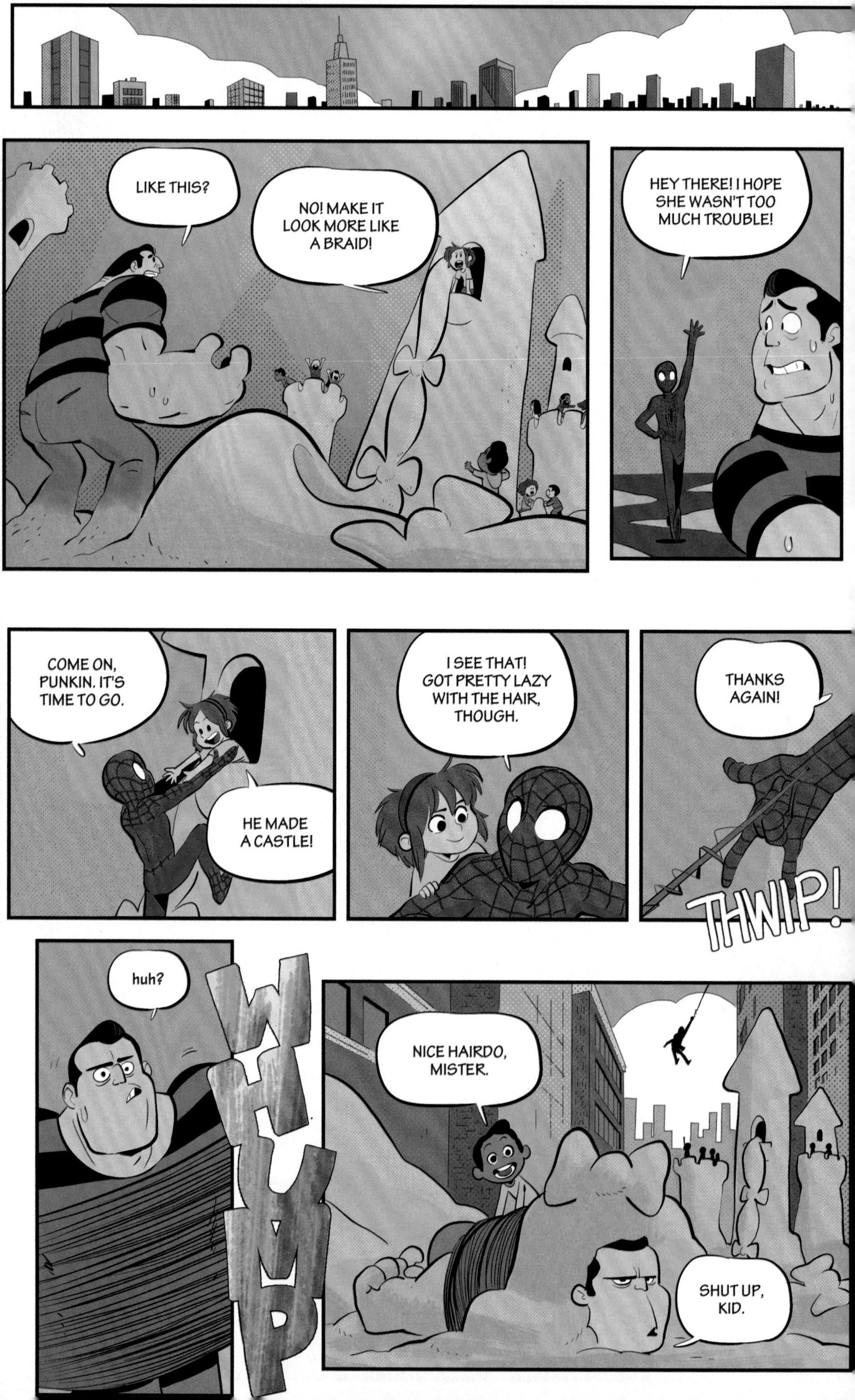
LIKE THIS?
NO! MAKE IT LOOK MORE LIKE A BRAID!
HEY THERE! I HOPE SHE WASN'T TOO MUCH TROUBLE!
COME ON, PUNKIN. IT'S TIME TO GO.
HE MADE A CASTLE!
I SEE THAT! GOT PRETTY LAZY WITH THE HAIR, THOUGH.
THANKS AGAIN!
THWIP!
huh?
WHUMP
NICE HAIRDO, MISTER.
SHUT UP, KID.

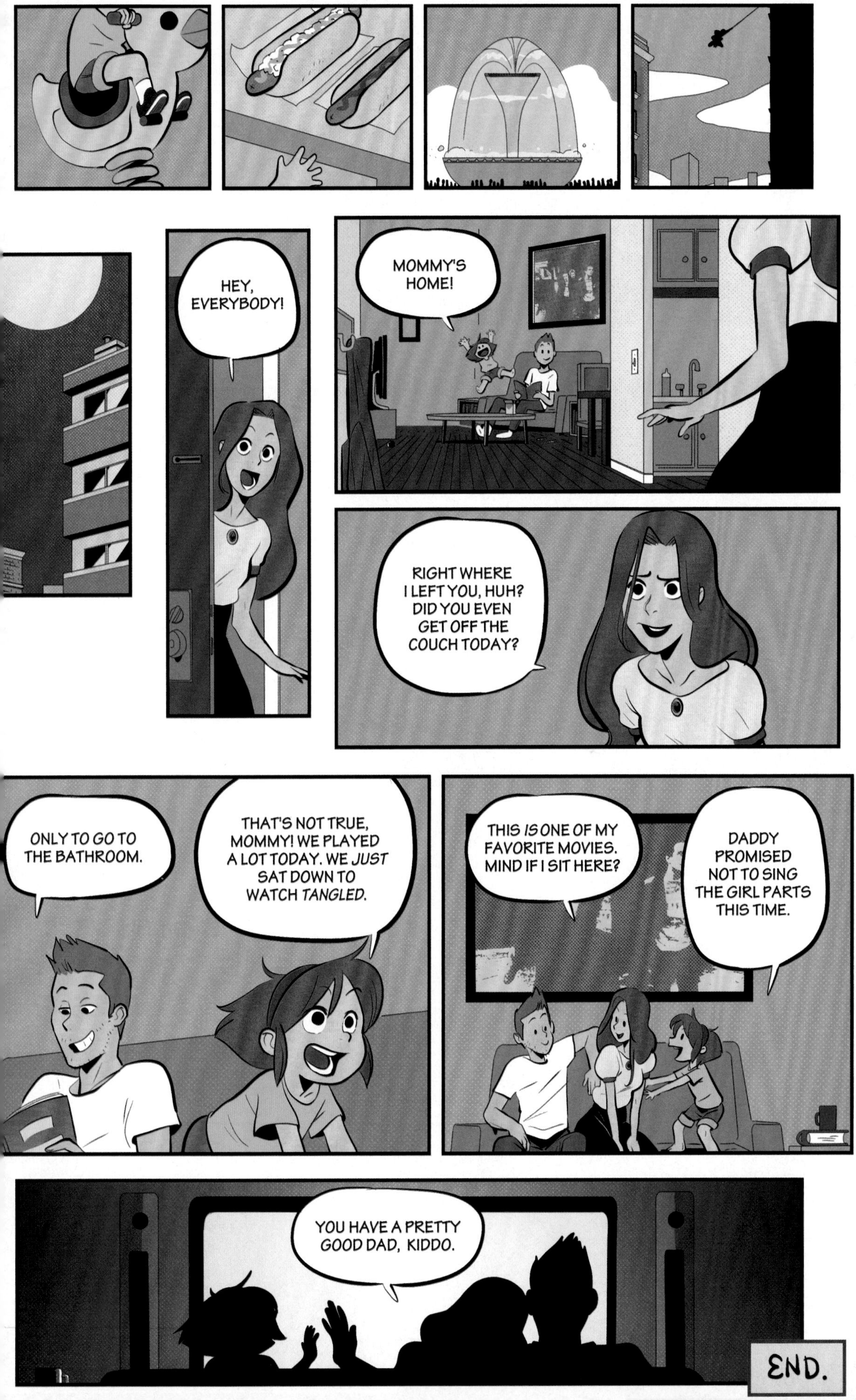
HEY, EVERYBODY!
MOMMY'S HOME!
RIGHT WHERE I LEFT YOU, HUH? DID YOU EVEN GET OFF THE COUCH TODAY?
ONLY TO GO TO THE BATHROOM.
THAT'S NOT TRUE, MOMMY! WE PLAYED A LOT TODAY. WE *JUST* SAT DOWN TO WATCH *TANGLED*.
THIS *IS* ONE OF MY FAVORITE MOVIES. MIND IF I SIT HERE?
DADDY PROMISED NOT TO SING THE GIRL PARTS THIS TIME.
YOU HAVE A PRETTY GOOD DAD, KIDDO.
END.

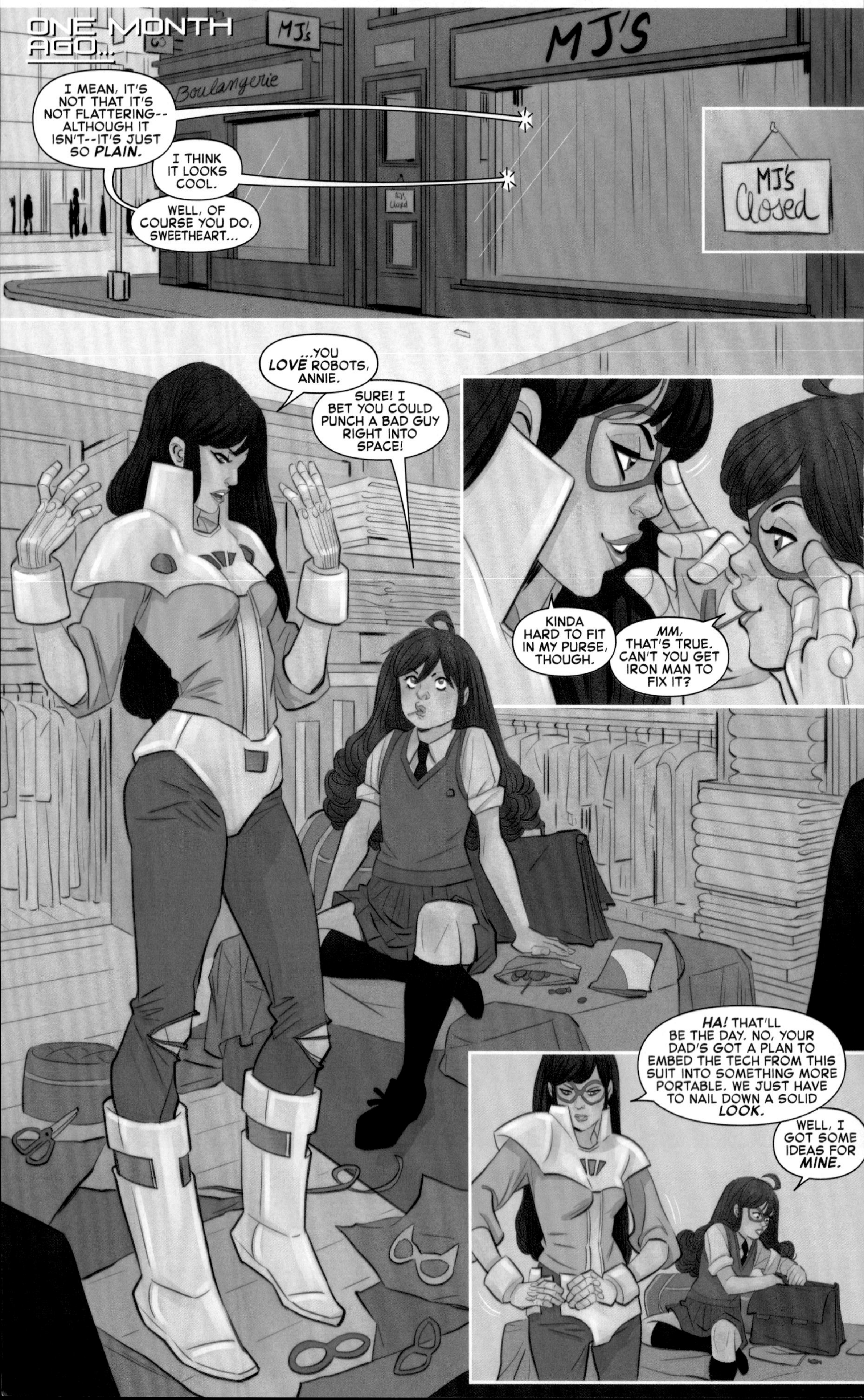

ONE MONTH AGO...
MJ's
Boulangerie
MJ'S
I MEAN, IT'S NOT THAT IT'S NOT FLATTERING--ALTHOUGH IT ISN'T--IT'S JUST SO PLAIN.
I THINK IT LOOKS COOL.
WELL, OF COURSE YOU DO, SWEETHEART...
MJ's Closed
...YOU LOVE ROBOTS, ANNIE.
SURE! I BET YOU COULD PUNCH A BAD GUY RIGHT INTO SPACE!
KINDA HARD TO FIT IN MY PURSE, THOUGH.
MM, THAT'S TRUE. CAN'T YOU GET IRON MAN TO FIX IT?
HA! THAT'LL BE THE DAY. NO, YOUR DAD'S GOT A PLAN TO EMBED THE TECH FROM THIS SUIT INTO SOMETHING MORE PORTABLE. WE JUST HAVE TO NAIL DOWN A SOLID LOOK.
WELL, I GOT SOME IDEAS FOR MINE.

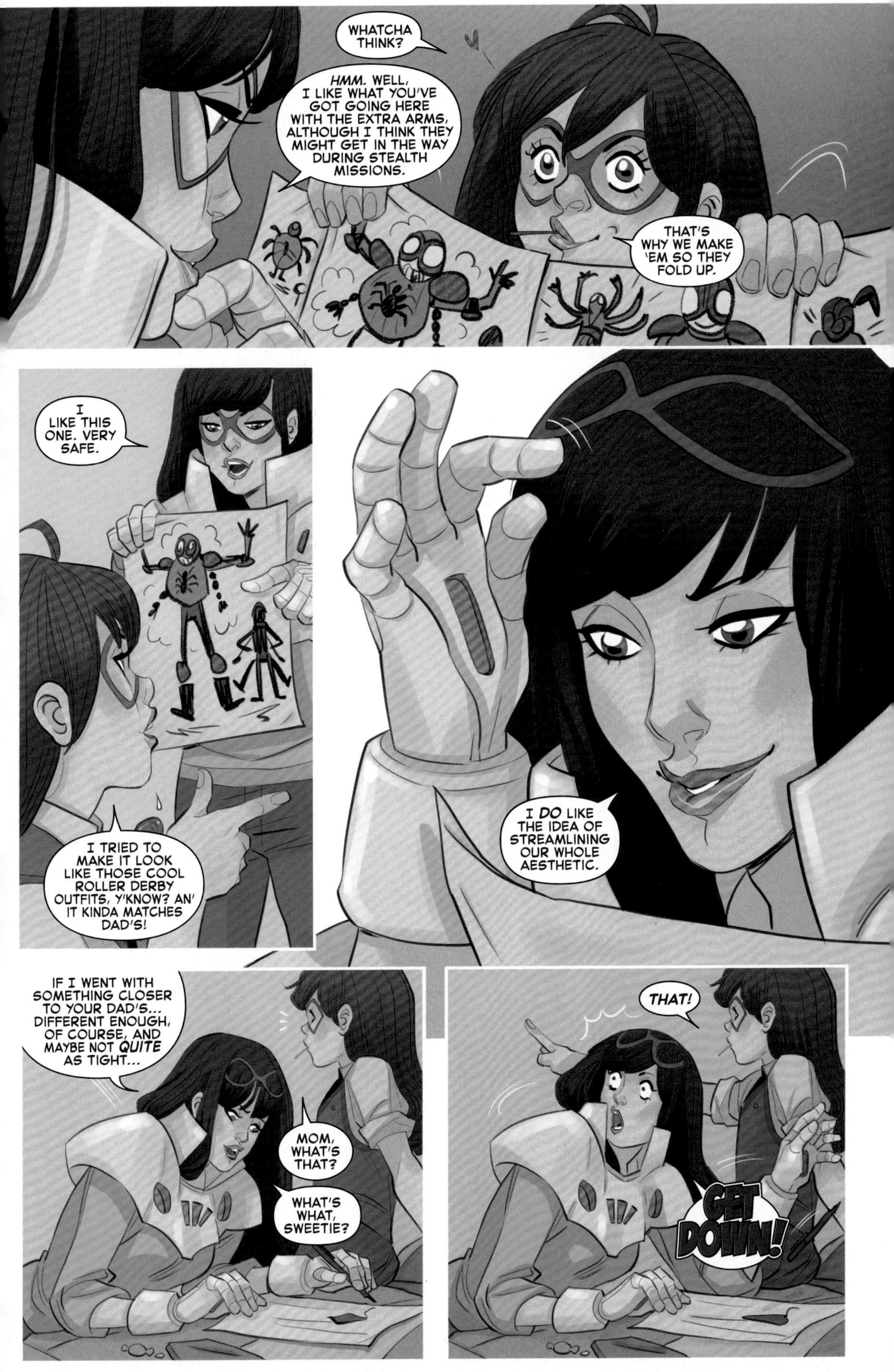
WHATCHA THINK?
HMM. WELL, I LIKE WHAT YOU'VE GOT GOING HERE WITH THE EXTRA ARMS, ALTHOUGH I THINK THEY MIGHT GET IN THE WAY DURING STEALTH MISSIONS.
THAT'S WHY WE MAKE 'EM SO THEY FOLD UP.
I LIKE THIS ONE. VERY SAFE.
I TRIED TO MAKE IT LOOK LIKE THOSE COOL ROLLER DERBY OUTFITS, Y'KNOW? AN' IT KINDA MATCHES DAD'S!
I DO LIKE THE IDEA OF STREAMLINING OUR WHOLE AESTHETIC.
IF I WENT WITH SOMETHING CLOSER TO YOUR DAD'S... DIFFERENT ENOUGH, OF COURSE, AND MAYBE NOT QUITE AS TIGHT...
MOM, WHAT'S THAT?
WHAT'S WHAT, SWEETIE?
THAT!
GET DOWN!

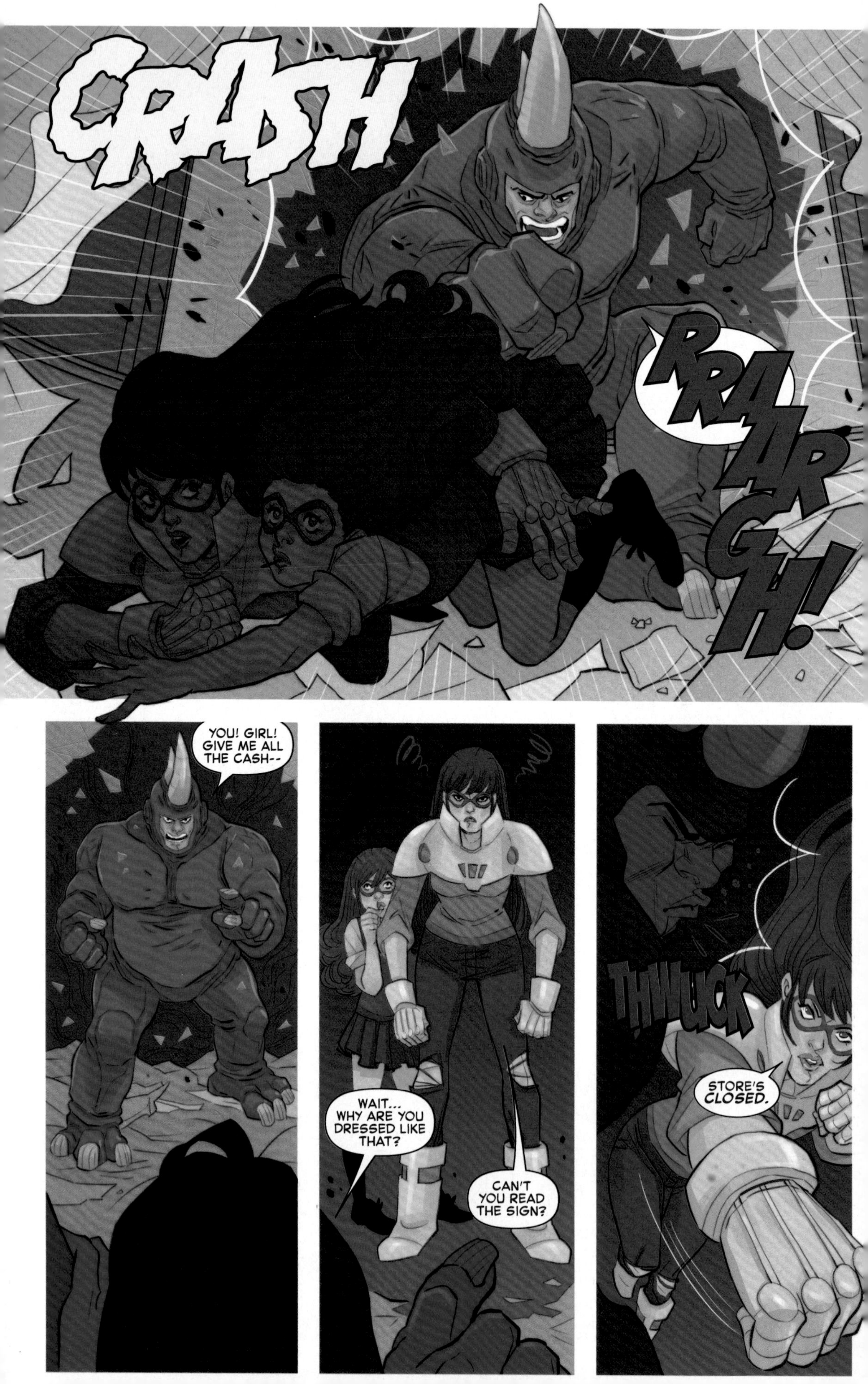
CRASH
RRAARGH!
YOU! GIRL! GIVE ME ALL THE CASH--
WAIT... WHY ARE YOU DRESSED LIKE THAT?
CAN'T YOU READ THE SIGN?
THWUCK
STORE'S CLOSED.

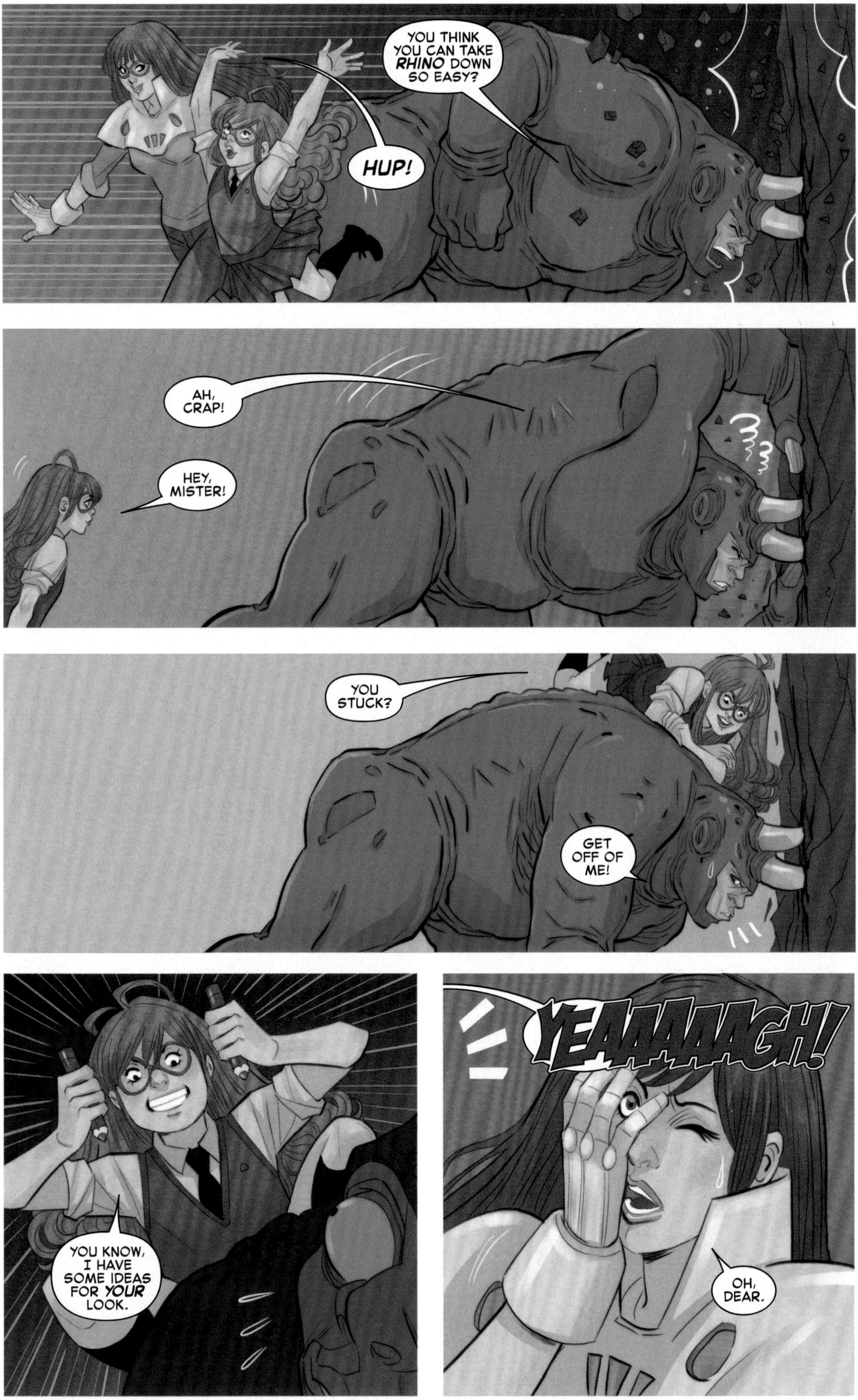

YOU THINK YOU CAN TAKE RHINO DOWN SO EASY?
HUP!
AH, CRAP!
HEY, MISTER!
YOU STUCK?
GET OFF OF ME!
YOU KNOW, I HAVE SOME IDEAS FOR YOUR LOOK.
YEAAAAAGH!
OH, DEAR.

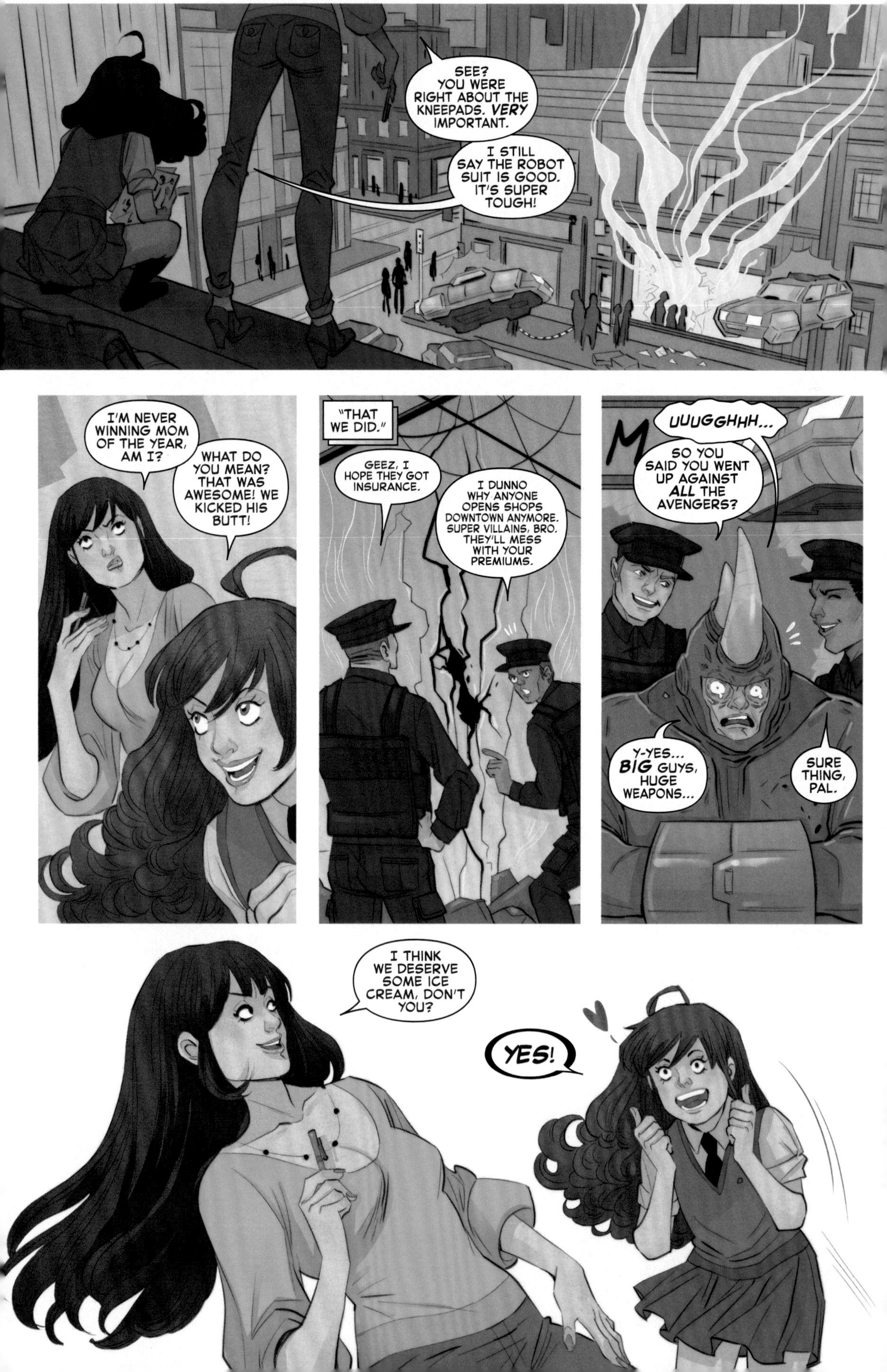
SEE? YOU WERE RIGHT ABOUT THE KNEEPADS. VERY IMPORTANT.
I STILL SAY THE ROBOT SUIT IS GOOD. IT'S SUPER TOUGH!
I'M NEVER WINNING MOM OF THE YEAR, AM I?
WHAT DO YOU MEAN? THAT WAS AWESOME! WE KICKED HIS BUTT!
"THAT WE DID."
GEEZ, I HOPE THEY GOT INSURANCE.
I DUNNO WHY ANYONE OPENS SHOPS DOWNTOWN ANYMORE. SUPER VILLAINS, BRO. THEY'LL MESS WITH YOUR PREMIUMS.
UUUGGHHH...
SO YOU SAID YOU WENT UP AGAINST ALL THE AVENGERS?
Y-YES... BIG GUYS, HUGE WEAPONS...
SURE THING, PAL.
I THINK WE DESERVE SOME ICE CREAM, DON'T YOU?
YES!

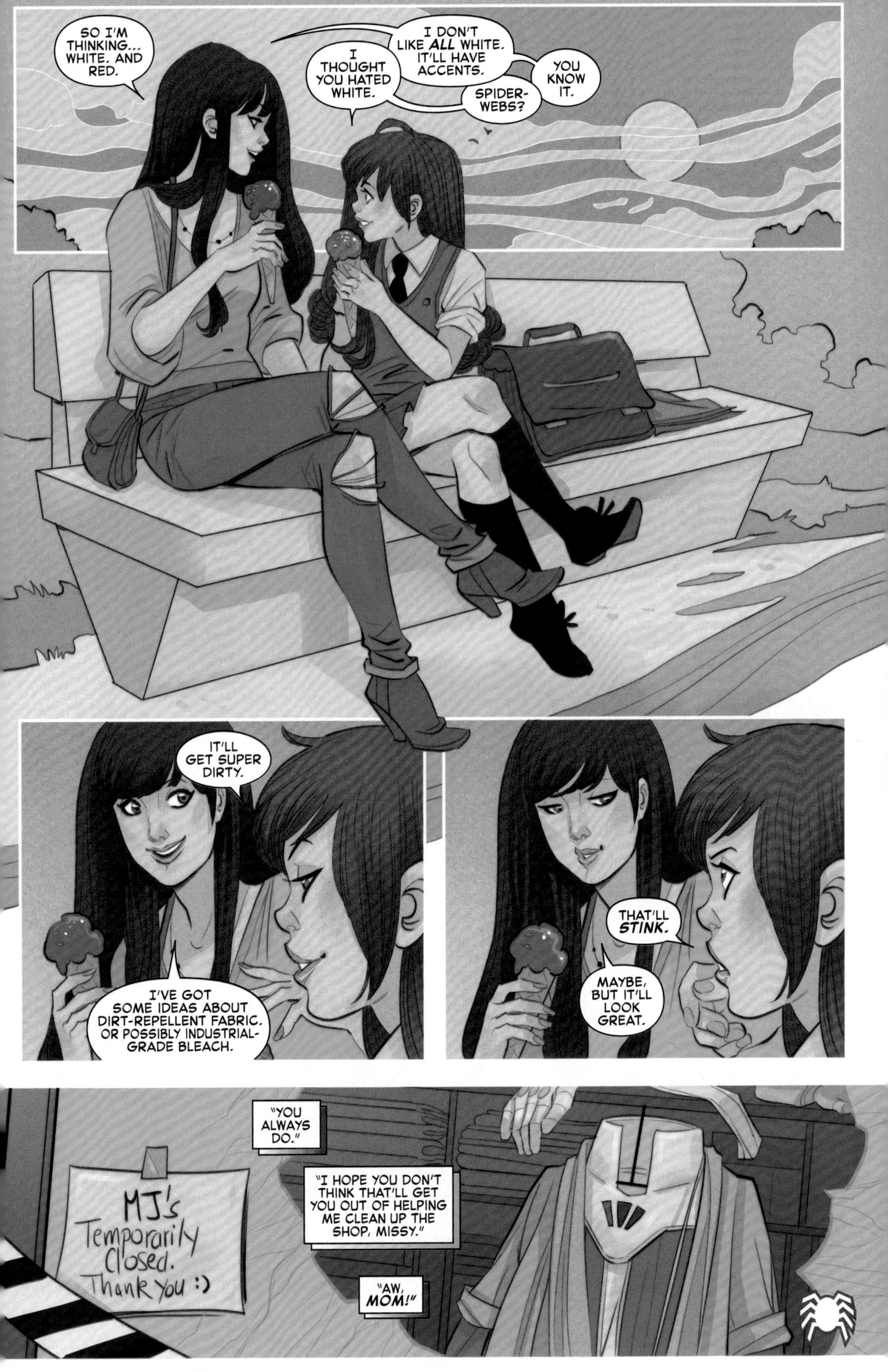
SO I'M THINKING... WHITE. AND RED.
I THOUGHT YOU HATED WHITE.
I DON'T LIKE ALL WHITE. IT'LL HAVE ACCENTS.
SPIDER-WEBS?
YOU KNOW IT.
IT'LL GET SUPER DIRTY.
I'VE GOT SOME IDEAS ABOUT DIRT-REPELLENT FABRIC. OR POSSIBLY INDUSTRIAL-GRADE BLEACH.
THAT'LL STINK.
MAYBE, BUT IT'LL LOOK GREAT.
"YOU ALWAYS DO."
MJ's Temporarily Closed. Thank You :)
"I HOPE YOU DON'T THINK THAT'LL GET YOU OUT OF HELPING ME CLEAN UP THE SHOP, MISSY."
"AW, MOM!"

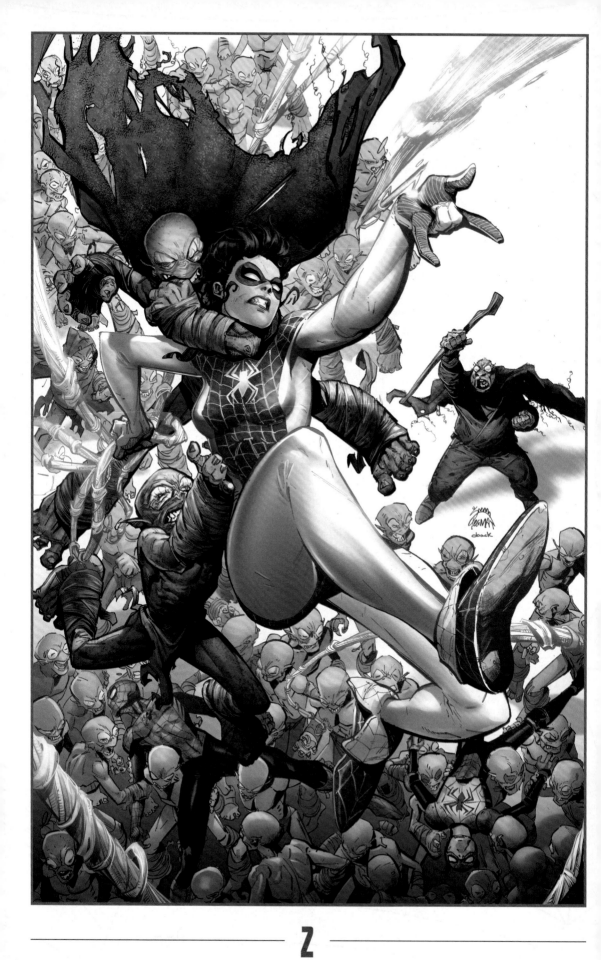

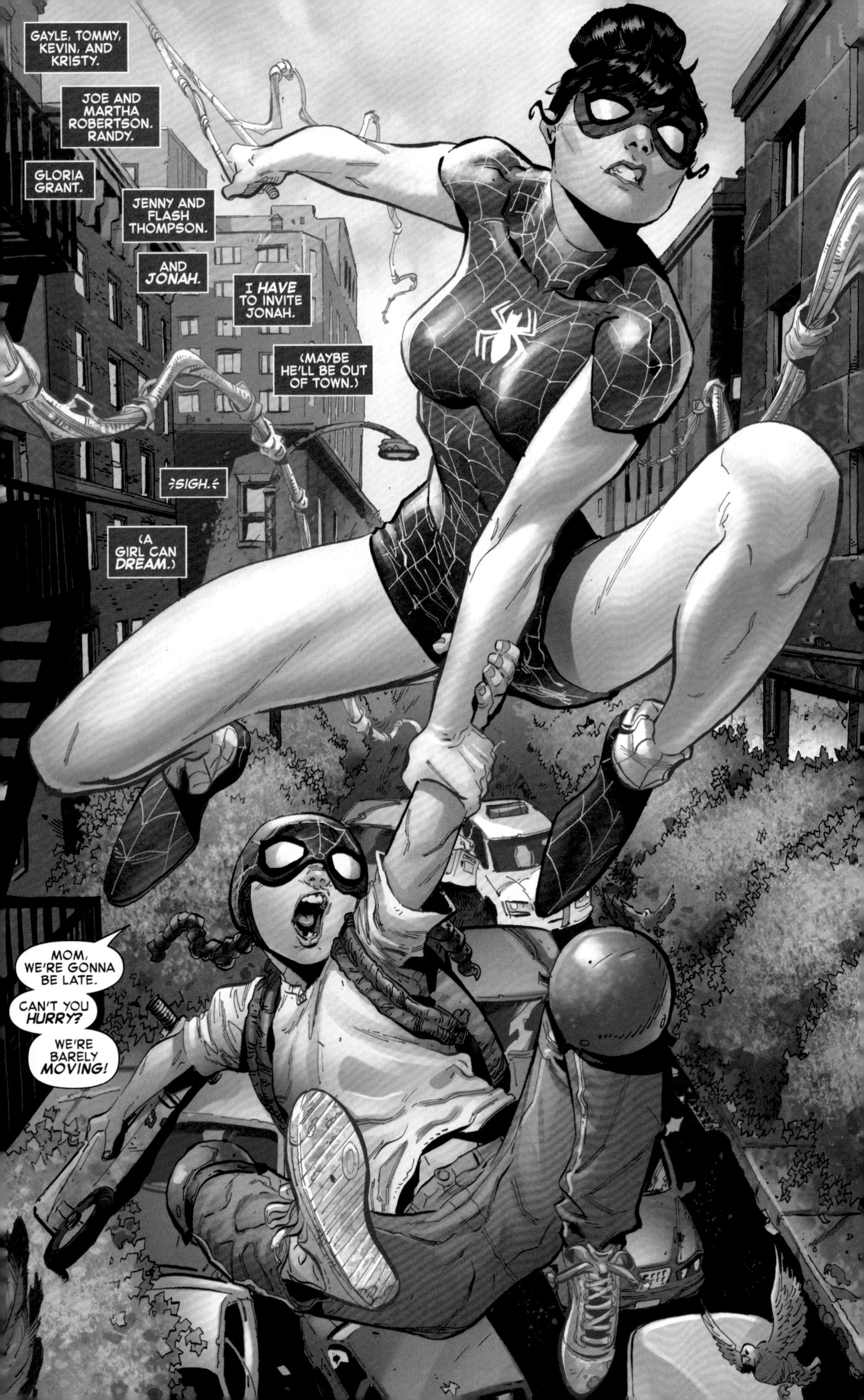
GAYLE, TOMMY, KEVIN, AND KRISTY.
JOE AND MARTHA ROBERTSON. RANDY.
GLORIA GRANT.
JENNY AND FLASH THOMPSON.
AND *JONAH*.
I *HAVE* TO INVITE JONAH.
(MAYBE HE'LL BE OUT OF TOWN.)
*SIGH.*
(A GIRL CAN *DREAM*.)
MOM, WE'RE GONNA BE LATE.
CAN'T YOU *HURRY?*
WE'RE BARELY *MOVING!*

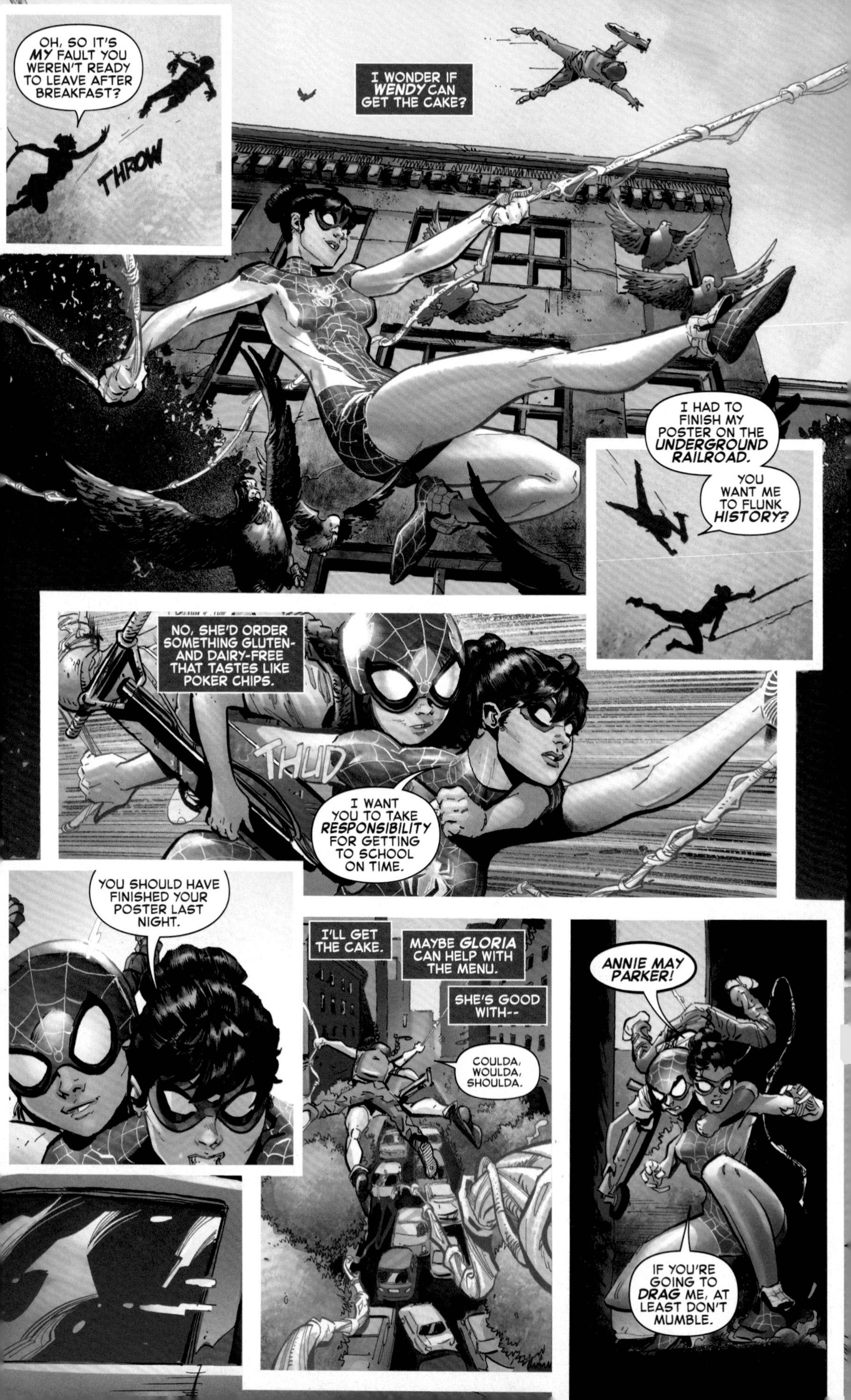

OH, SO IT'S MY FAULT YOU WEREN'T READY TO LEAVE AFTER BREAKFAST?
THROW
I WONDER IF WENDY CAN GET THE CAKE?
I HAD TO FINISH MY POSTER ON THE UNDERGROUND RAILROAD.
YOU WANT ME TO FLUNK HISTORY?
NO, SHE'D ORDER SOMETHING GLUTEN- AND DAIRY-FREE THAT TASTES LIKE POKER CHIPS.
THUD
I WANT YOU TO TAKE RESPONSIBILITY FOR GETTING TO SCHOOL ON TIME.
YOU SHOULD HAVE FINISHED YOUR POSTER LAST NIGHT.
I'LL GET THE CAKE.
MAYBE GLORIA CAN HELP WITH THE MENU.
SHE'S GOOD WITH--
COULDA, WOULDA, SHOULDA.
ANNIE MAY PARKER!
IF YOU'RE GOING TO DRAG ME, AT LEAST DON'T MUMBLE.

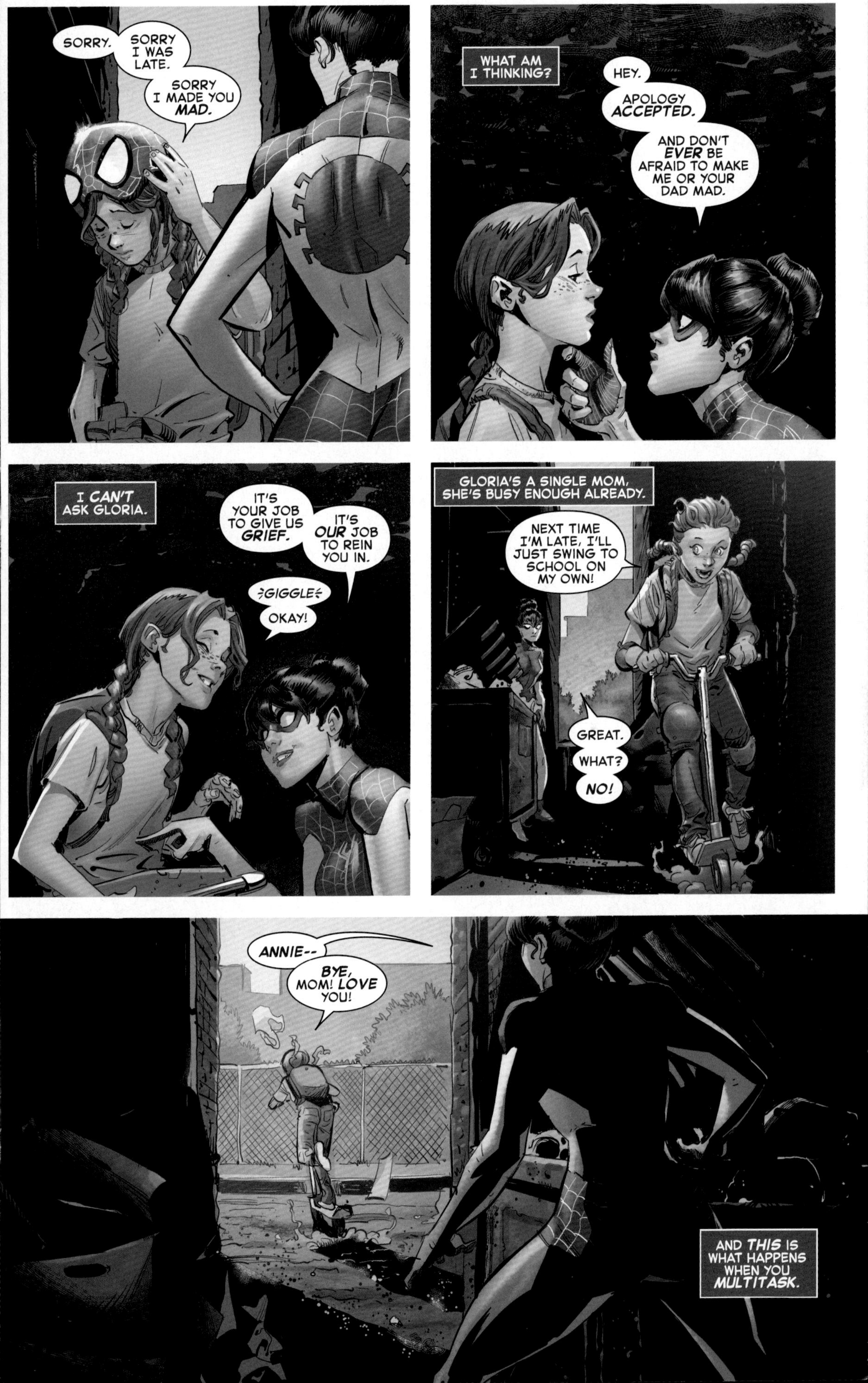
SORRY.
SORRY I WAS LATE.
SORRY I MADE YOU MAD.
WHAT AM I THINKING?
HEY.
APOLOGY ACCEPTED.
AND DON'T EVER BE AFRAID TO MAKE ME OR YOUR DAD MAD.
I CAN'T ASK GLORIA.
IT'S YOUR JOB TO GIVE US GRIEF.
IT'S OUR JOB TO REIN YOU IN.
GIGGLE
OKAY!
GLORIA'S A SINGLE MOM, SHE'S BUSY ENOUGH ALREADY.
NEXT TIME I'M LATE, I'LL JUST SWING TO SCHOOL ON MY OWN!
GREAT.
WHAT?
NO!
ANNIE--
BYE, MOM! LOVE YOU!
AND THIS IS WHAT HAPPENS WHEN YOU MULTITASK.

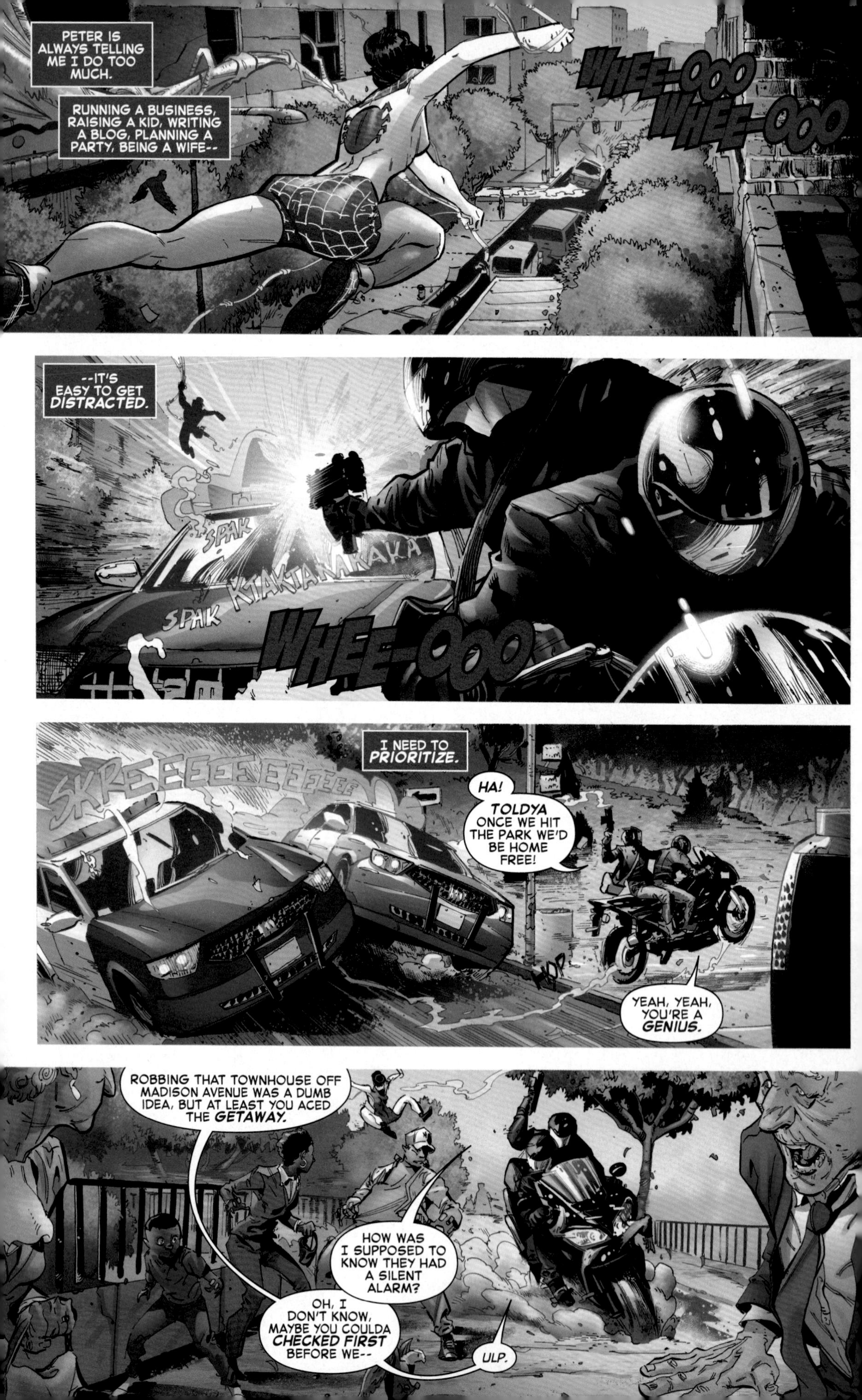
PETER IS ALWAYS TELLING ME I DO TOO MUCH.
RUNNING A BUSINESS, RAISING A KID, WRITING A BLOG, PLANNING A PARTY, BEING A WIFE--
WHEE-OOO WHEE-OOO
--IT'S EASY TO GET DISTRACTED.
SPAK
KTAKTAKAKAKA
SPAK
WHEE-OOO
I NEED TO PRIORITIZE.
SKREEEEEEEEEEE
HA! TOLDYA ONCE WE HIT THE PARK WE'D BE HOME FREE!
HOP
YEAH, YEAH, YOU'RE A GENIUS.
ROBBING THAT TOWNHOUSE OFF MADISON AVENUE WAS A DUMB IDEA, BUT AT LEAST YOU ACED THE GETAWAY.
HOW WAS I SUPPOSED TO KNOW THEY HAD A SILENT ALARM?
OH, I DON'T KNOW, MAYBE YOU COULDA CHECKED FIRST BEFORE WE--
ULP.

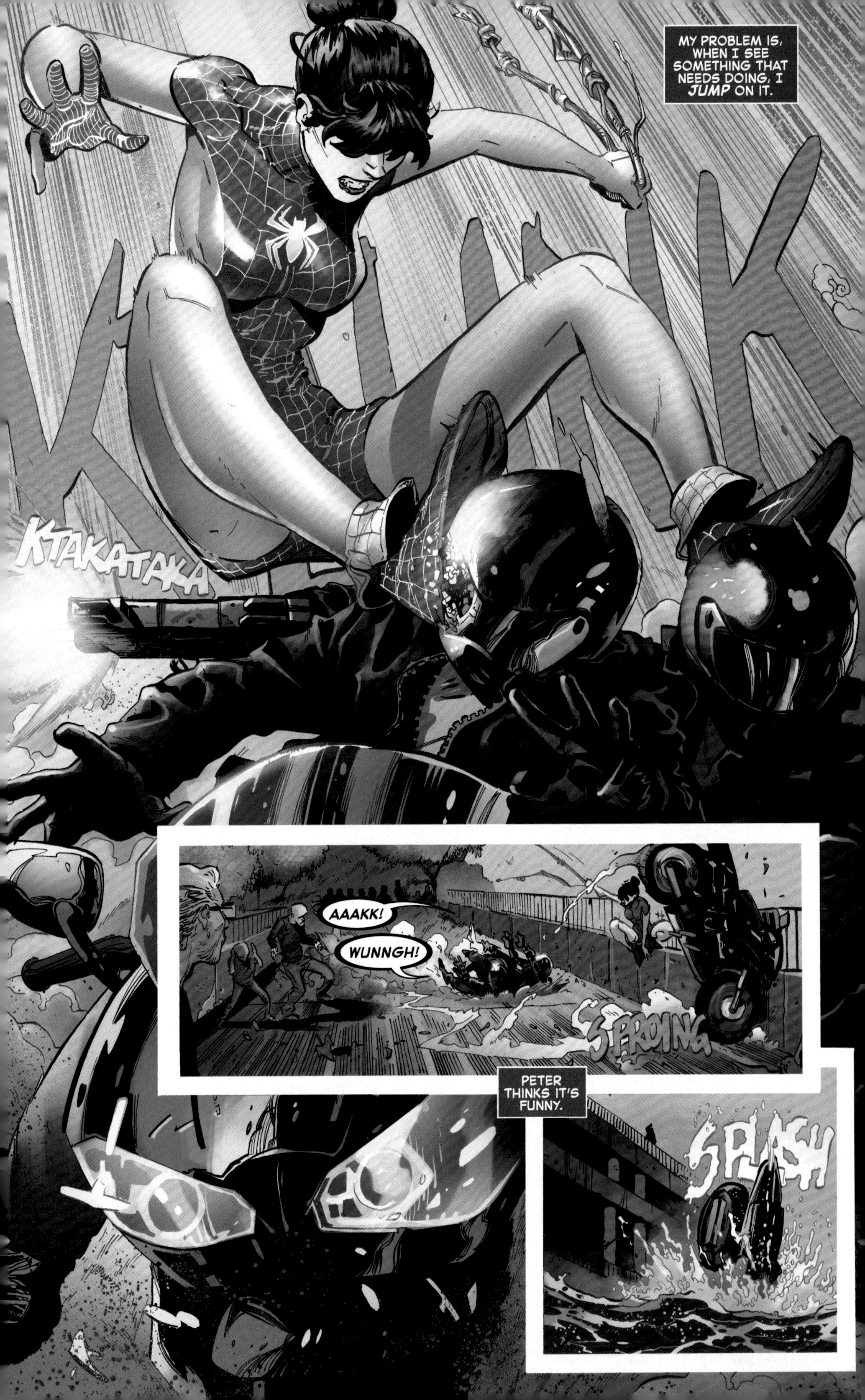
MY PROBLEM IS, WHEN I SEE SOMETHING THAT NEEDS DOING, I JUMP ON IT.
KTAKATAKA
AAAKK!
WUNNGH!
SPROING
PETER THINKS IT'S FUNNY.
SPLASH

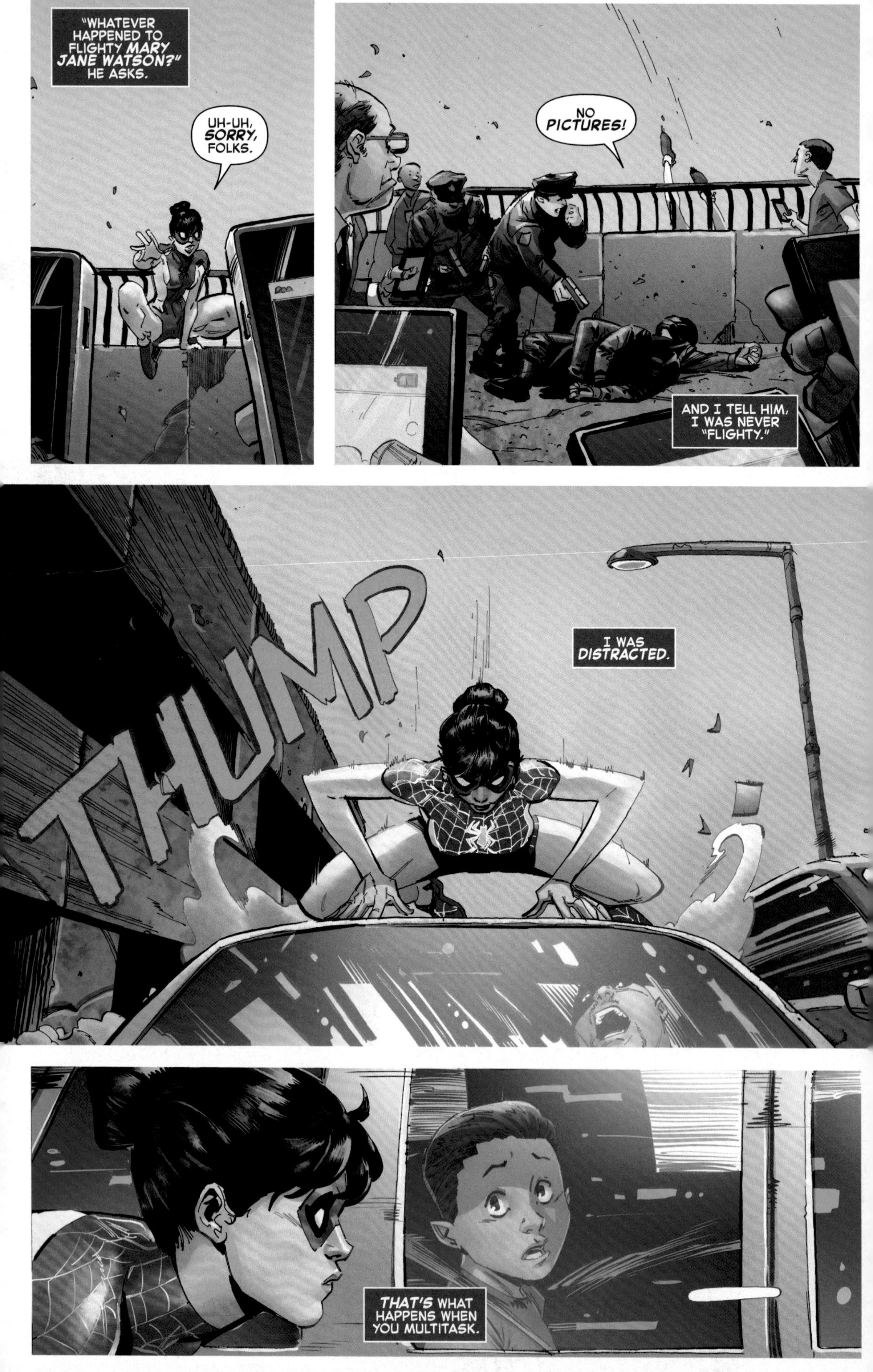
"WHATEVER HAPPENED TO FLIGHTY MARY JANE WATSON?" HE ASKS.
UH-UH, SORRY, FOLKS.
NO PICTURES!
AND I TELL HIM, I WAS NEVER "FLIGHTY."
THUMP
I WAS DISTRACTED.
THAT'S WHAT HAPPENS WHEN YOU MULTITASK.

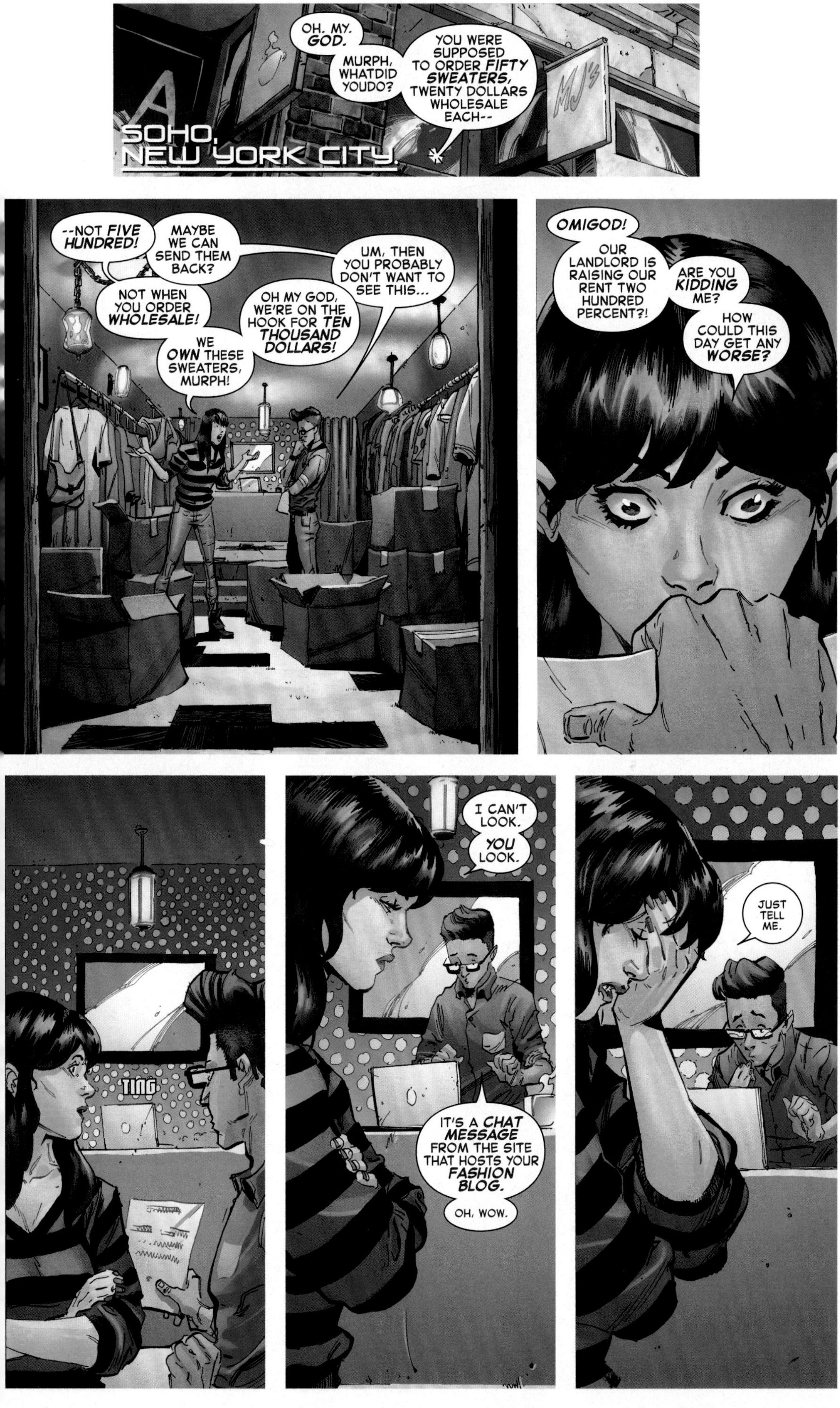

SOHO, NEW YORK CITY.
OH. MY. GOD.
MURPH, WHATDID YOUDO?
YOU WERE SUPPOSED TO ORDER FIFTY SWEATERS, TWENTY DOLLARS WHOLESALE EACH--
MJ's
--NOT FIVE HUNDRED!
MAYBE WE CAN SEND THEM BACK?
NOT WHEN YOU ORDER WHOLESALE!
WE OWN THESE SWEATERS, MURPH!
OH MY GOD, WE'RE ON THE HOOK FOR TEN THOUSAND DOLLARS!
UM, THEN YOU PROBABLY DON'T WANT TO SEE THIS...
OMIGOD!
OUR LANDLORD IS RAISING OUR RENT TWO HUNDRED PERCENT?!
ARE YOU KIDDING ME?
HOW COULD THIS DAY GET ANY WORSE?
TING
I CAN'T LOOK.
YOU LOOK.
IT'S A CHAT MESSAGE FROM THE SITE THAT HOSTS YOUR FASHION BLOG.
OH, WOW.
JUST TELL ME.

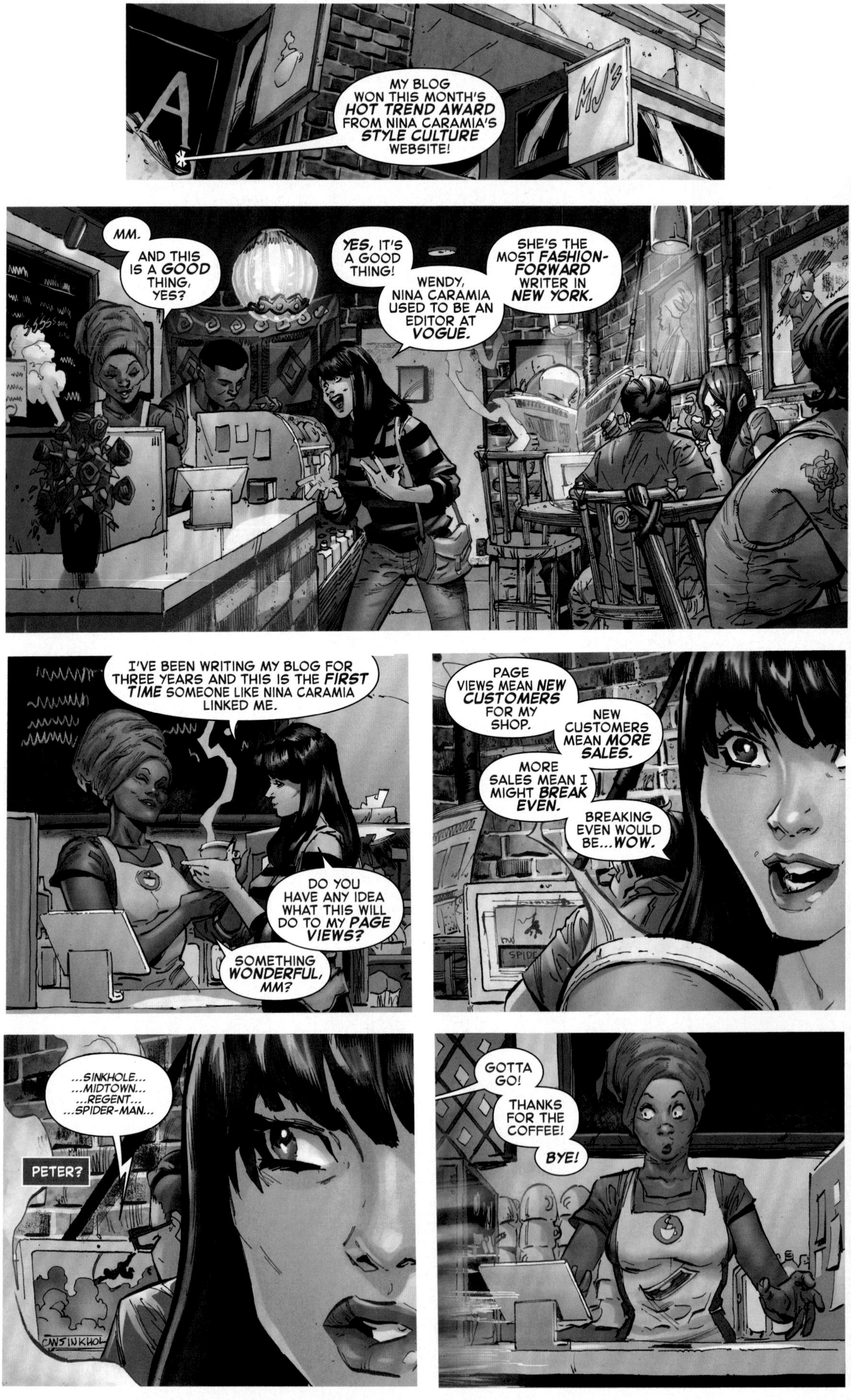
MJ's
MY BLOG WON THIS MONTH'S **HOT TREND AWARD** FROM NINA CARAMIA'S **STYLE CULTURE** WEBSITE!
MM.
AND THIS IS A **GOOD** THING, YES?
**YES,** IT'S A GOOD THING!
WENDY, NINA CARAMIA USED TO BE AN EDITOR AT **VOGUE.**
SHE'S THE MOST **FASHION-FORWARD** WRITER IN **NEW YORK.**
I'VE BEEN WRITING MY BLOG FOR THREE YEARS AND THIS IS THE **FIRST TIME** SOMEONE LIKE NINA CARAMIA LINKED ME.
DO YOU HAVE ANY IDEA WHAT THIS WILL DO TO MY **PAGE VIEWS?**
SOMETHING **WONDERFUL,** MM?
PAGE VIEWS MEAN **NEW CUSTOMERS** FOR MY SHOP.
NEW CUSTOMERS MEAN **MORE SALES.**
MORE SALES MEAN I MIGHT **BREAK EVEN.**
BREAKING EVEN WOULD BE...**WOW.**
...SINKHOLE...
...MIDTOWN...
...REGENT...
...SPIDER-MAN...
PETER?
GOTTA GO!
THANKS FOR THE COFFEE!
**BYE!**

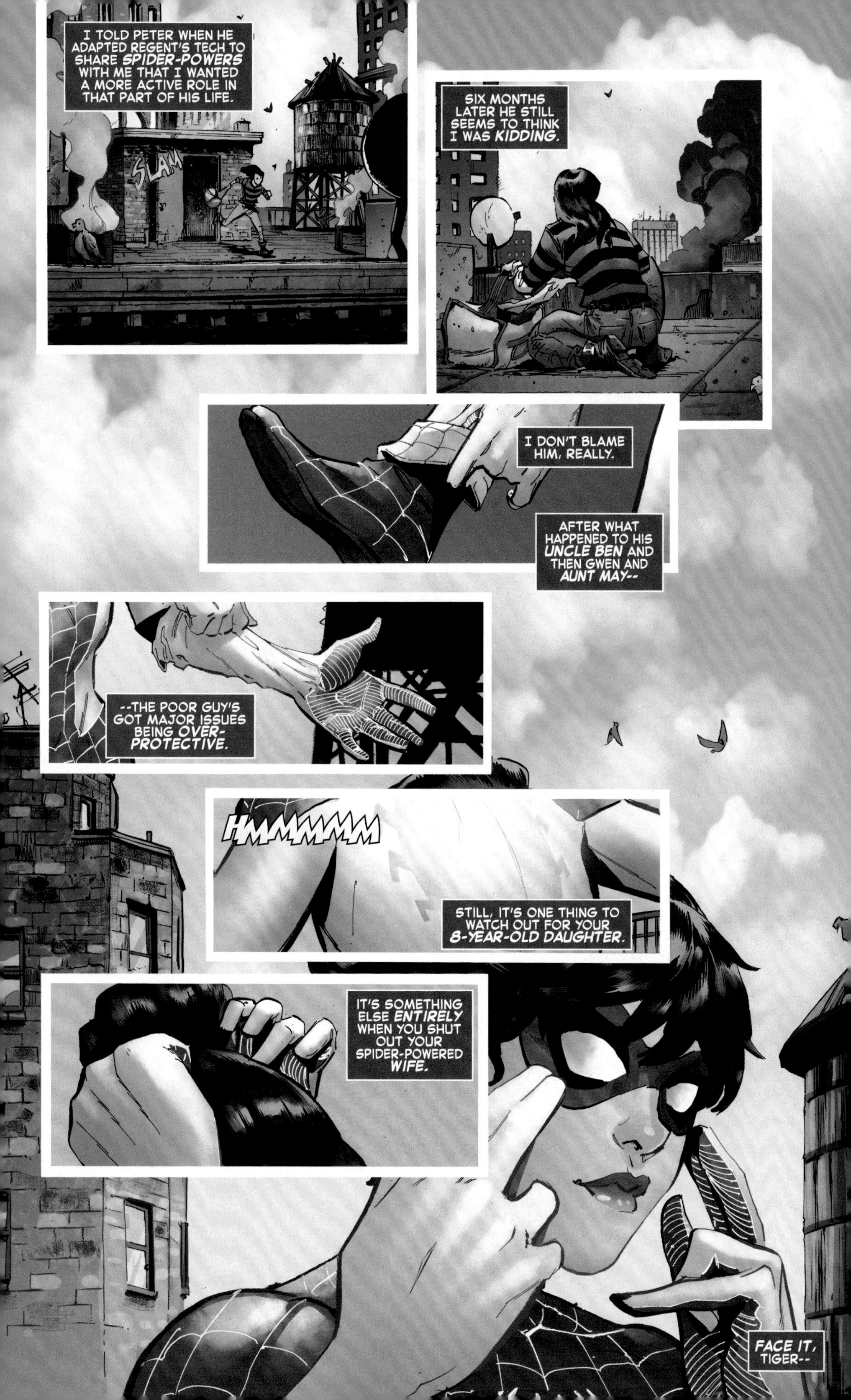
I TOLD PETER WHEN HE ADAPTED REGENT'S TECH TO SHARE SPIDER-POWERS WITH ME THAT I WANTED A MORE ACTIVE ROLE IN THAT PART OF HIS LIFE.
SLAM
SIX MONTHS LATER HE STILL SEEMS TO THINK I WAS KIDDING.
I DON'T BLAME HIM, REALLY.
AFTER WHAT HAPPENED TO HIS UNCLE BEN AND THEN GWEN AND AUNT MAY--
--THE POOR GUY'S GOT MAJOR ISSUES BEING OVER-PROTECTIVE.
HMMMMM
STILL, IT'S ONE THING TO WATCH OUT FOR YOUR 8-YEAR-OLD DAUGHTER.
IT'S SOMETHING ELSE ENTIRELY WHEN YOU SHUT OUT YOUR SPIDER-POWERED WIFE.
FACE IT, TIGER--

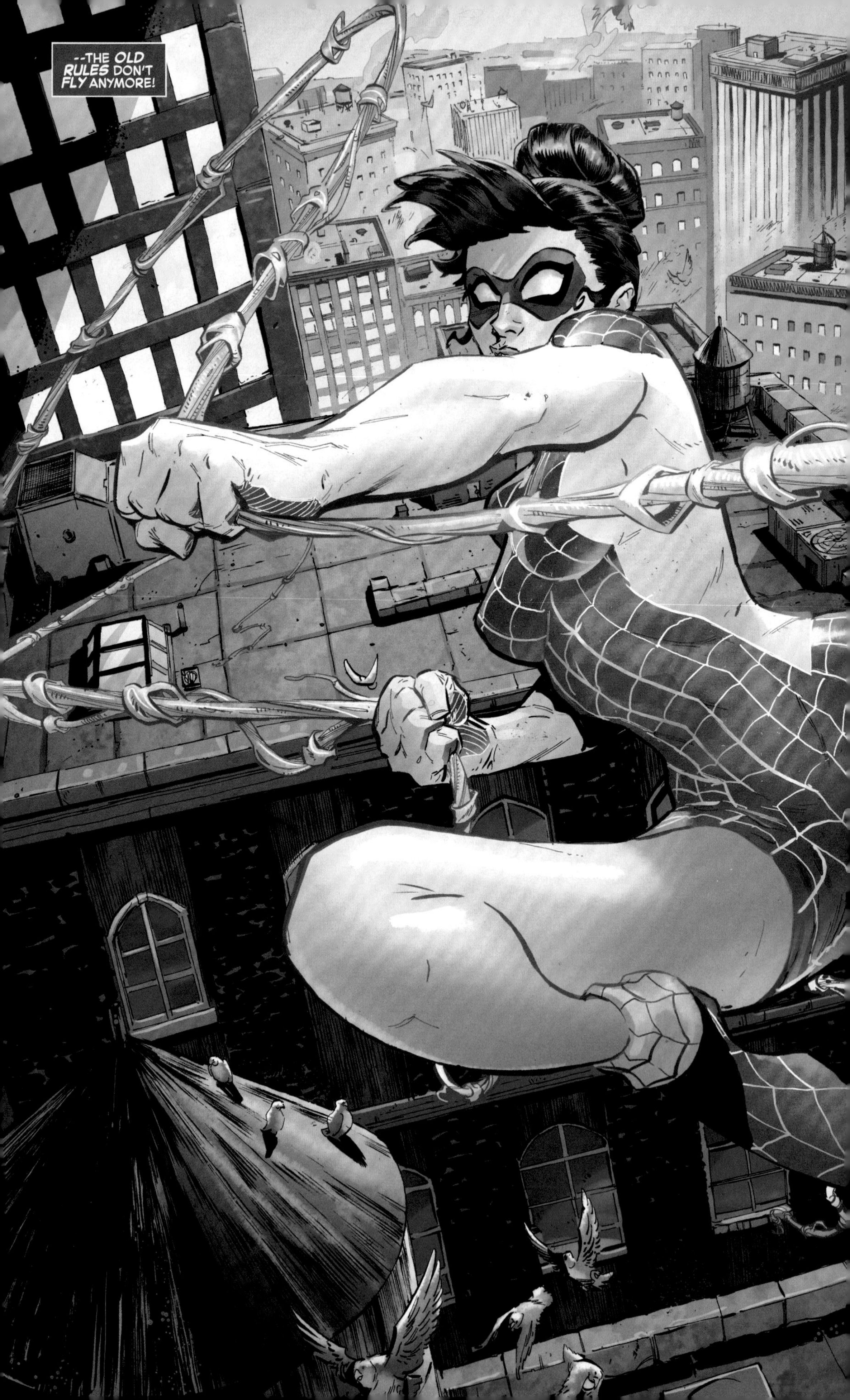
--THE OLD RULES DON'T FLY ANYMORE!

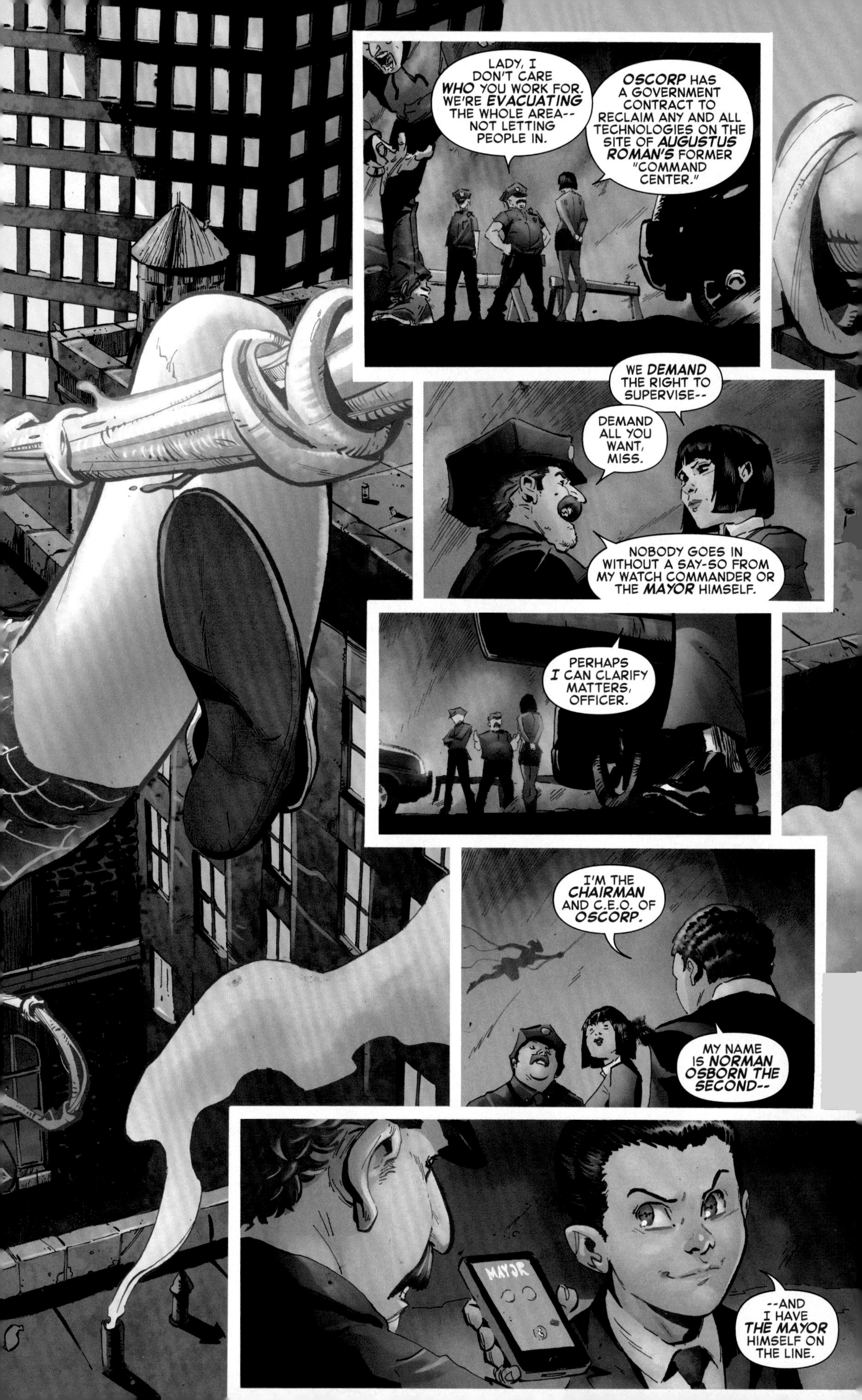
LADY, I DON'T CARE WHO YOU WORK FOR. WE'RE EVACUATING THE WHOLE AREA-- NOT LETTING PEOPLE IN.
OSCORP HAS A GOVERNMENT CONTRACT TO RECLAIM ANY AND ALL TECHNOLOGIES ON THE SITE OF AUGUSTUS ROMAN'S FORMER "COMMAND CENTER."
WE DEMAND THE RIGHT TO SUPERVISE--
DEMAND ALL YOU WANT, MISS.
NOBODY GOES IN WITHOUT A SAY-SO FROM MY WATCH COMMANDER OR THE MAYOR HIMSELF.
PERHAPS I CAN CLARIFY MATTERS, OFFICER.
I'M THE CHAIRMAN AND C.E.O. OF OSCORP.
MY NAME IS NORMAN OSBORN THE SECOND--
MAYOR
--AND I HAVE THE MAYOR HIMSELF ON THE LINE.

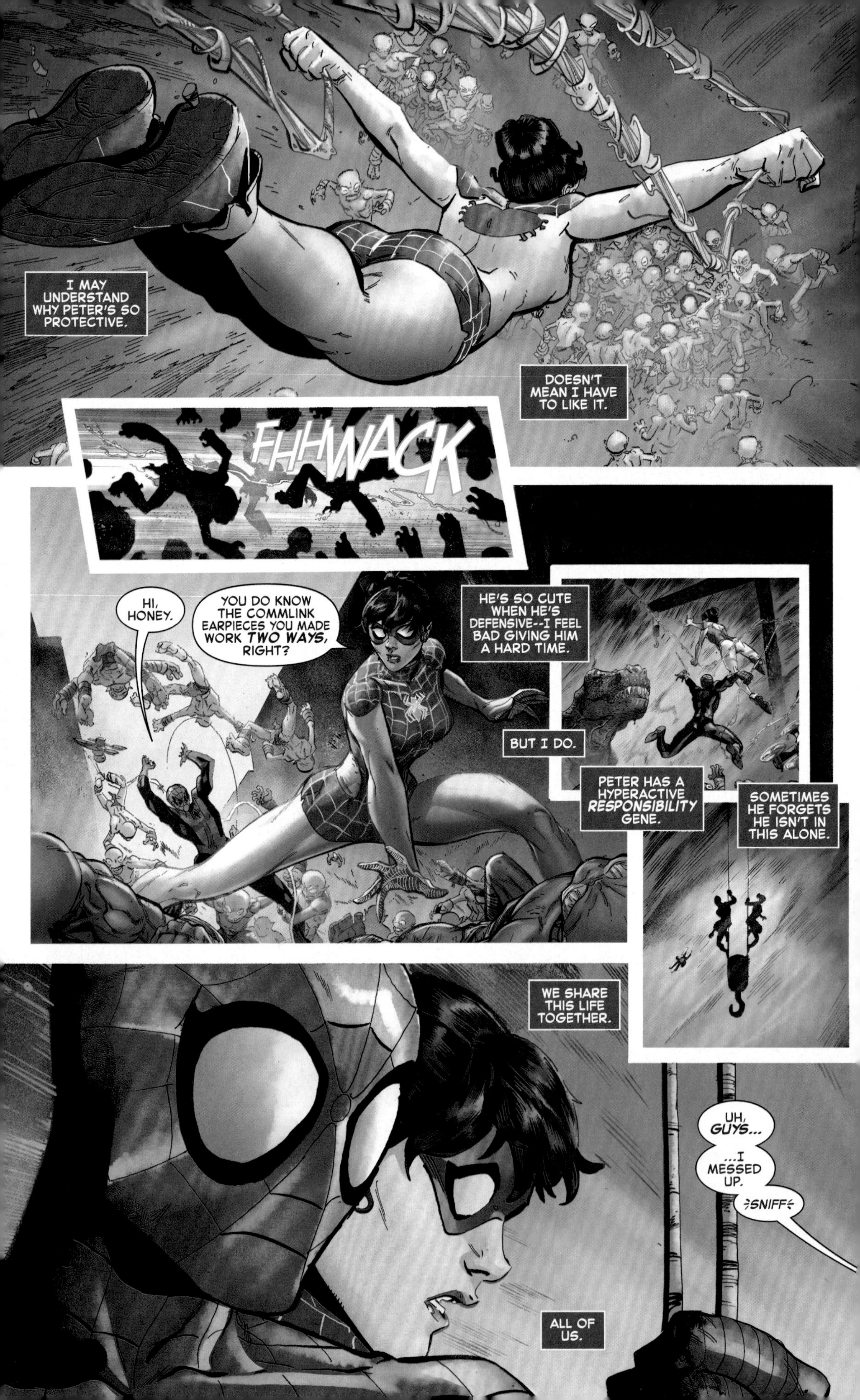
I MAY UNDERSTAND WHY PETER'S SO PROTECTIVE.
DOESN'T MEAN I HAVE TO LIKE IT.
FHHWACK
HI, HONEY.
YOU DO KNOW THE COMMLINK EARPIECES YOU MADE WORK TWO WAYS, RIGHT?
HE'S SO CUTE WHEN HE'S DEFENSIVE--I FEEL BAD GIVING HIM A HARD TIME.
BUT I DO.
PETER HAS A HYPERACTIVE RESPONSIBILITY GENE.
SOMETIMES HE FORGETS HE ISN'T IN THIS ALONE.
WE SHARE THIS LIFE TOGETHER.
UH, GUYS...
...I MESSED UP.
SNIFF
ALL OF US.

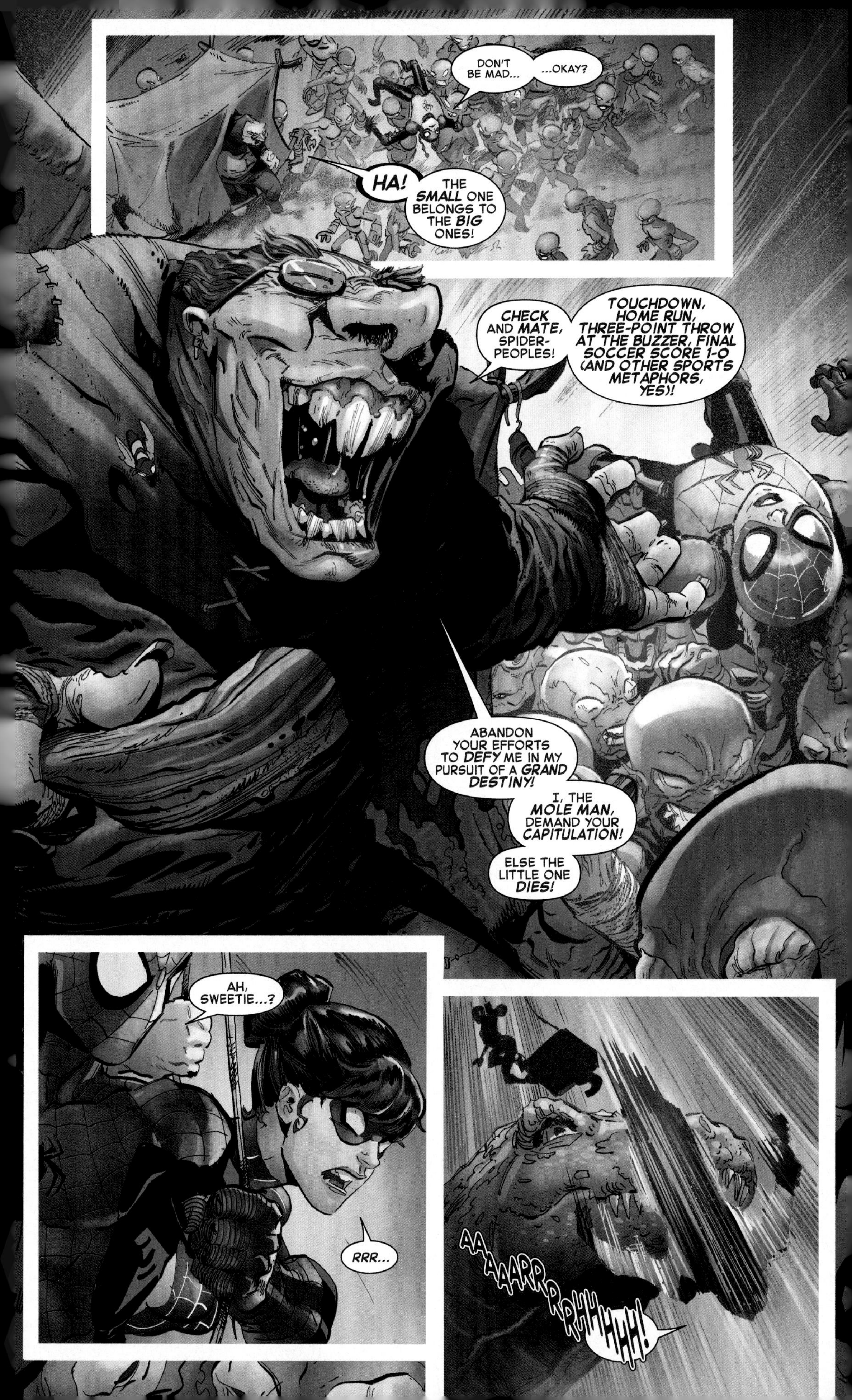
DON'T BE MAD...
...OKAY?
HA!
THE SMALL ONE BELONGS TO THE BIG ONES!
CHECK AND MATE, SPIDER-PEOPLES!
TOUCHDOWN, HOME RUN, THREE-POINT THROW AT THE BUZZER, FINAL SOCCER SCORE 1-0 (AND OTHER SPORTS METAPHORS, YES)!
ABANDON YOUR EFFORTS TO DEFY ME IN MY PURSUIT OF A GRAND DESTINY!
I, THE MOLE MAN, DEMAND YOUR CAPITULATION!
ELSE THE LITTLE ONE DIES!
AH, SWEETIE...?
RRR...
AAAAARRRRHHHHH!

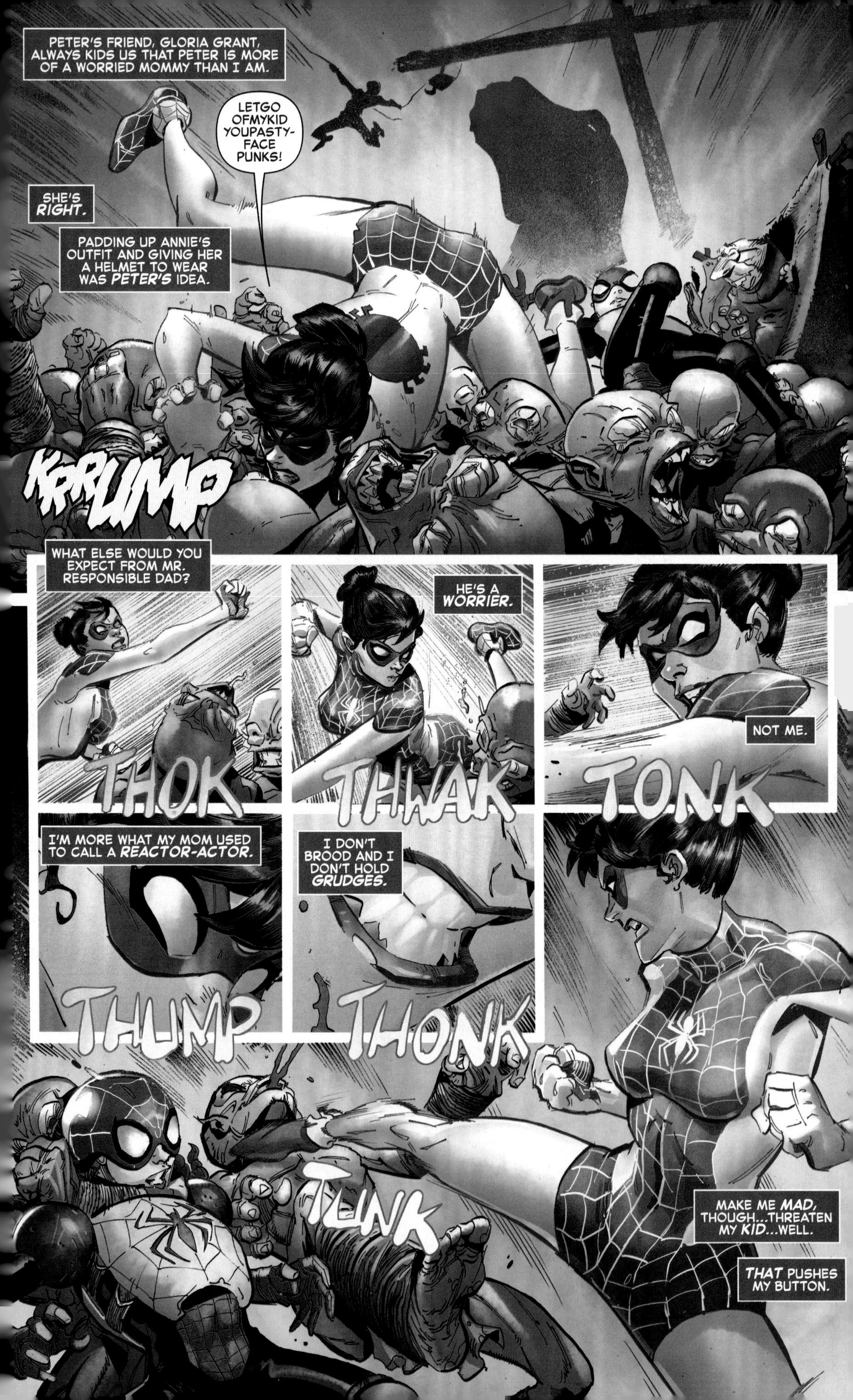
PETER'S FRIEND, GLORIA GRANT, ALWAYS KIDS US THAT PETER IS MORE OF A WORRIED MOMMY THAN I AM.
LETGO OFMYKID YOUPASTY-FACE PUNKS!
SHE'S *RIGHT.*
PADDING UP ANNIE'S OUTFIT AND GIVING HER A HELMET TO WEAR WAS *PETER'S* IDEA.
KRRUMP
WHAT ELSE WOULD YOU EXPECT FROM MR. RESPONSIBLE DAD?
THOK
HE'S A *WORRIER.*
THWAK
NOT ME.
TONK
I'M MORE WHAT MY MOM USED TO CALL A *REACTOR-ACTOR.*
THUMP
I DON'T BROOD AND I DON'T HOLD *GRUDGES.*
THONK
TUNK
MAKE ME *MAD,* THOUGH...THREATEN MY *KID*...WELL.
*THAT* PUSHES MY BUTTON.

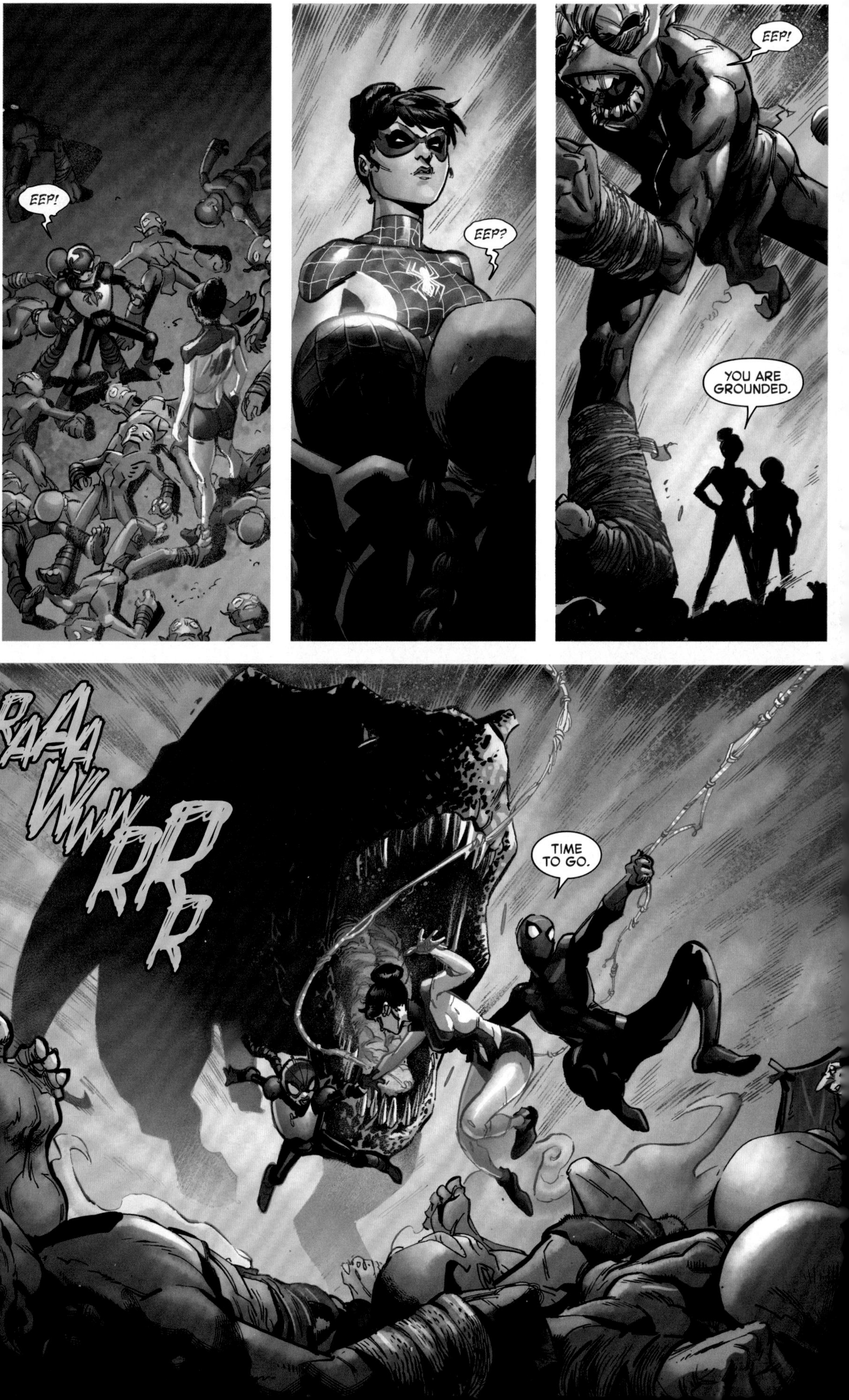
EEP!
EEP?
EEP!
YOU ARE GROUNDED.
RAAAWWWRRRR
TIME TO GO.

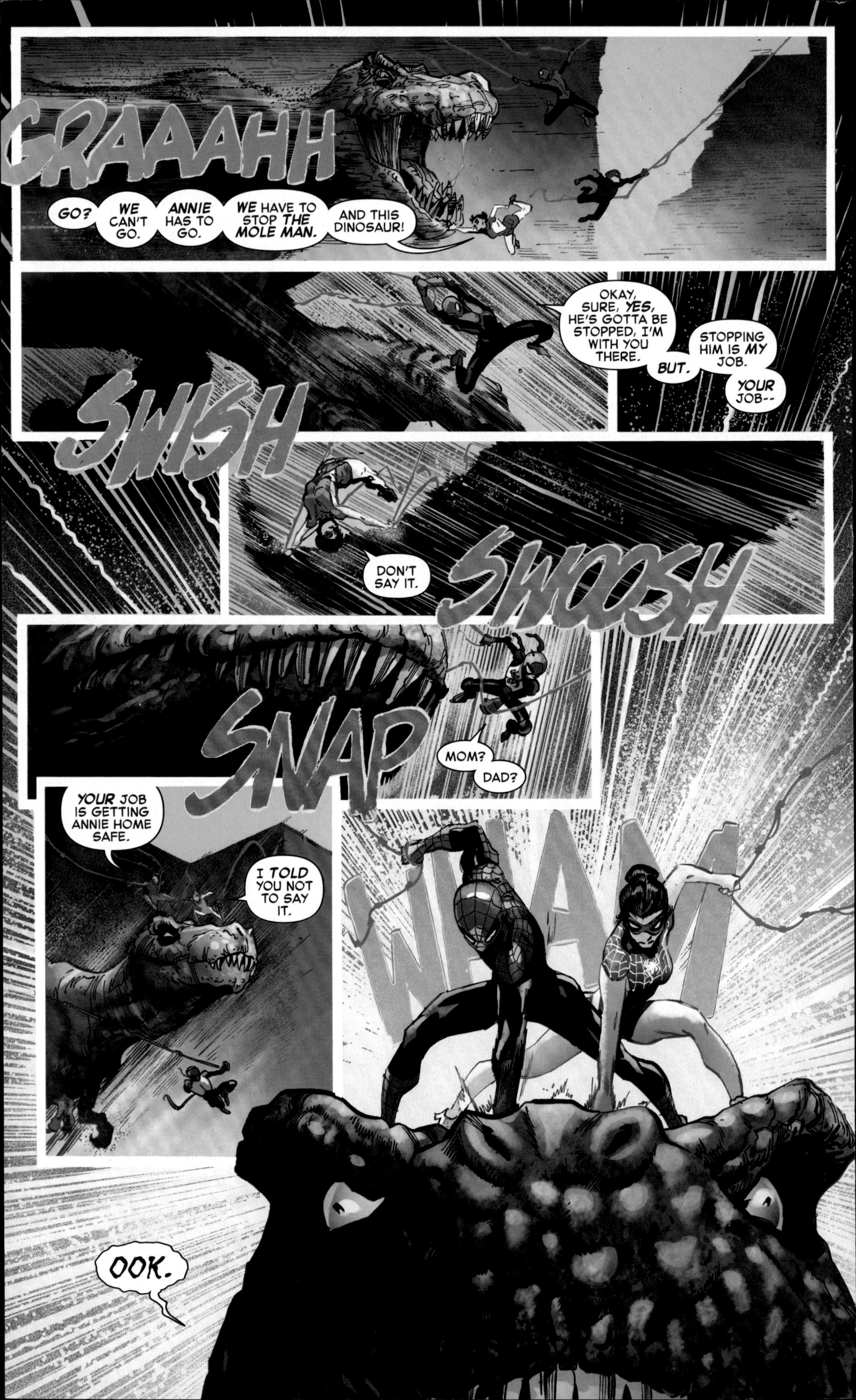
GRAAAHH
GO?
WE CAN'T GO.
ANNIE HAS TO GO.
WE HAVE TO STOP THE MOLE MAN.
AND THIS DINOSAUR!
OKAY, SURE, YES, HE'S GOTTA BE STOPPED, I'M WITH YOU THERE.
BUT.
STOPPING HIM IS MY JOB.
YOUR JOB--
SWISH
DON'T SAY IT.
SWOOSH
SNAP
MOM?
DAD?
YOUR JOB IS GETTING ANNIE HOME SAFE.
I TOLD YOU NOT TO SAY IT.
WHAM
OOK.

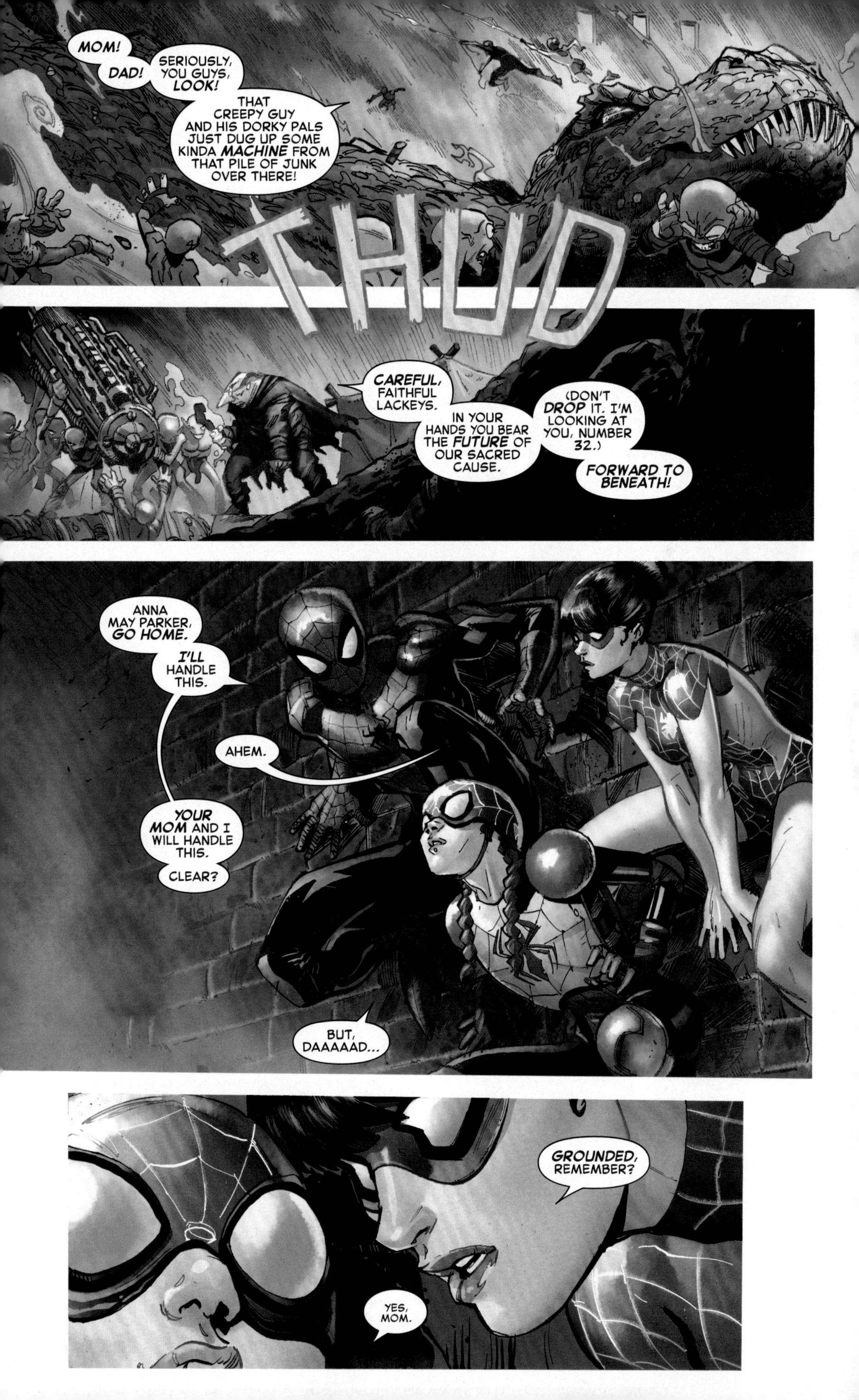
MOM!
DAD!
SERIOUSLY, YOU GUYS, LOOK!
THAT CREEPY GUY AND HIS DORKY PALS JUST DUG UP SOME KINDA MACHINE FROM THAT PILE OF JUNK OVER THERE!
THUD
CAREFUL, FAITHFUL LACKEYS.
IN YOUR HANDS YOU BEAR THE FUTURE OF OUR SACRED CAUSE.
(DON'T DROP IT. I'M LOOKING AT YOU, NUMBER 32.)
FORWARD TO BENEATH!
ANNA MAY PARKER, GO HOME.
I'LL HANDLE THIS.
AHEM.
YOUR MOM AND I WILL HANDLE THIS.
CLEAR?
BUT, DAAAAAD...
GROUNDED, REMEMBER?
YES, MOM.

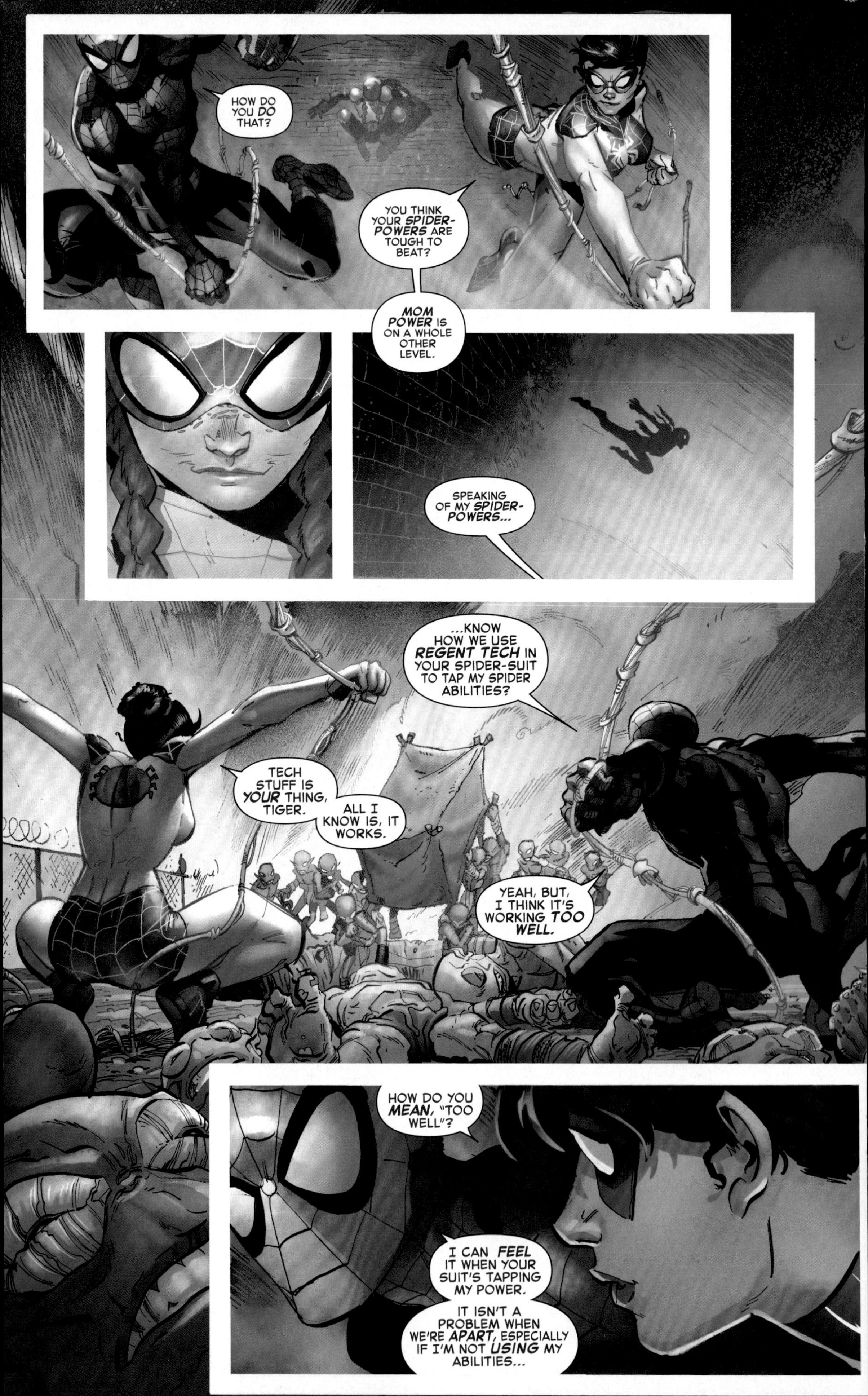
HOW DO YOU DO THAT?
YOU THINK YOUR SPIDER-POWERS ARE TOUGH TO BEAT?
MOM POWER IS ON A WHOLE OTHER LEVEL.
SPEAKING OF MY SPIDER-POWERS...
...KNOW HOW WE USE REGENT TECH IN YOUR SPIDER-SUIT TO TAP MY SPIDER ABILITIES?
TECH STUFF IS YOUR THING, TIGER.
ALL I KNOW IS, IT WORKS.
YEAH, BUT, I THINK IT'S WORKING TOO WELL.
HOW DO YOU MEAN, "TOO WELL"?
I CAN FEEL IT WHEN YOUR SUIT'S TAPPING MY POWER.
IT ISN'T A PROBLEM WHEN WE'RE APART, ESPECIALLY IF I'M NOT USING MY ABILITIES...

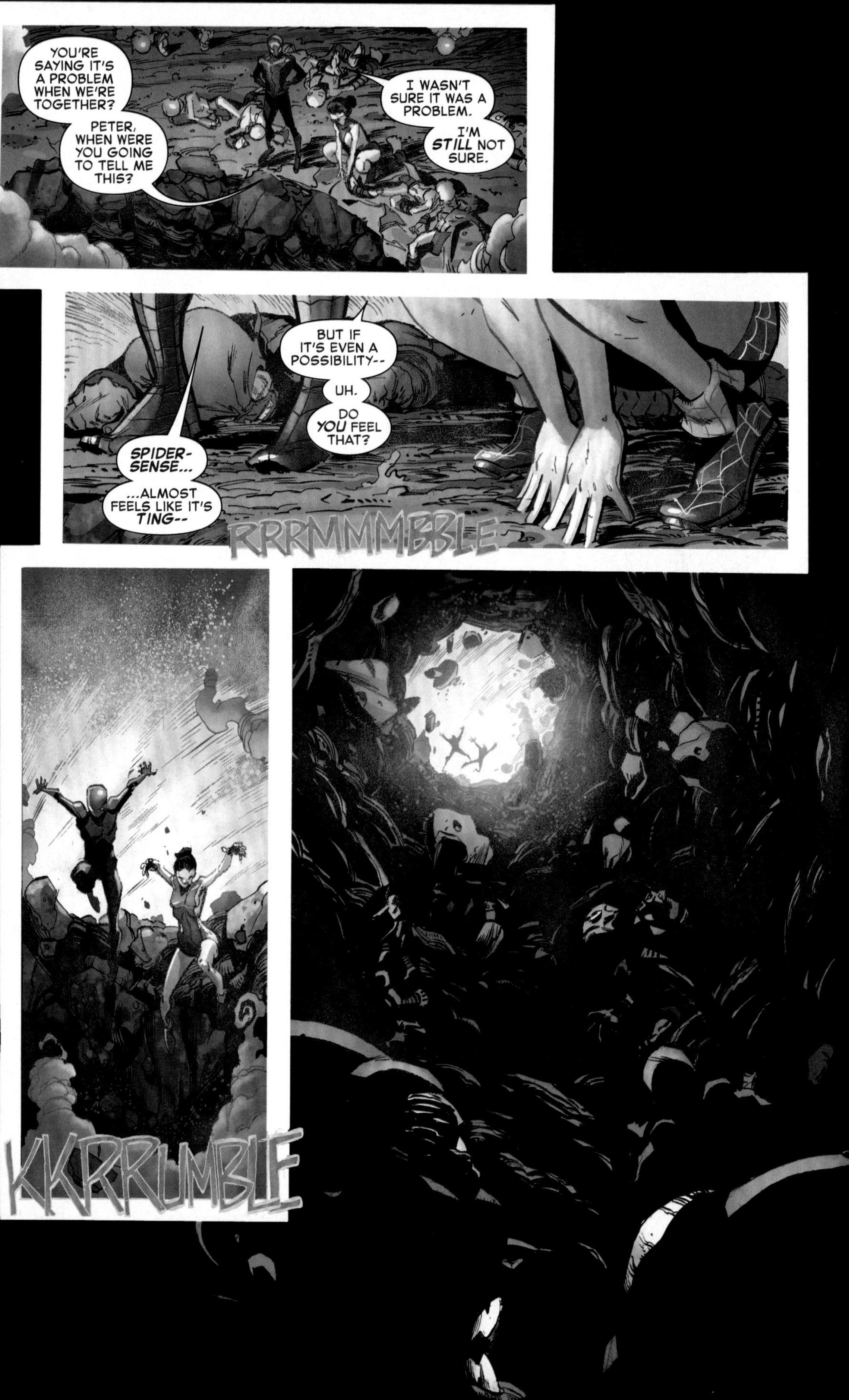
YOU'RE SAYING IT'S A PROBLEM WHEN WE'RE TOGETHER?
PETER, WHEN WERE YOU GOING TO TELL ME THIS?
I WASN'T SURE IT WAS A PROBLEM.
I'M STILL NOT SURE.
BUT IF IT'S EVEN A POSSIBILITY--
UH.
DO YOU FEEL THAT?
SPIDER-SENSE...
...ALMOST FEELS LIKE IT'S TING--
RRRMMMBBLE
KKRRUMBLE

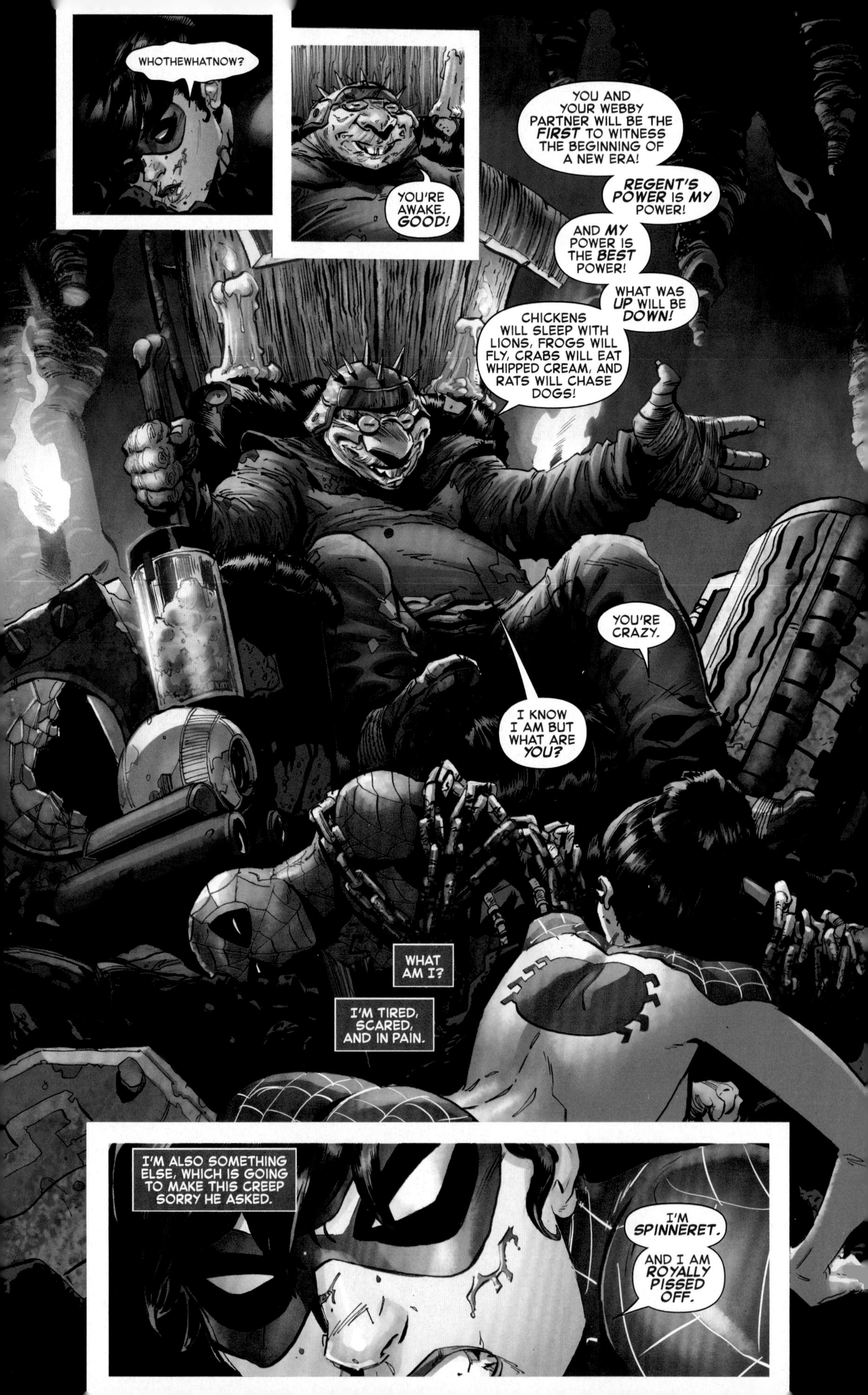
WHOTHEWHATNOW?
YOU'RE AWAKE. GOOD!
YOU AND YOUR WEBBY PARTNER WILL BE THE FIRST TO WITNESS THE BEGINNING OF A NEW ERA!
REGENT'S POWER IS MY POWER!
AND MY POWER IS THE BEST POWER!
WHAT WAS UP WILL BE DOWN!
CHICKENS WILL SLEEP WITH LIONS, FROGS WILL FLY, CRABS WILL EAT WHIPPED CREAM, AND RATS WILL CHASE DOGS!
YOU'RE CRAZY.
I KNOW I AM BUT WHAT ARE YOU?
WHAT AM I?
I'M TIRED, SCARED, AND IN PAIN.
I'M ALSO SOMETHING ELSE, WHICH IS GOING TO MAKE THIS CREEP SORRY HE ASKED.
I'M SPINNERET.
AND I AM ROYALLY PISSED OFF.

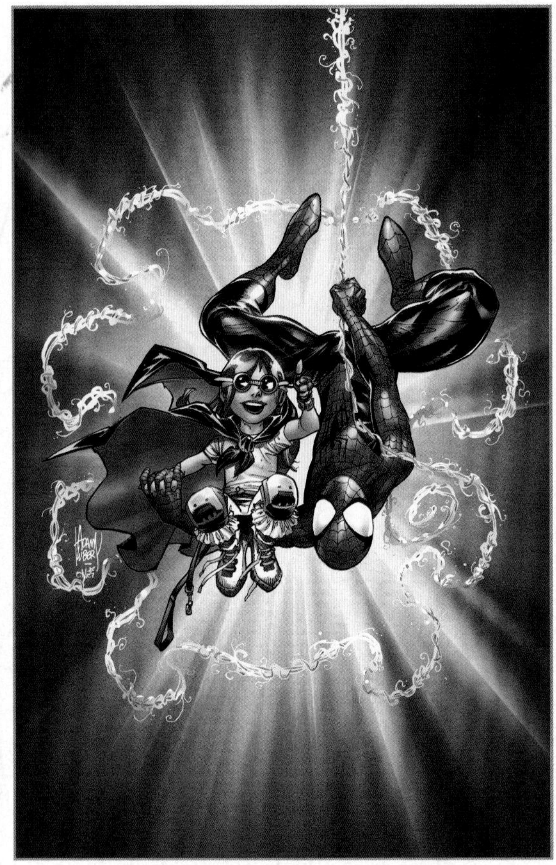

1 variant by **ADAM KUBERT** & **NEI RUFFINO**

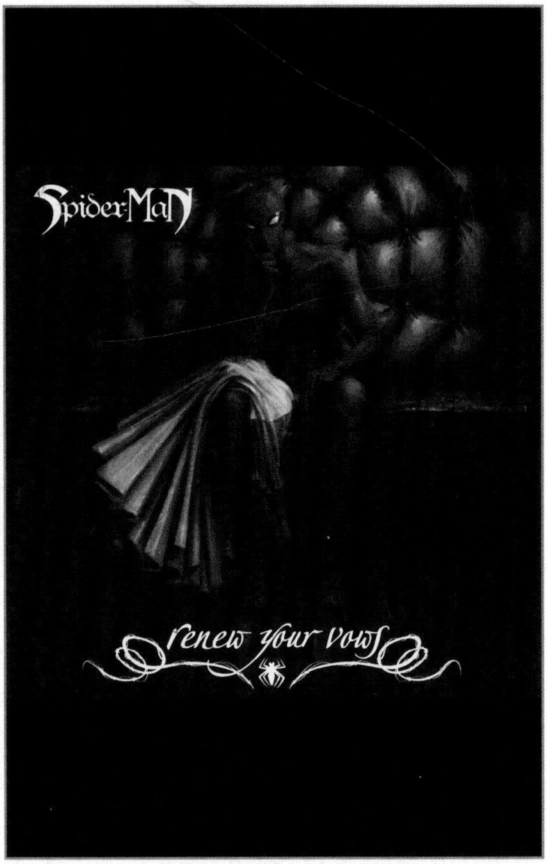

Spider-Man
renew your vows


1 hip-hop variant by **SAM SPRATT**

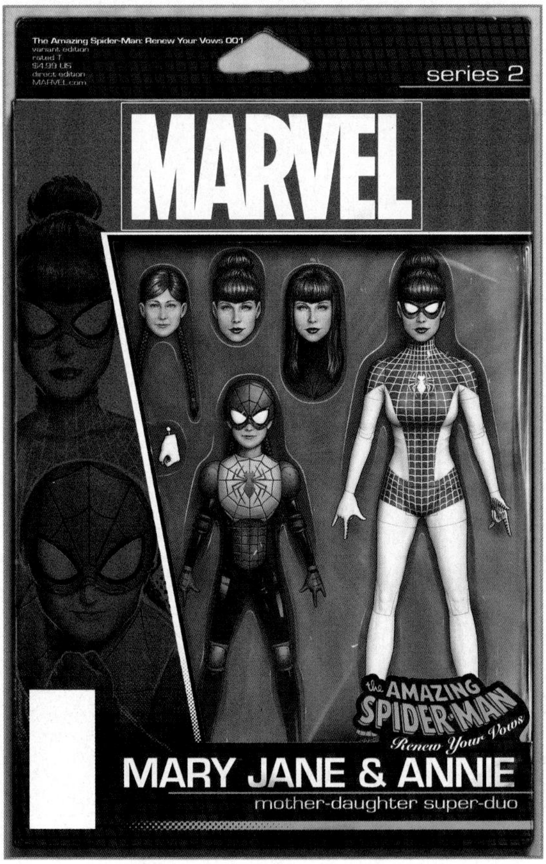

The Amazing Spider-Man: Renew Your Vows 001
variant edition
rated T
$4.99 US
direct edition
MARVEL.com
series 2
MARVEL
the AMAZING SPIDER-MAN
Renew Your Vows
MARY JANE & ANNIE
mother-daughter super-duo


1 action figure variant by **JOHN TYLER CHRISTOPHER**

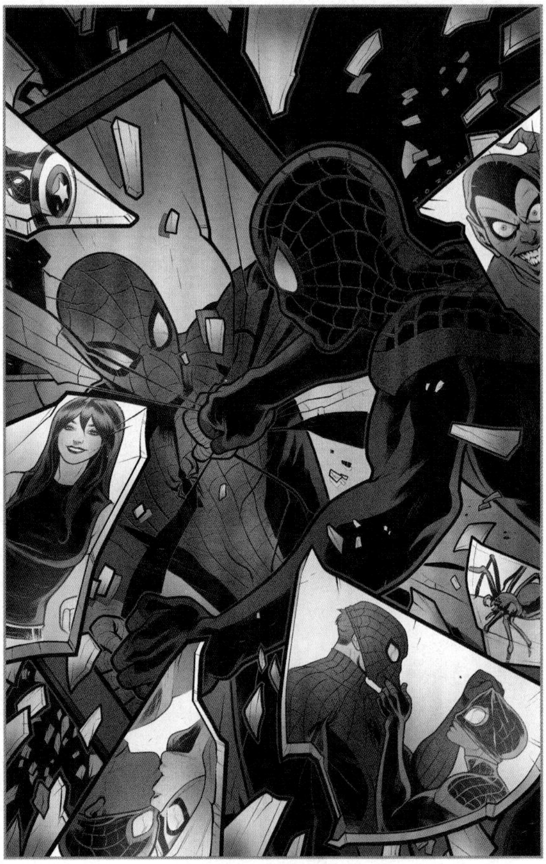

1 variant by **ELIZABETH TORQUE**

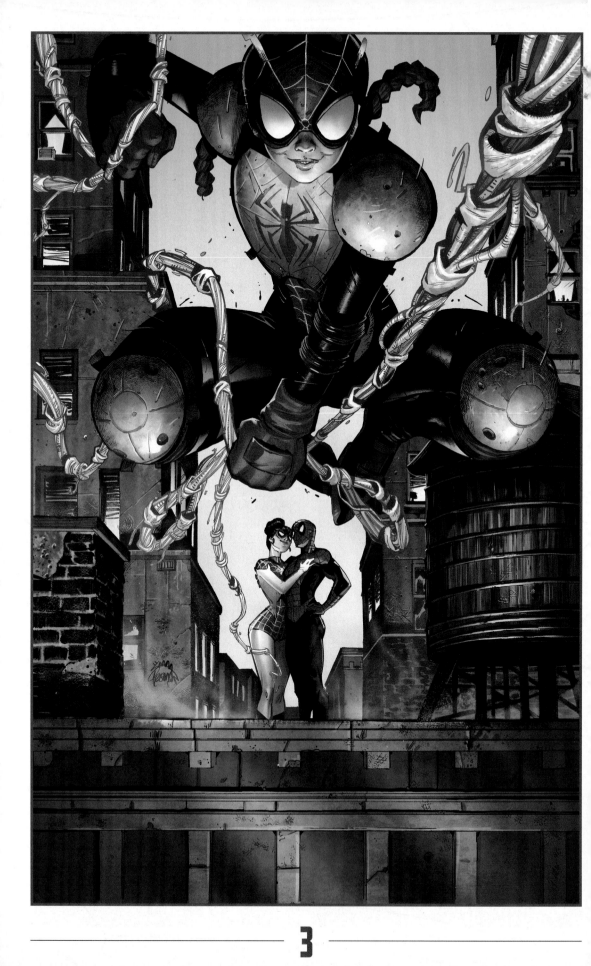

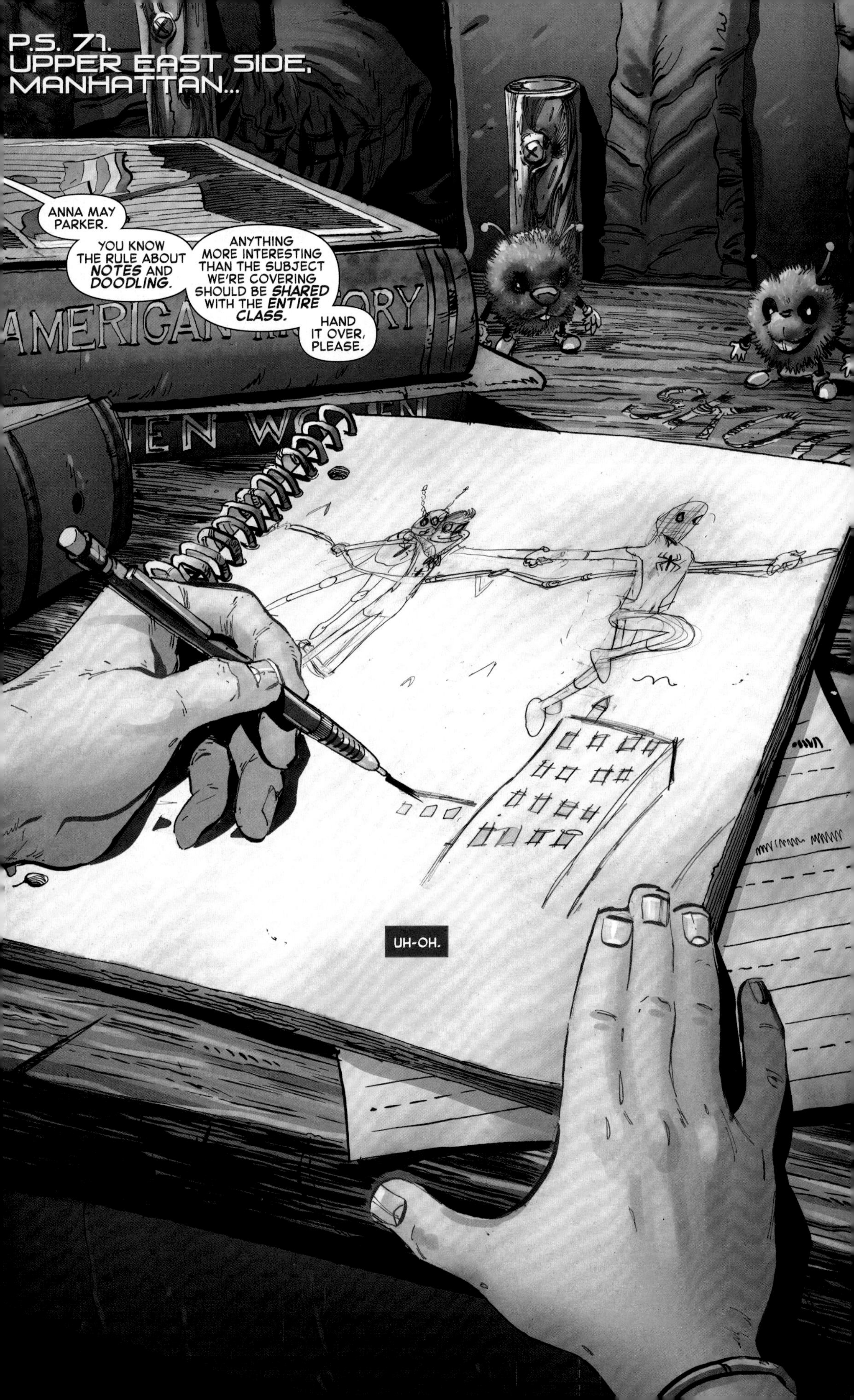

P.S. 71. UPPER EAST SIDE, MANHATTAN...
ANNA MAY PARKER.
YOU KNOW THE RULE ABOUT NOTES AND DOODLING.
ANYTHING MORE INTERESTING THAN THE SUBJECT WE'RE COVERING SHOULD BE SHARED WITH THE ENTIRE CLASS.
HAND IT OVER, PLEASE.
UH-OH.

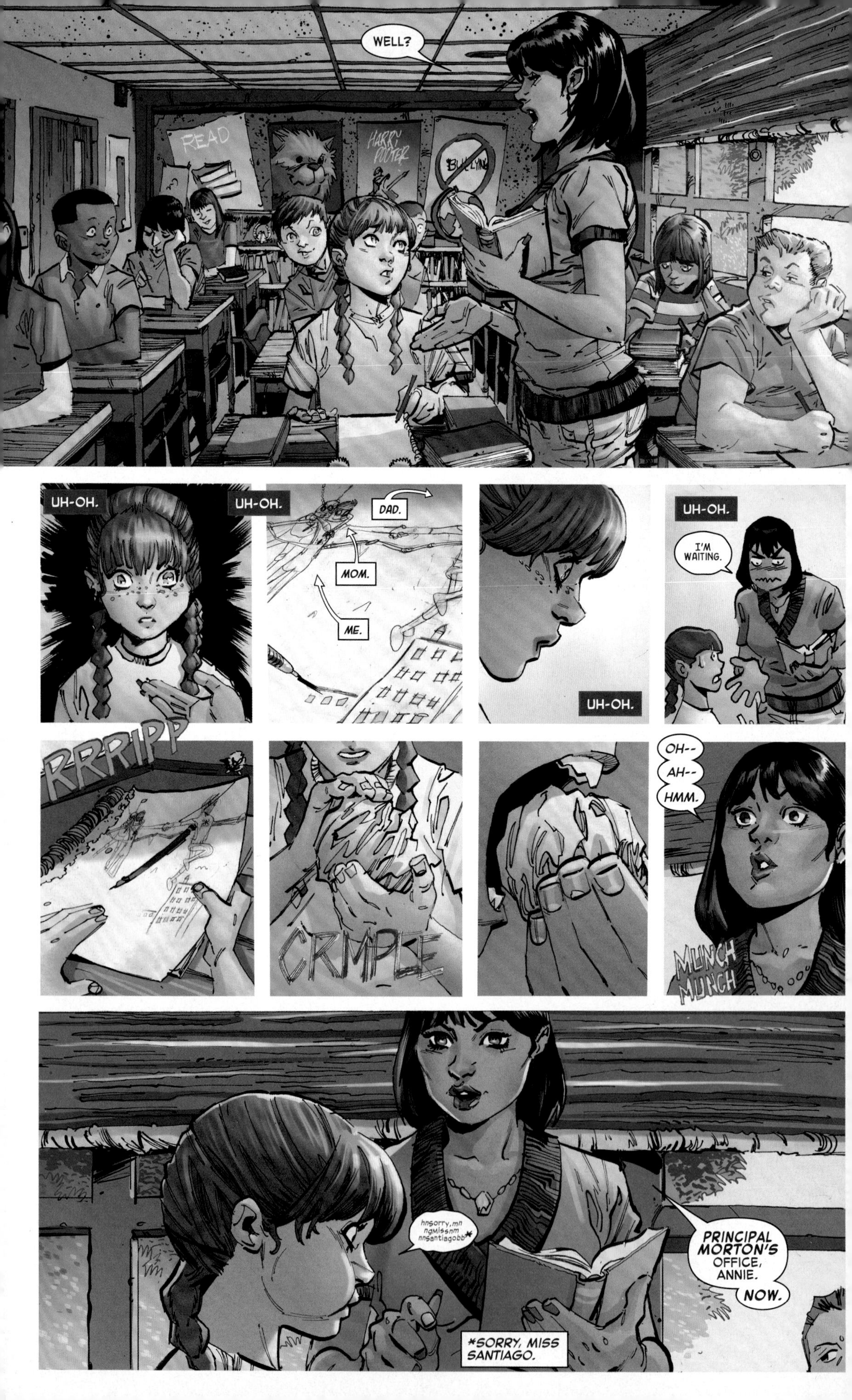
WELL?
READ
HARRY POOTER
BULLYING
UH-OH.
UH-OH.
DAD.
MOM.
ME.
UH-OH.
UH-OH.
I'M WAITING.
RRRIPP
CRMPLE
OH--
AH--
HMM.
MUNCH MUNCH
hnsorry,mn ngmissnm nnsantiagobb*
PRINCIPAL MORTON'S OFFICE, ANNIE.
NOW.
*SORRY, MISS SANTIAGO.

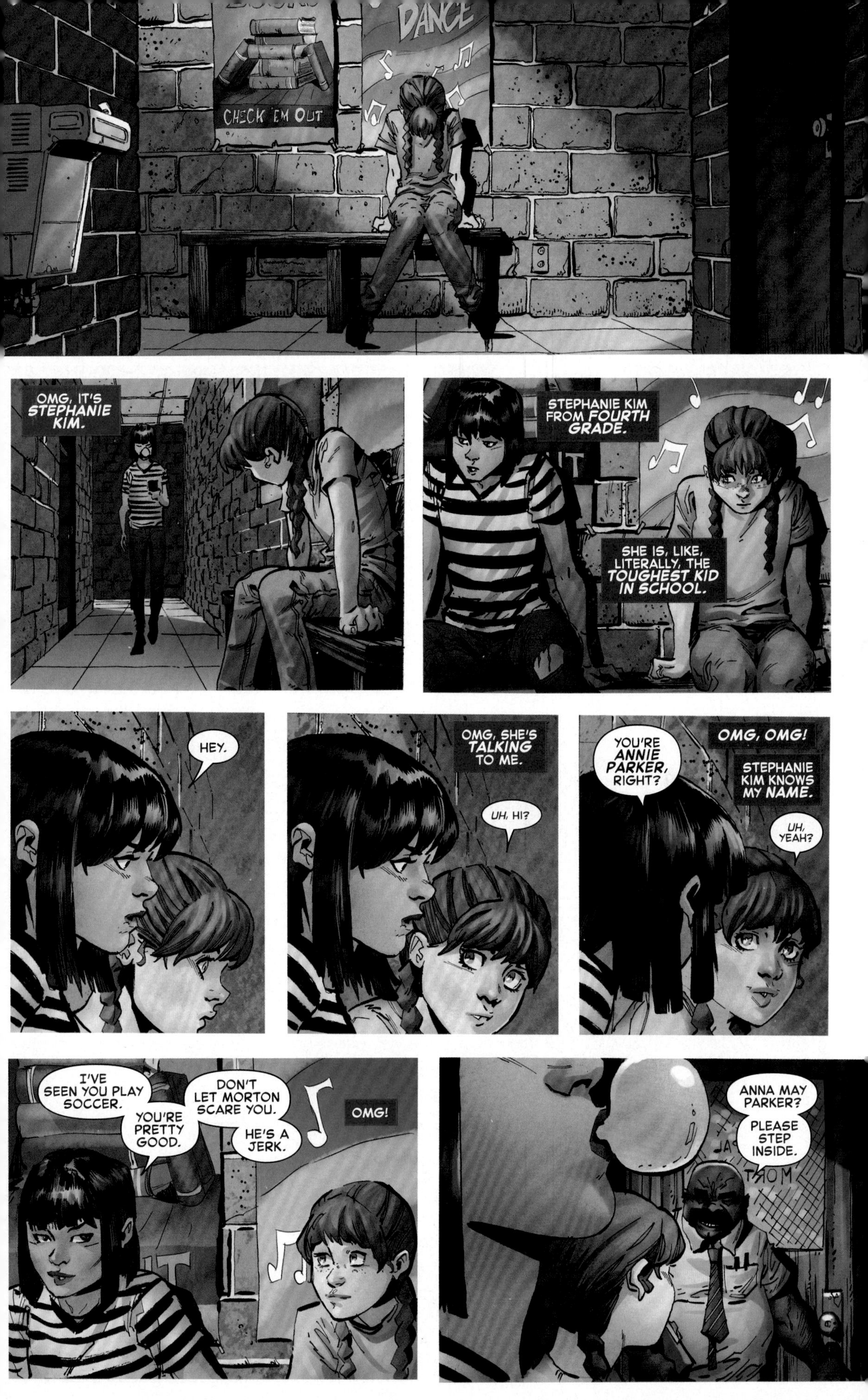
CHECK 'EM OUT
DANCE
OMG, IT'S STEPHANIE KIM.
STEPHANIE KIM FROM FOURTH GRADE.
SHE IS, LIKE, LITERALLY, THE TOUGHEST KID IN SCHOOL.
HEY.
OMG, SHE'S TALKING TO ME.
UH, HI?
YOU'RE ANNIE PARKER, RIGHT?
OMG, OMG!
STEPHANIE KIM KNOWS MY NAME.
UH, YEAH?
I'VE SEEN YOU PLAY SOCCER.
YOU'RE PRETTY GOOD.
DON'T LET MORTON SCARE YOU.
HE'S A JERK.
OMG!
ANNA MAY PARKER?
PLEASE STEP INSIDE.

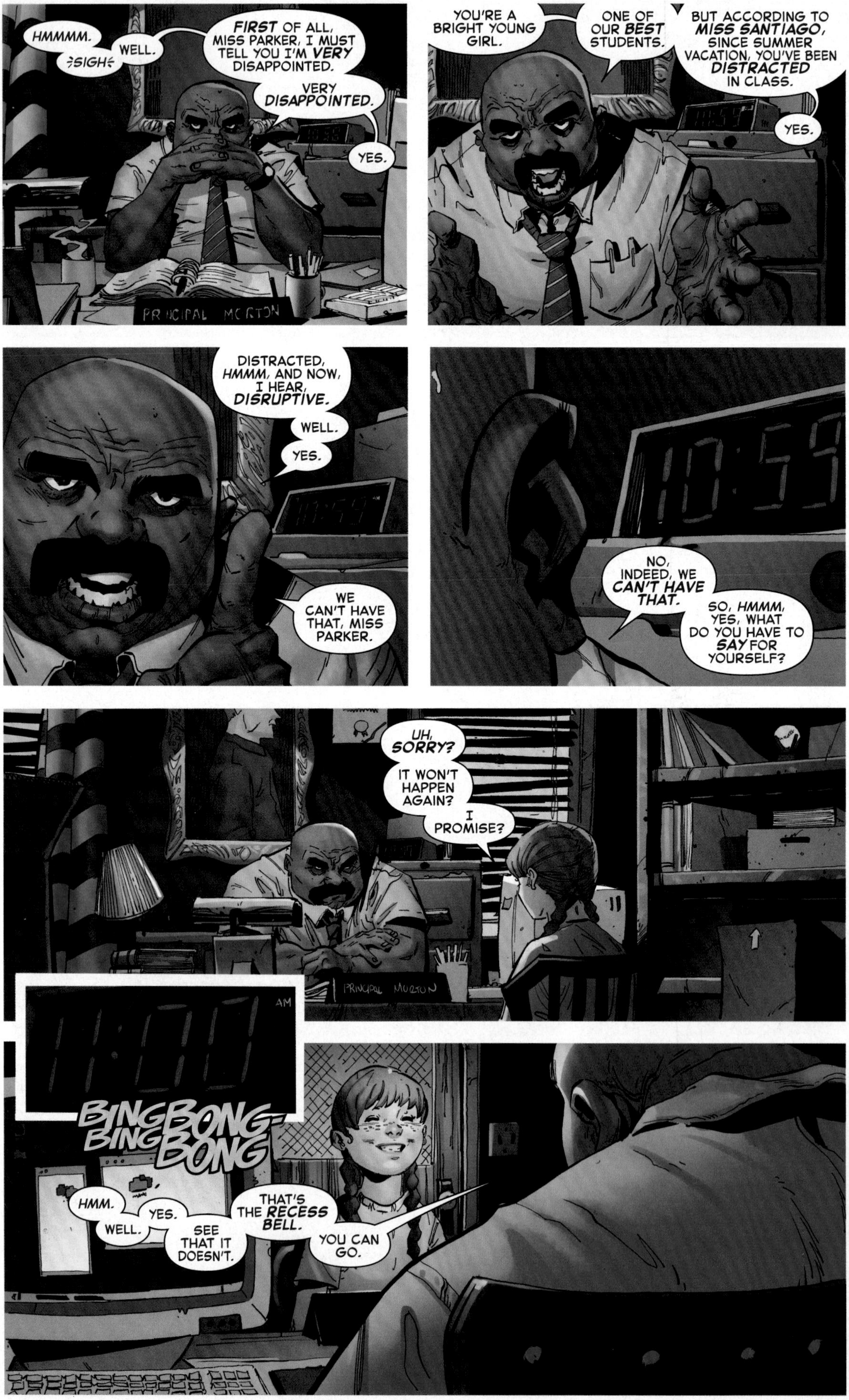
HMMMM.
>SIGH<
WELL.
FIRST OF ALL, MISS PARKER, I MUST TELL YOU I'M VERY DISAPPOINTED.
VERY DISAPPOINTED.
YES.
PRINCIPAL MORTON
YOU'RE A BRIGHT YOUNG GIRL.
ONE OF OUR BEST STUDENTS.
BUT ACCORDING TO MISS SANTIAGO, SINCE SUMMER VACATION, YOU'VE BEEN DISTRACTED IN CLASS.
YES.
DISTRACTED, HMMM, AND NOW, I HEAR, DISRUPTIVE.
WELL.
YES.
WE CAN'T HAVE THAT, MISS PARKER.
NO, INDEED, WE CAN'T HAVE THAT.
SO, HMMM, YES, WHAT DO YOU HAVE TO SAY FOR YOURSELF?
UH, SORRY?
IT WON'T HAPPEN AGAIN?
I PROMISE?
PRINCIPAL MORTON
AM
BINGBONG BINGBONG
HMM.
WELL.
YES.
SEE THAT IT DOESN'T.
THAT'S THE RECESS BELL.
YOU CAN GO.

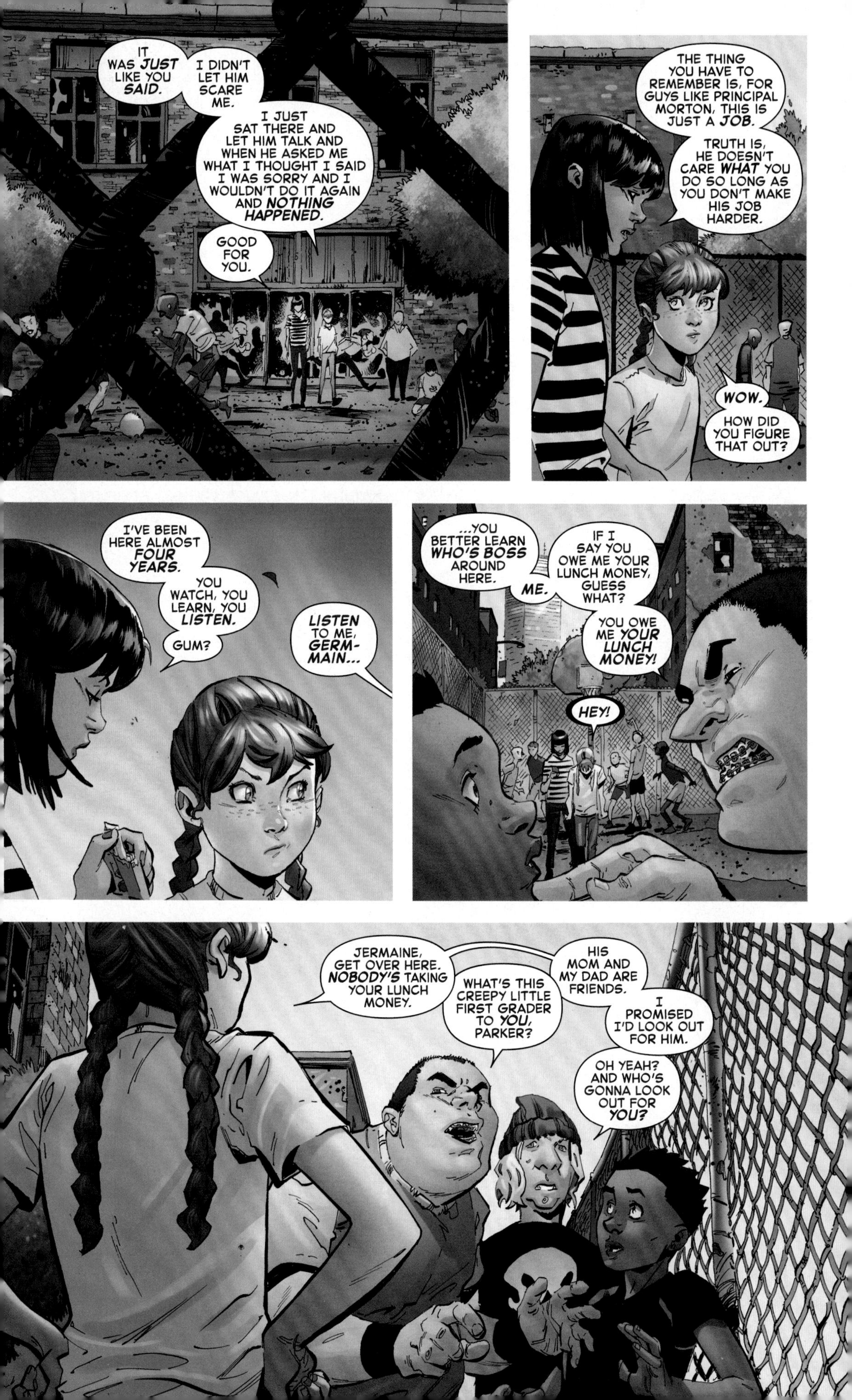
IT WAS JUST LIKE YOU SAID.
I DIDN'T LET HIM SCARE ME.
I JUST SAT THERE AND LET HIM TALK AND WHEN HE ASKED ME WHAT I THOUGHT I SAID I WAS SORRY AND I WOULDN'T DO IT AGAIN AND NOTHING HAPPENED.
GOOD FOR YOU.
THE THING YOU HAVE TO REMEMBER IS, FOR GUYS LIKE PRINCIPAL MORTON, THIS IS JUST A JOB.
TRUTH IS, HE DOESN'T CARE WHAT YOU DO SO LONG AS YOU DON'T MAKE HIS JOB HARDER.
WOW.
HOW DID YOU FIGURE THAT OUT?
I'VE BEEN HERE ALMOST FOUR YEARS.
YOU WATCH, YOU LEARN, YOU LISTEN.
GUM?
LISTEN TO ME, GERMMAIN...
...YOU BETTER LEARN WHO'S BOSS AROUND HERE.
ME.
IF I SAY YOU OWE ME YOUR LUNCH MONEY, GUESS WHAT?
YOU OWE ME YOUR LUNCH MONEY!
HEY!
JERMAINE, GET OVER HERE. NOBODY'S TAKING YOUR LUNCH MONEY.
WHAT'S THIS CREEPY LITTLE FIRST GRADER TO YOU, PARKER?
HIS MOM AND MY DAD ARE FRIENDS.
I PROMISED I'D LOOK OUT FOR HIM.
OH YEAH? AND WHO'S GONNA LOOK OUT FOR YOU?

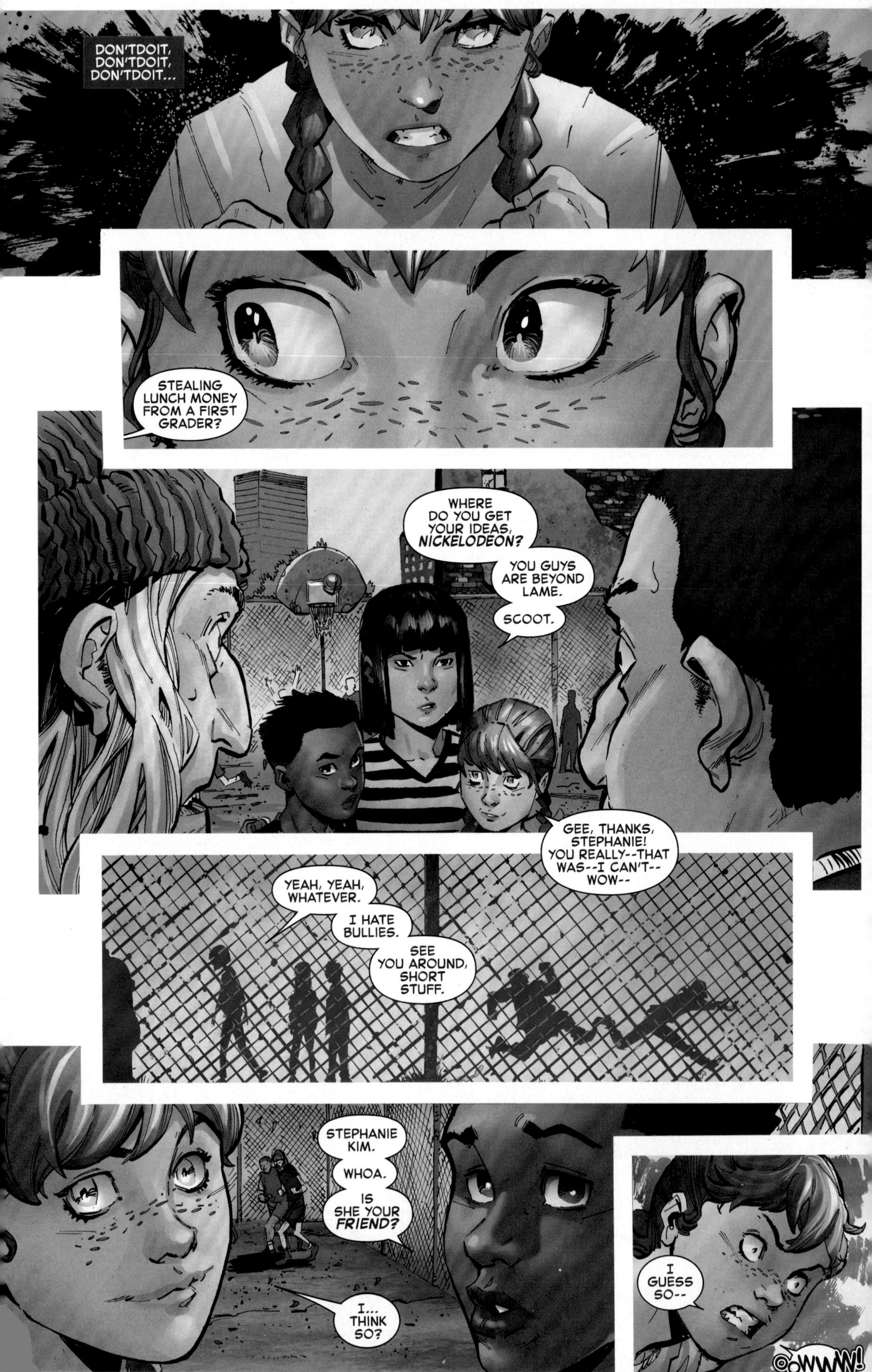
DON'TDOIT, DON'TDOIT, DON'TDOIT...
STEALING LUNCH MONEY FROM A FIRST GRADER?
WHERE DO YOU GET YOUR IDEAS, *NICKELODEON?*
YOU GUYS ARE BEYOND LAME.
SCOOT.
GEE, THANKS, STEPHANIE! YOU REALLY--THAT WAS--I CAN'T-- WOW--
YEAH, YEAH, WHATEVER.
I HATE BULLIES.
SEE YOU AROUND, SHORT STUFF.
STEPHANIE KIM.
WHOA.
IS SHE YOUR *FRIEND?*
I... THINK SO?
I GUESS SO--
OWWW!

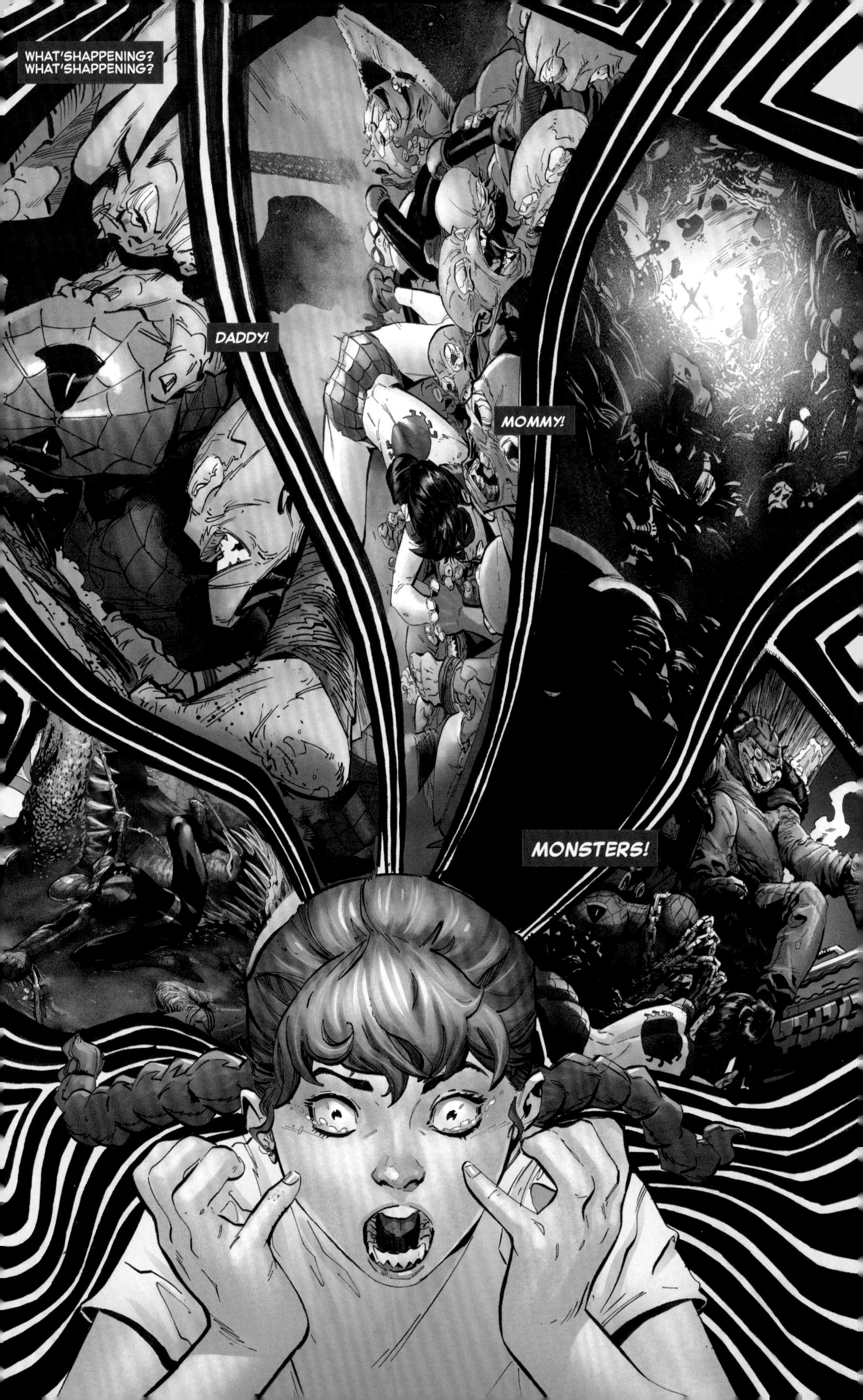
WHAT'SHAPPENING?
WHAT'SHAPPENING?
DADDY!
MOMMY!
MONSTERS!

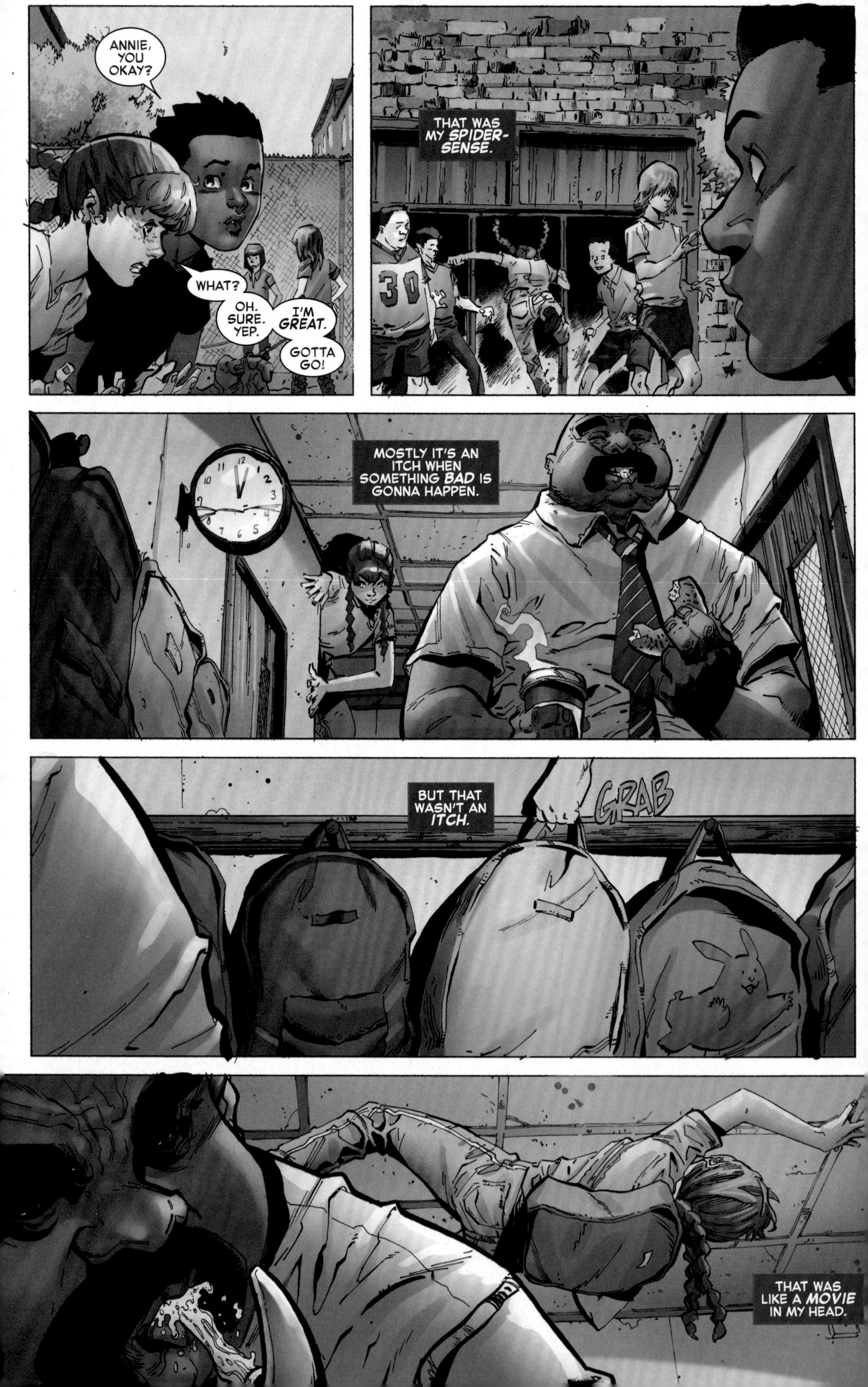
ANNIE, YOU OKAY?
WHAT?
OH. SURE. YEP.
I'M GREAT.
GOTTA GO!
THAT WAS MY SPIDER-SENSE.
MOSTLY IT'S AN ITCH WHEN SOMETHING BAD IS GONNA HAPPEN.
BUT THAT WASN'T AN ITCH.
GRAB
THAT WAS LIKE A MOVIE IN MY HEAD.

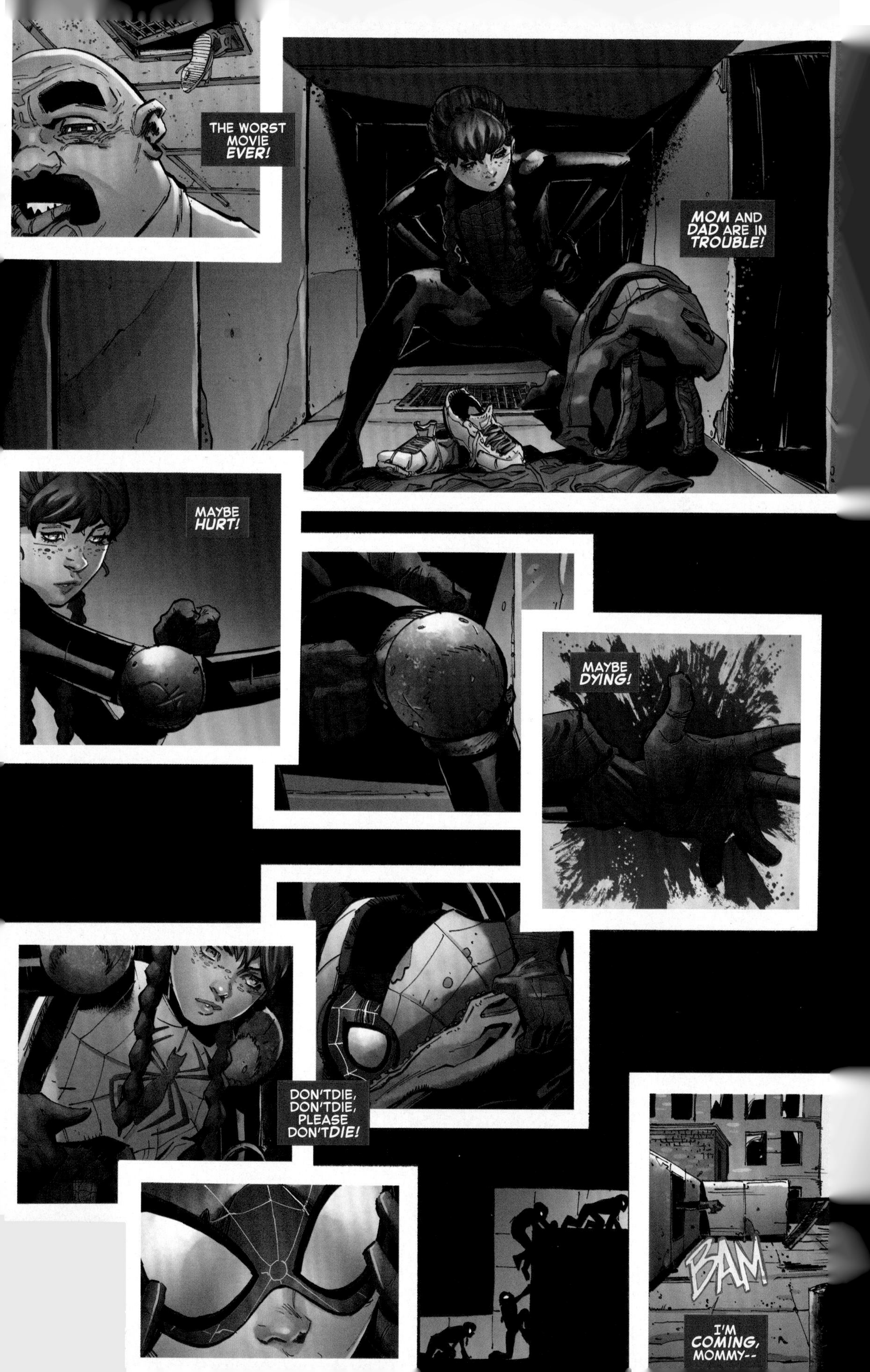
THE WORST MOVIE EVER!
MOM AND DAD ARE IN TROUBLE!
MAYBE HURT!
MAYBE DYING!
DON'TDIE, DON'TDIE, PLEASE DON'TDIE!
BAM
I'M COMING, MOMMY--

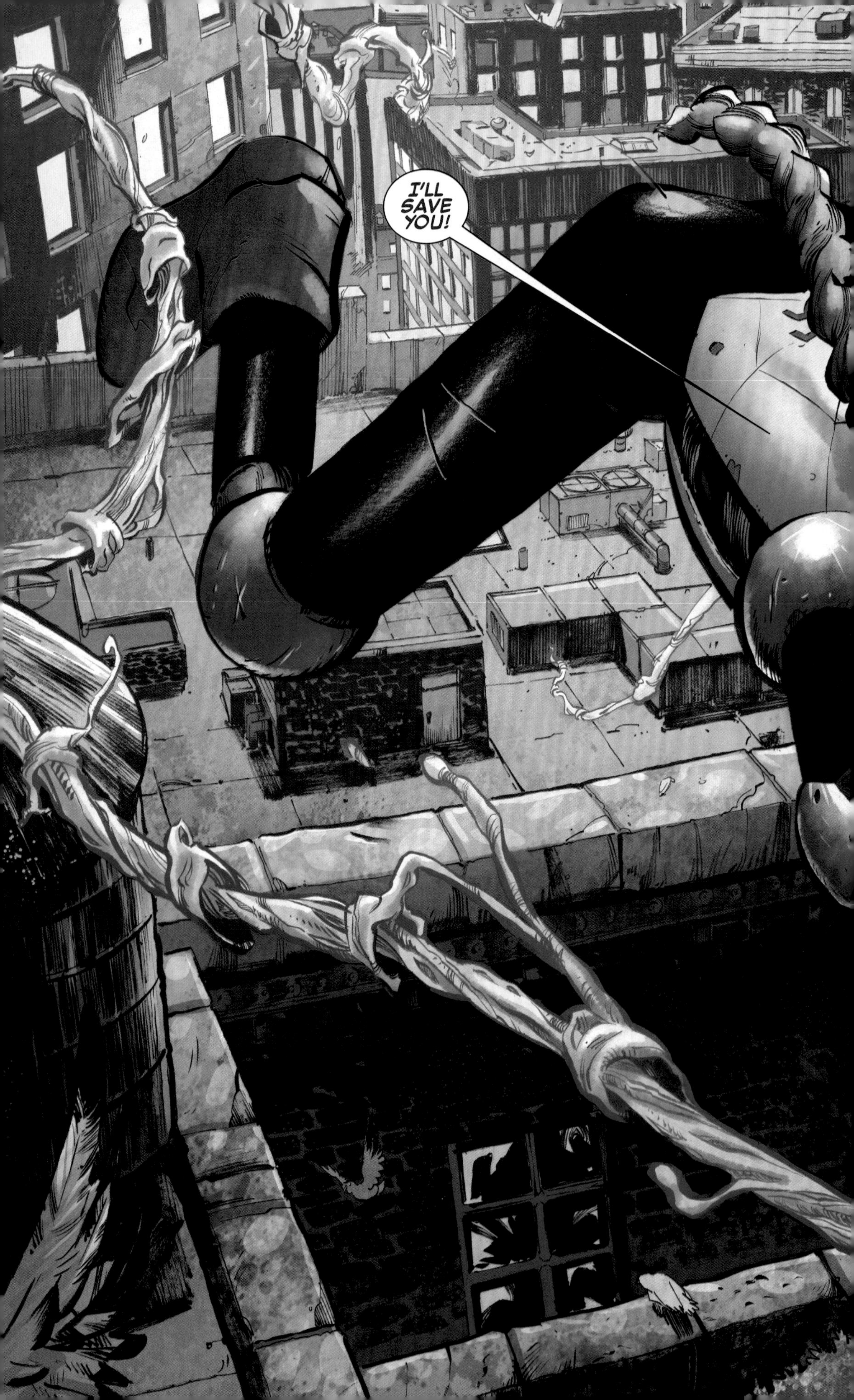
I'LL SAVE YOU!

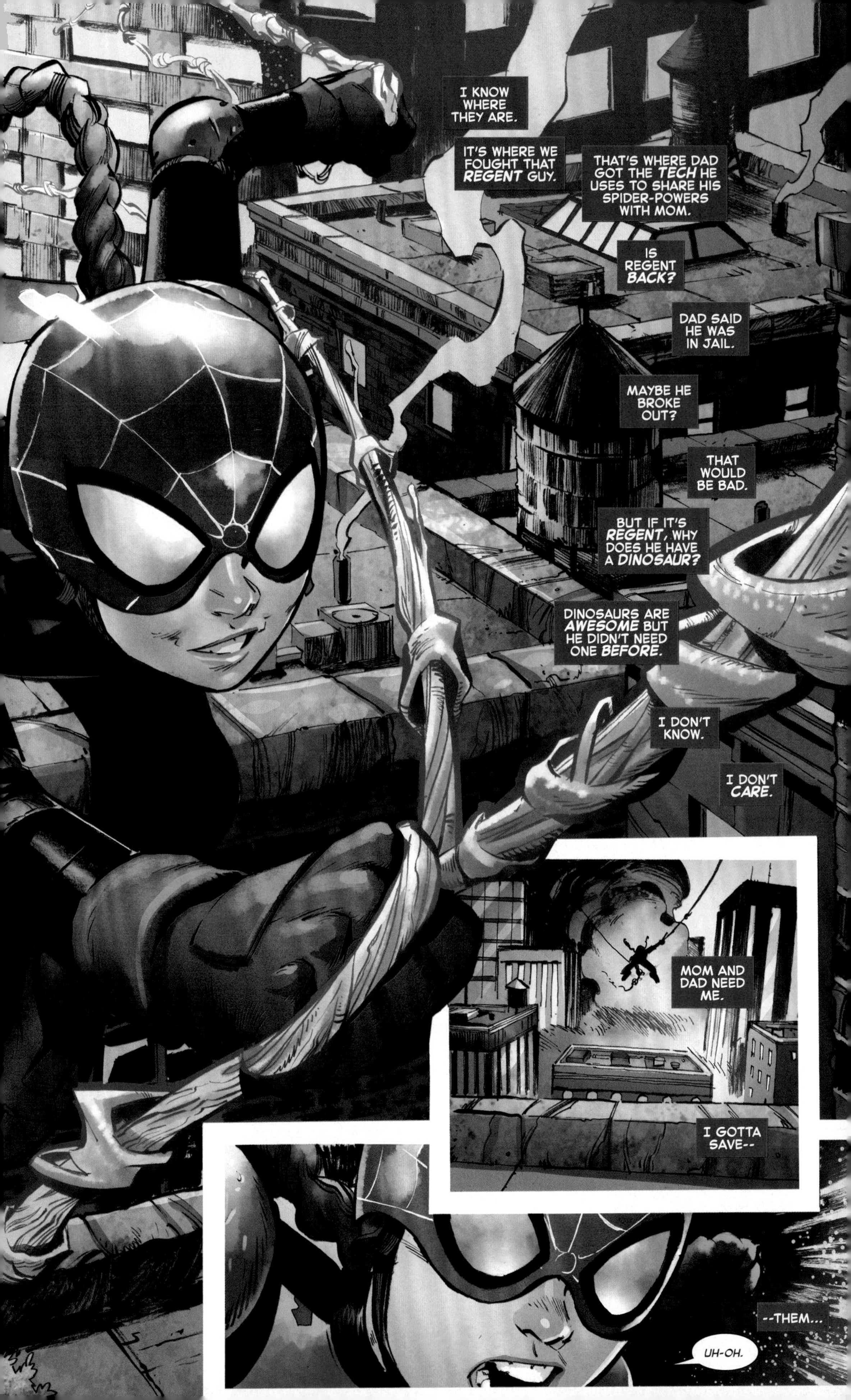
I KNOW WHERE THEY ARE.
IT'S WHERE WE FOUGHT THAT *REGENT* GUY.
THAT'S WHERE DAD GOT THE *TECH* HE USES TO SHARE HIS SPIDER-POWERS WITH MOM.
IS REGENT *BACK?*
DAD SAID HE WAS IN JAIL.
MAYBE HE BROKE OUT?
THAT WOULD BE BAD.
BUT IF IT'S *REGENT,* WHY DOES HE HAVE A *DINOSAUR?*
DINOSAURS ARE *AWESOME* BUT HE DIDN'T NEED ONE *BEFORE.*
I DON'T KNOW.
I DON'T *CARE.*
MOM AND DAD NEED ME.
I GOTTA SAVE--
--THEM...
UH-OH.

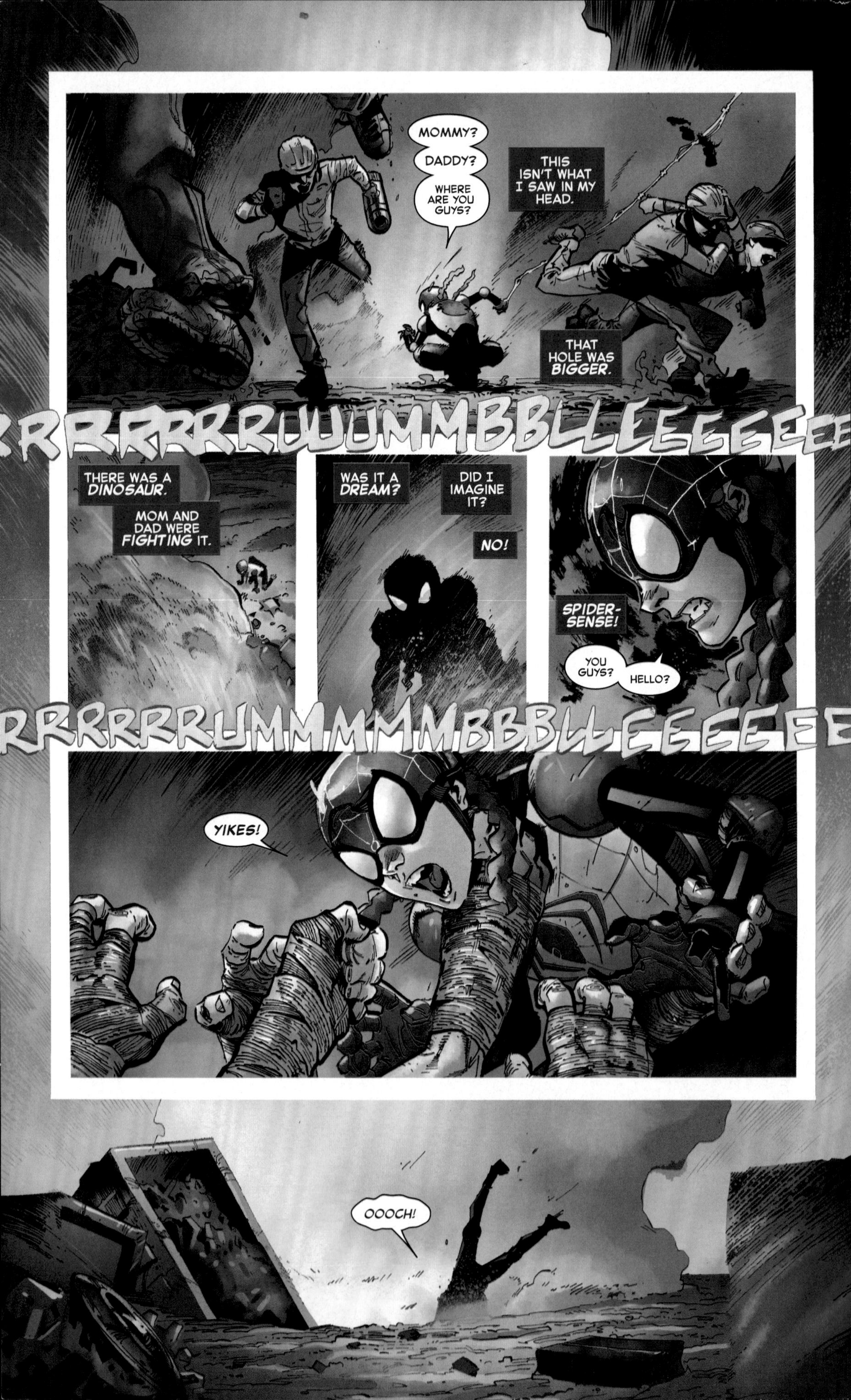
MOMMY?
DADDY?
WHERE ARE YOU GUYS?
THIS ISN'T WHAT I SAW IN MY HEAD.
THAT HOLE WAS BIGGER.
RRRRRRRUUUUMMBBLLEEEEEE
THERE WAS A DINOSAUR.
MOM AND DAD WERE FIGHTING IT.
WAS IT A DREAM?
DID I IMAGINE IT?
NO!
SPIDER-SENSE!
YOU GUYS?
HELLO?
RRRRRRRUMMMMMMBBBLLEEEEEE
YIKES!
OOOCH!

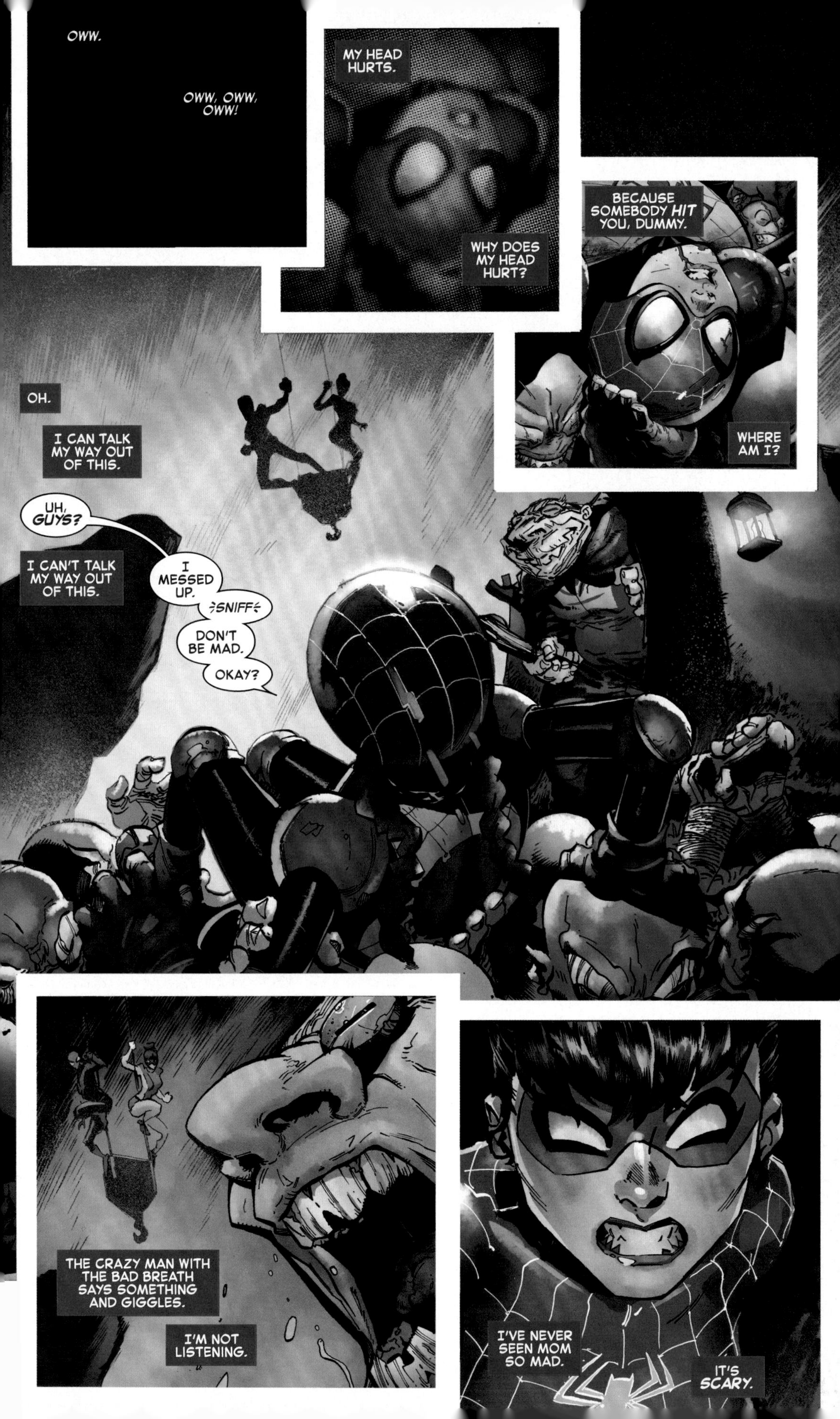
OWW.
OWW, OWW, OWW!
MY HEAD HURTS.
WHY DOES MY HEAD HURT?
BECAUSE SOMEBODY HIT YOU, DUMMY.
WHERE AM I?
OH.
I CAN TALK MY WAY OUT OF THIS.
UH, GUYS?
I CAN'T TALK MY WAY OUT OF THIS.
I MESSED UP.
SNIFF
DON'T BE MAD.
OKAY?
THE CRAZY MAN WITH THE BAD BREATH SAYS SOMETHING AND GIGGLES.
I'M NOT LISTENING.
I'VE NEVER SEEN MOM SO MAD.
IT'S SCARY.

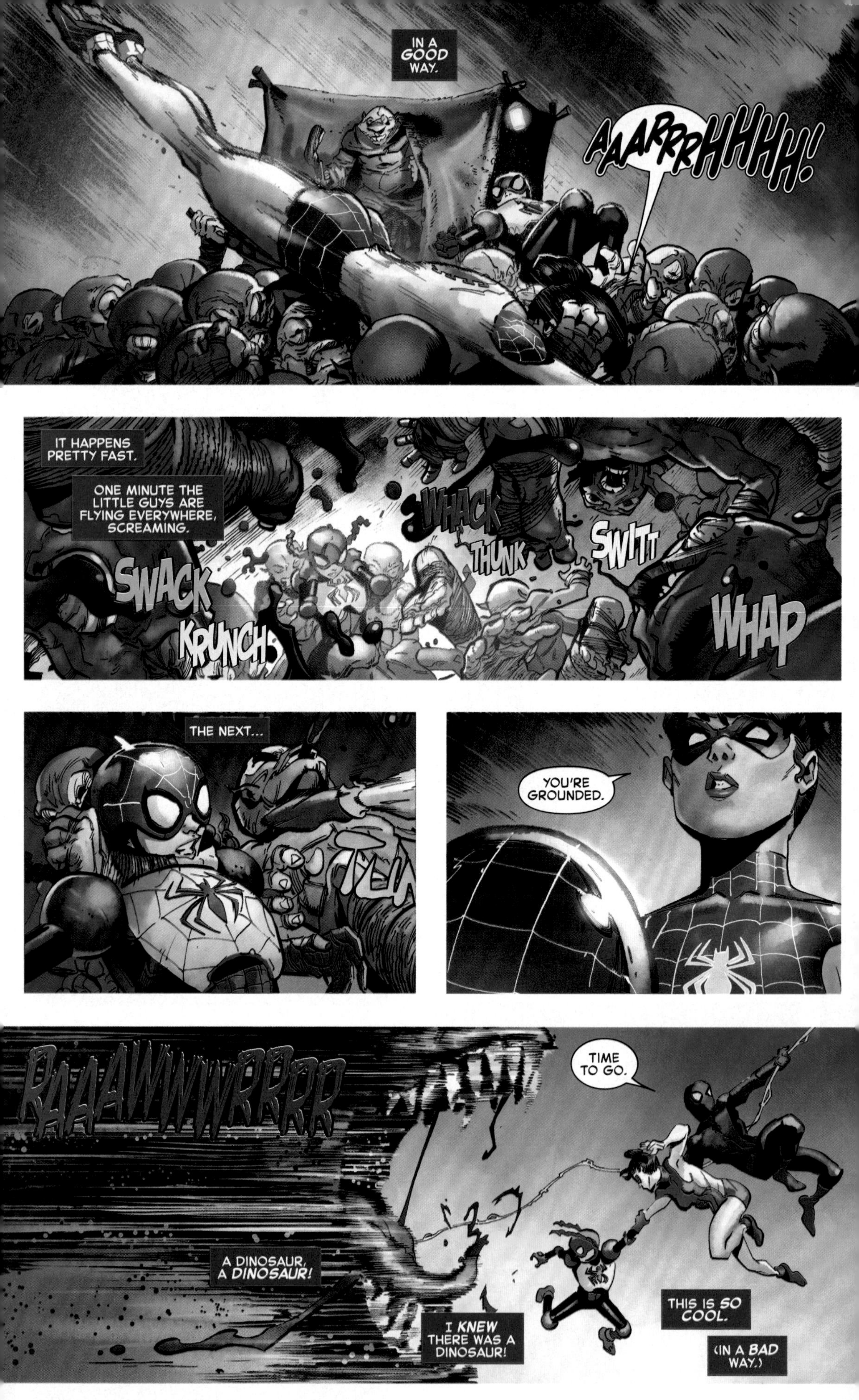

IN A *GOOD* WAY.
AAARRRHHHHH!
IT HAPPENS PRETTY FAST.
ONE MINUTE THE LITTLE GUYS ARE FLYING EVERYWHERE, SCREAMING.
WHACK
THUNK
SWITT
SWACK
KRUNCH
WHAP
THE NEXT...
YOU'RE GROUNDED.
RAAAWWWRRRR
TIME TO GO.
A DINOSAUR, A *DINOSAUR!*
I *KNEW* THERE WAS A DINOSAUR!
THIS IS *SO COOL.*
(IN A *BAD* WAY.)

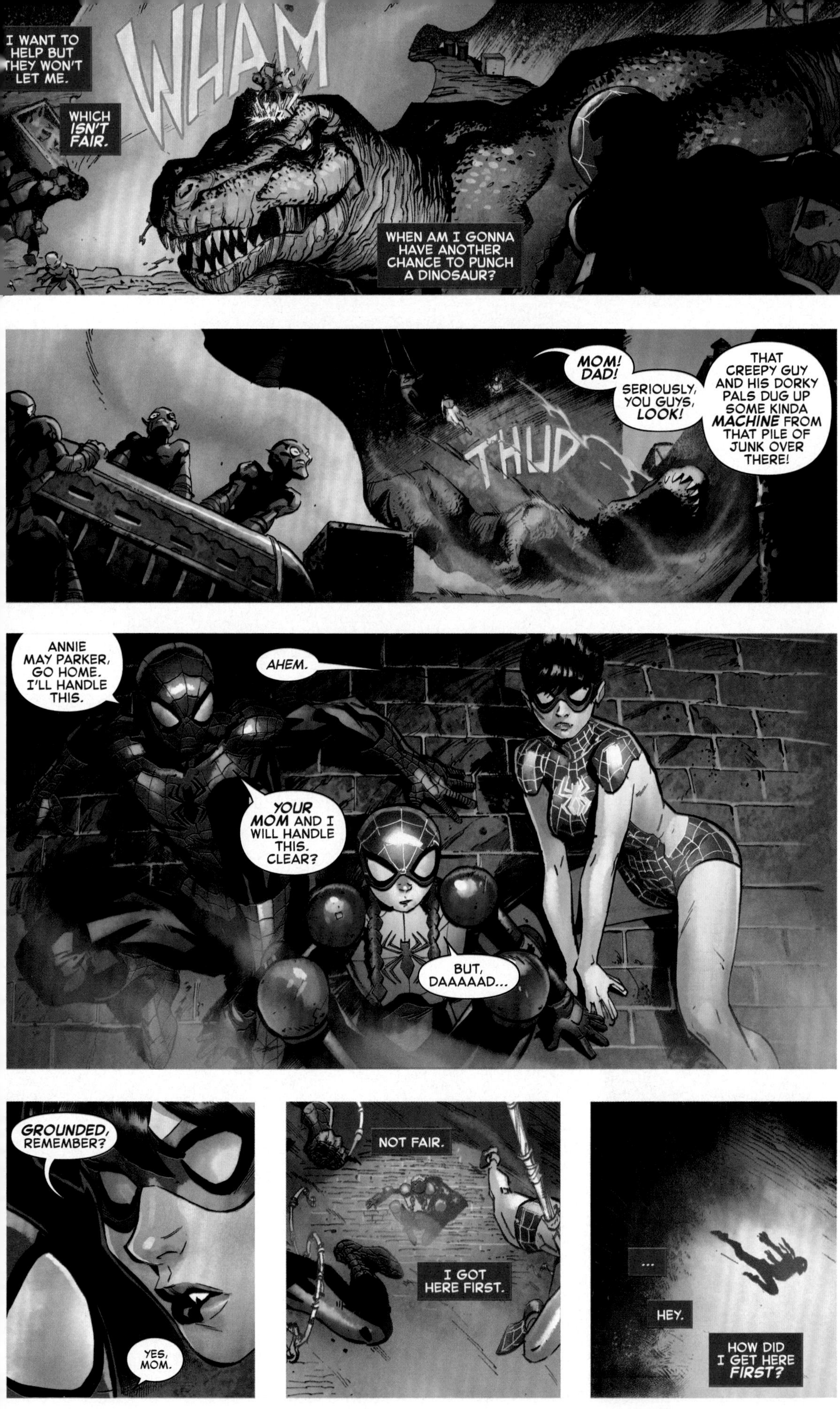
I WANT TO HELP BUT THEY WON'T LET ME.
WHAM
WHICH *ISN'T* *FAIR*.
WHEN AM I GONNA HAVE ANOTHER CHANCE TO PUNCH A DINOSAUR?
*MOM! DAD!*
SERIOUSLY, YOU GUYS, *LOOK!*
THUD
THAT CREEPY GUY AND HIS DORKY PALS DUG UP SOME KINDA *MACHINE* FROM THAT PILE OF JUNK OVER THERE!
ANNIE MAY PARKER, GO HOME. I'LL HANDLE THIS.
AHEM.
*YOUR MOM* AND I WILL HANDLE THIS. CLEAR?
BUT, DAAAAAD...
*GROUNDED*, REMEMBER?
YES, MOM.
NOT FAIR.
I GOT HERE FIRST.
...
HEY.
HOW DID I GET HERE *FIRST?*

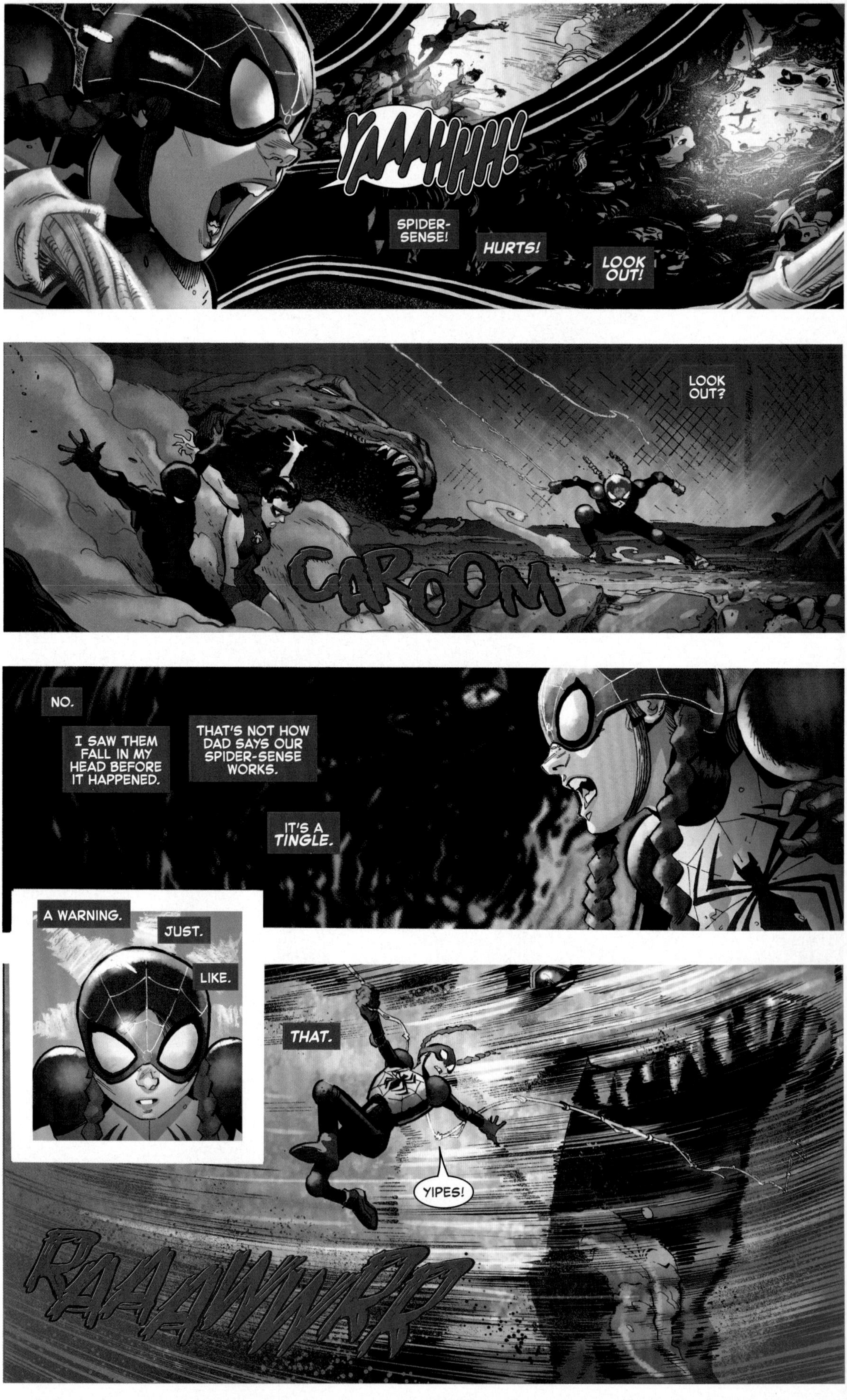
YAAAHHH!
SPIDER-SENSE!
HURTS!
LOOK OUT!
LOOK OUT?
CAROOM
NO.
I SAW THEM FALL IN MY HEAD BEFORE IT HAPPENED.
THAT'S NOT HOW DAD SAYS OUR SPIDER-SENSE WORKS.
IT'S A TINGLE.
A WARNING.
JUST.
LIKE.
THAT.
YIPES!
RAAAWWRR

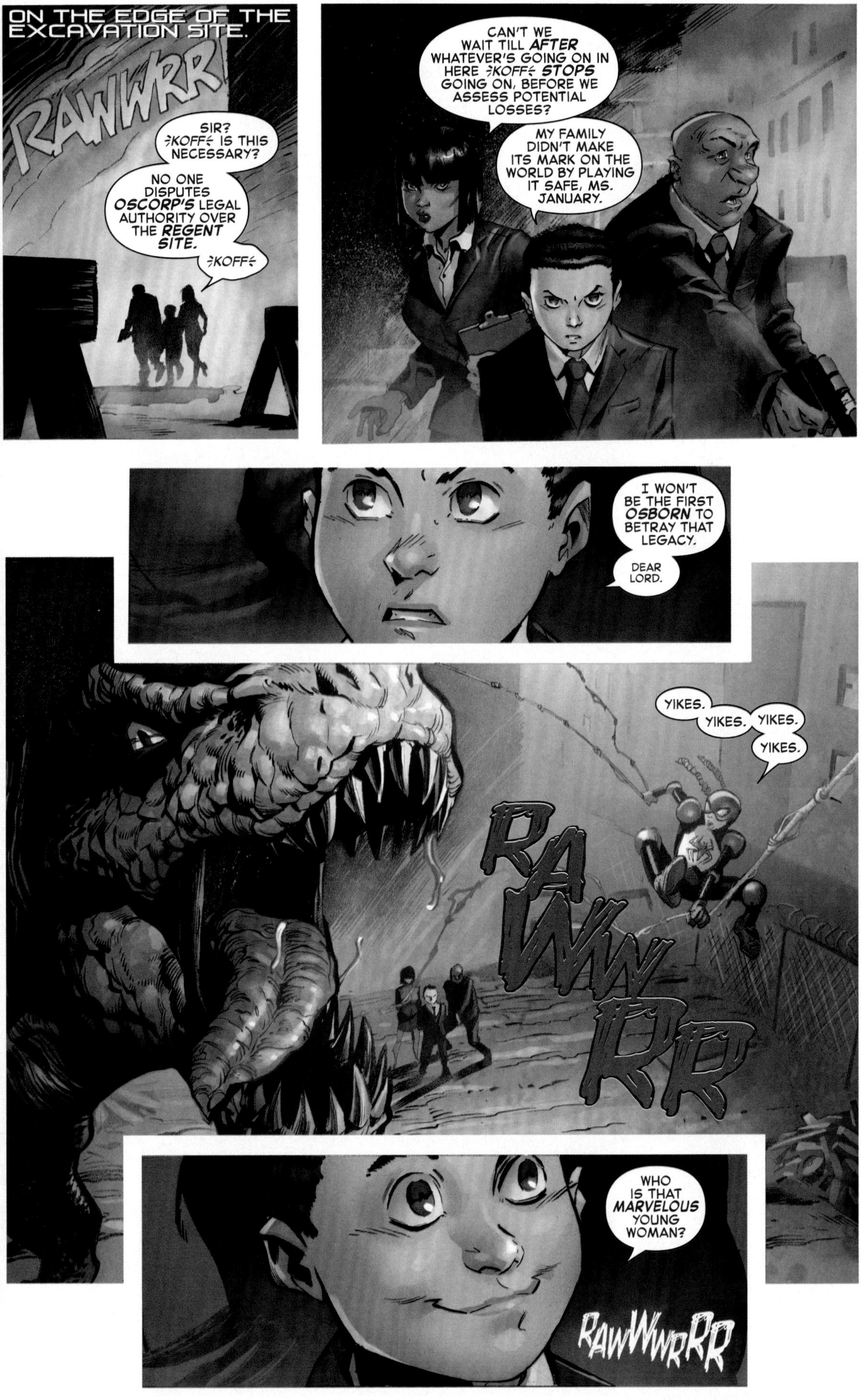
ON THE EDGE OF THE EXCAVATION SITE.
RAWWRR
SIR? ≠KOFF≠ IS THIS NECESSARY?
NO ONE DISPUTES OSCORP'S LEGAL AUTHORITY OVER THE REGENT SITE.
≠KOFF≠
CAN'T WE WAIT TILL AFTER WHATEVER'S GOING ON IN HERE ≠KOFF≠ STOPS GOING ON, BEFORE WE ASSESS POTENTIAL LOSSES?
MY FAMILY DIDN'T MAKE ITS MARK ON THE WORLD BY PLAYING IT SAFE, MS. JANUARY.
I WON'T BE THE FIRST OSBORN TO BETRAY THAT LEGACY.
DEAR LORD.
YIKES.
YIKES.
YIKES.
YIKES.
RAWWRR
WHO IS THAT MARVELOUS YOUNG WOMAN?
RAWWWRRR

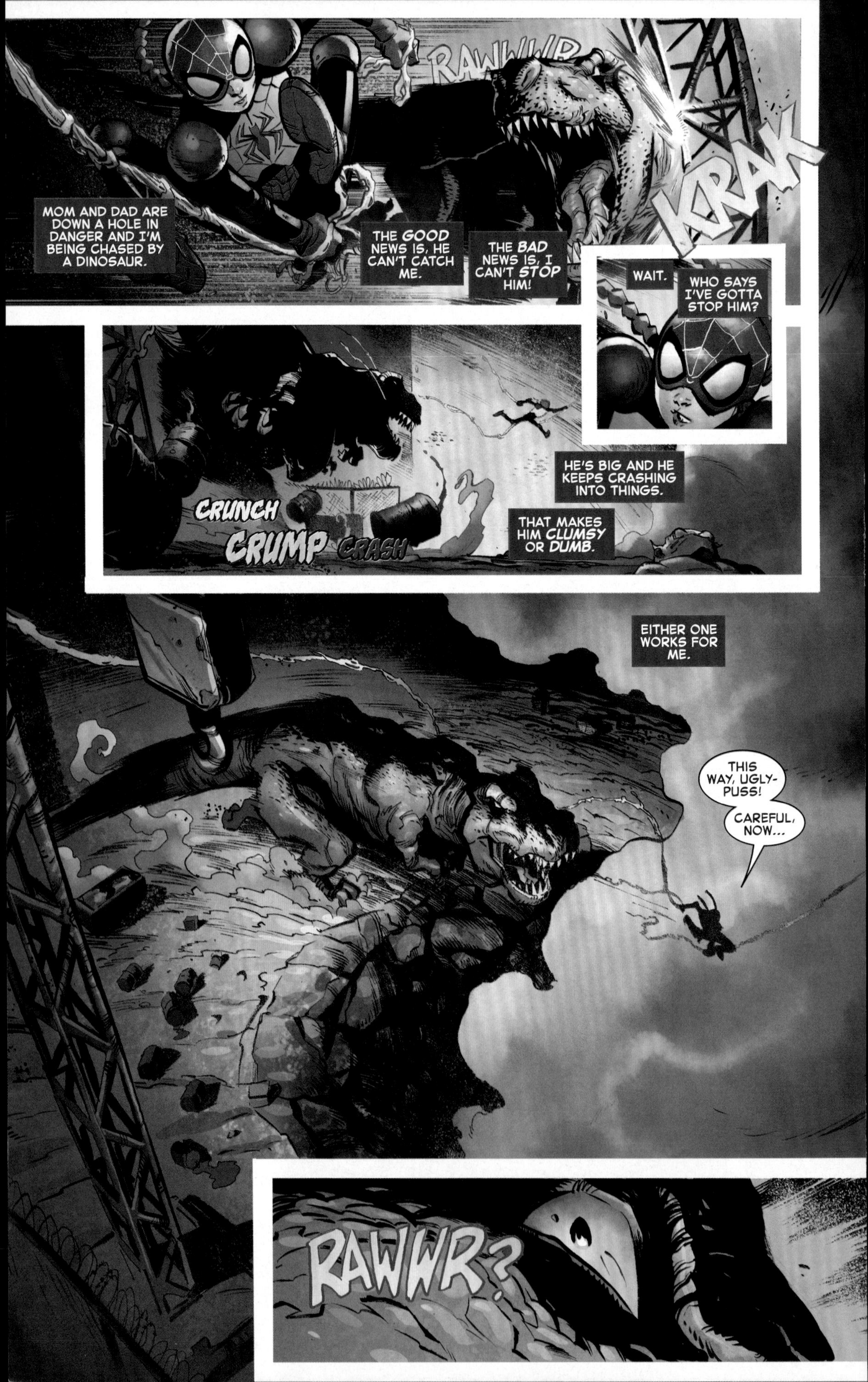

RAWWWR
MOM AND DAD ARE DOWN A HOLE IN DANGER AND I'M BEING CHASED BY A DINOSAUR.
THE GOOD NEWS IS, HE CAN'T CATCH ME.
THE BAD NEWS IS, I CAN'T STOP HIM!
KRAK
WAIT.
WHO SAYS I'VE GOTTA STOP HIM?
HE'S BIG AND HE KEEPS CRASHING INTO THINGS.
THAT MAKES HIM CLUMSY OR DUMB.
CRUNCH
CRUMP
CRASH
EITHER ONE WORKS FOR ME.
THIS WAY, UGLY-PUSS!
CAREFUL, NOW...
RAWWR?

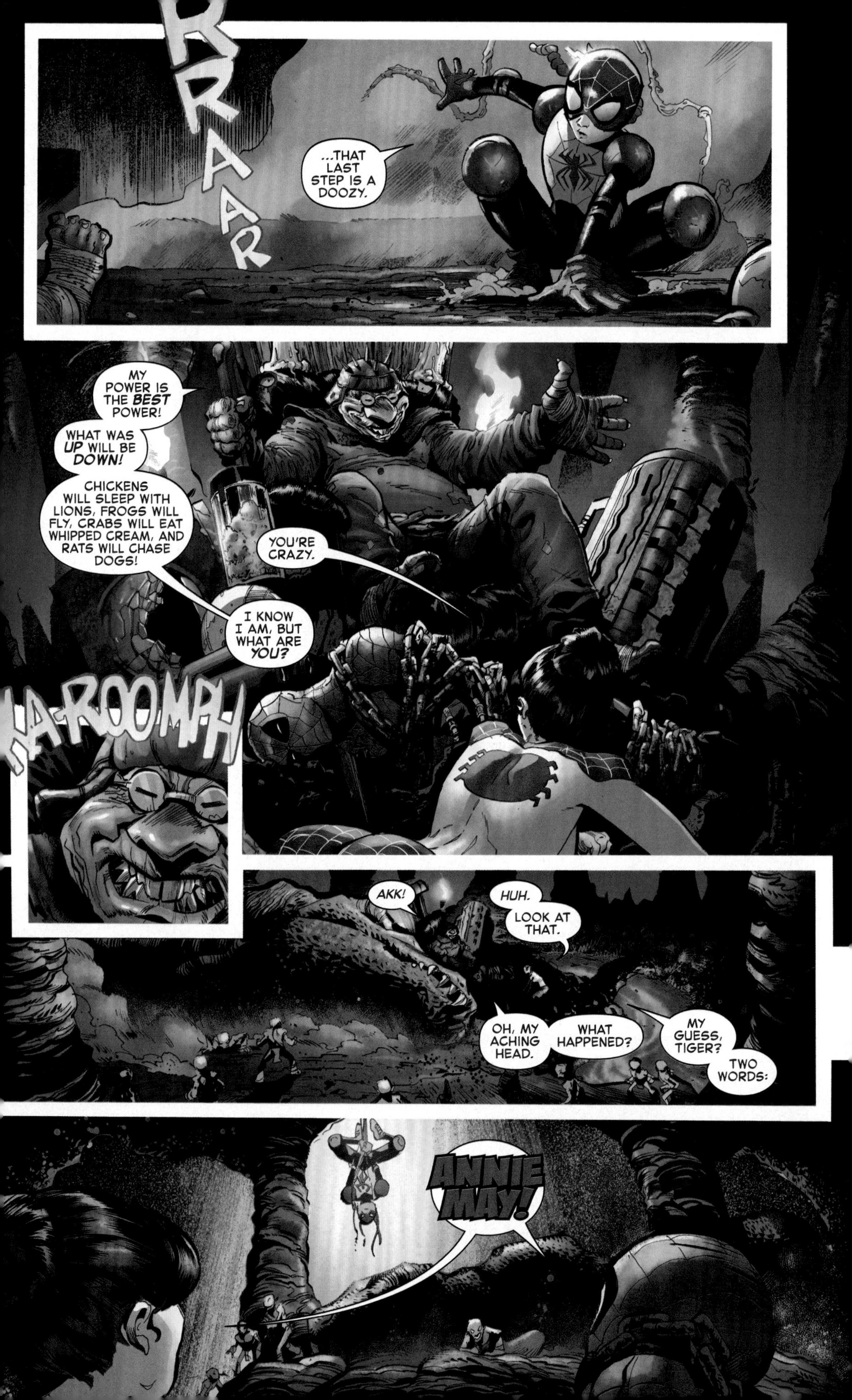
RRAAR
...THAT LAST STEP IS A DOOZY.
MY POWER IS THE BEST POWER!
WHAT WAS UP WILL BE DOWN!
CHICKENS WILL SLEEP WITH LIONS, FROGS WILL FLY, CRABS WILL EAT WHIPPED CREAM, AND RATS WILL CHASE DOGS!
YOU'RE CRAZY.
I KNOW I AM, BUT WHAT ARE YOU?
KA-ROOMPH
AKK!
HUH.
LOOK AT THAT.
OH, MY ACHING HEAD.
WHAT HAPPENED?
MY GUESS, TIGER?
TWO WORDS:
ANNIE MAY!

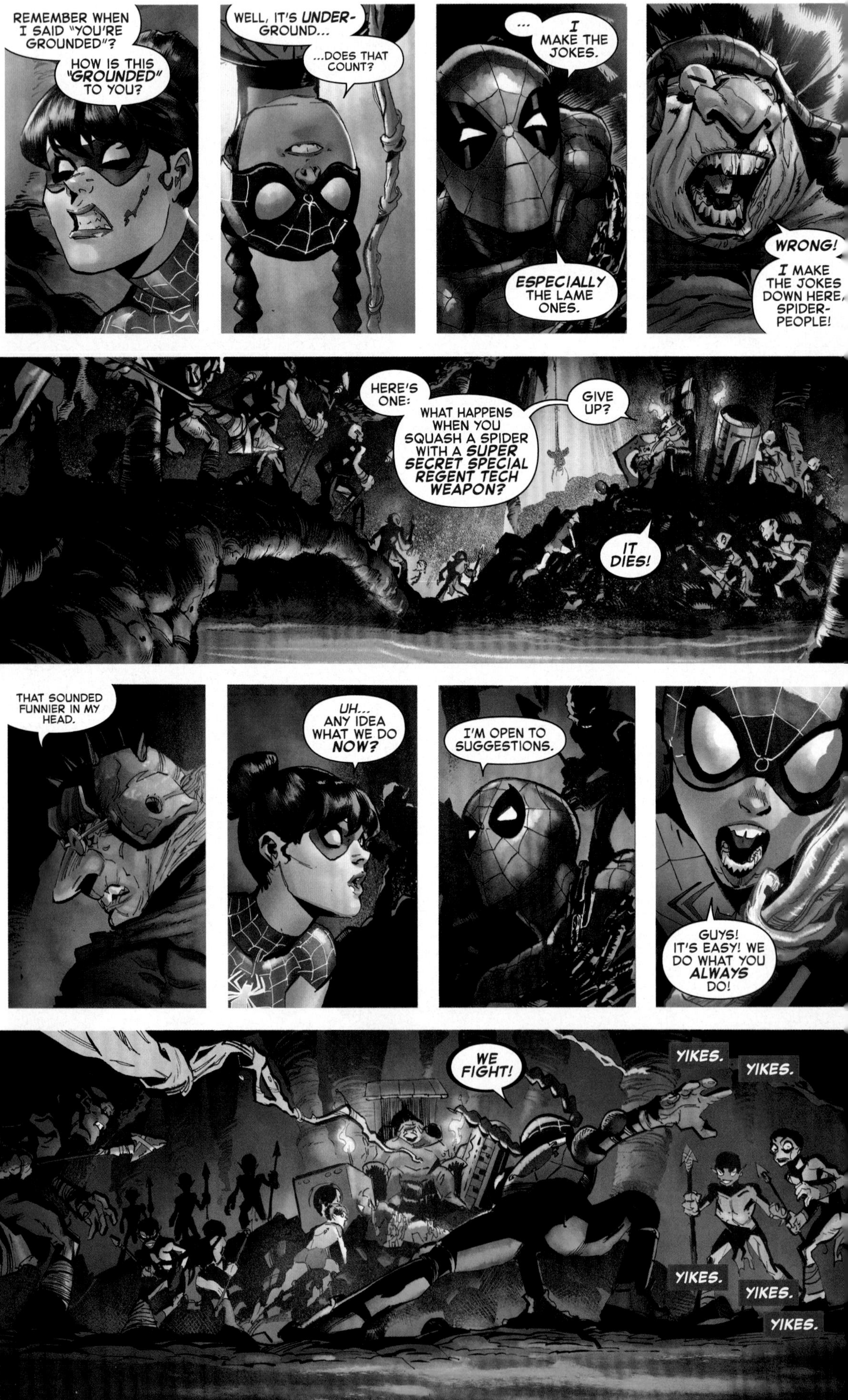
REMEMBER WHEN I SAID "YOU'RE GROUNDED"?
HOW IS THIS "GROUNDED" TO YOU?
WELL, IT'S UNDER-GROUND...
...DOES THAT COUNT?
...
I MAKE THE JOKES.
ESPECIALLY THE LAME ONES.
WRONG! I MAKE THE JOKES DOWN HERE, SPIDER-PEOPLE!
HERE'S ONE:
WHAT HAPPENS WHEN YOU SQUASH A SPIDER WITH A SUPER SECRET SPECIAL REGENT TECH WEAPON?
GIVE UP?
IT DIES!
THAT SOUNDED FUNNIER IN MY HEAD.
UH... ANY IDEA WHAT WE DO NOW?
I'M OPEN TO SUGGESTIONS.
GUYS! IT'S EASY! WE DO WHAT YOU ALWAYS DO!
WE FIGHT!
YIKES.
YIKES.
YIKES.
YIKES.
YIKES.

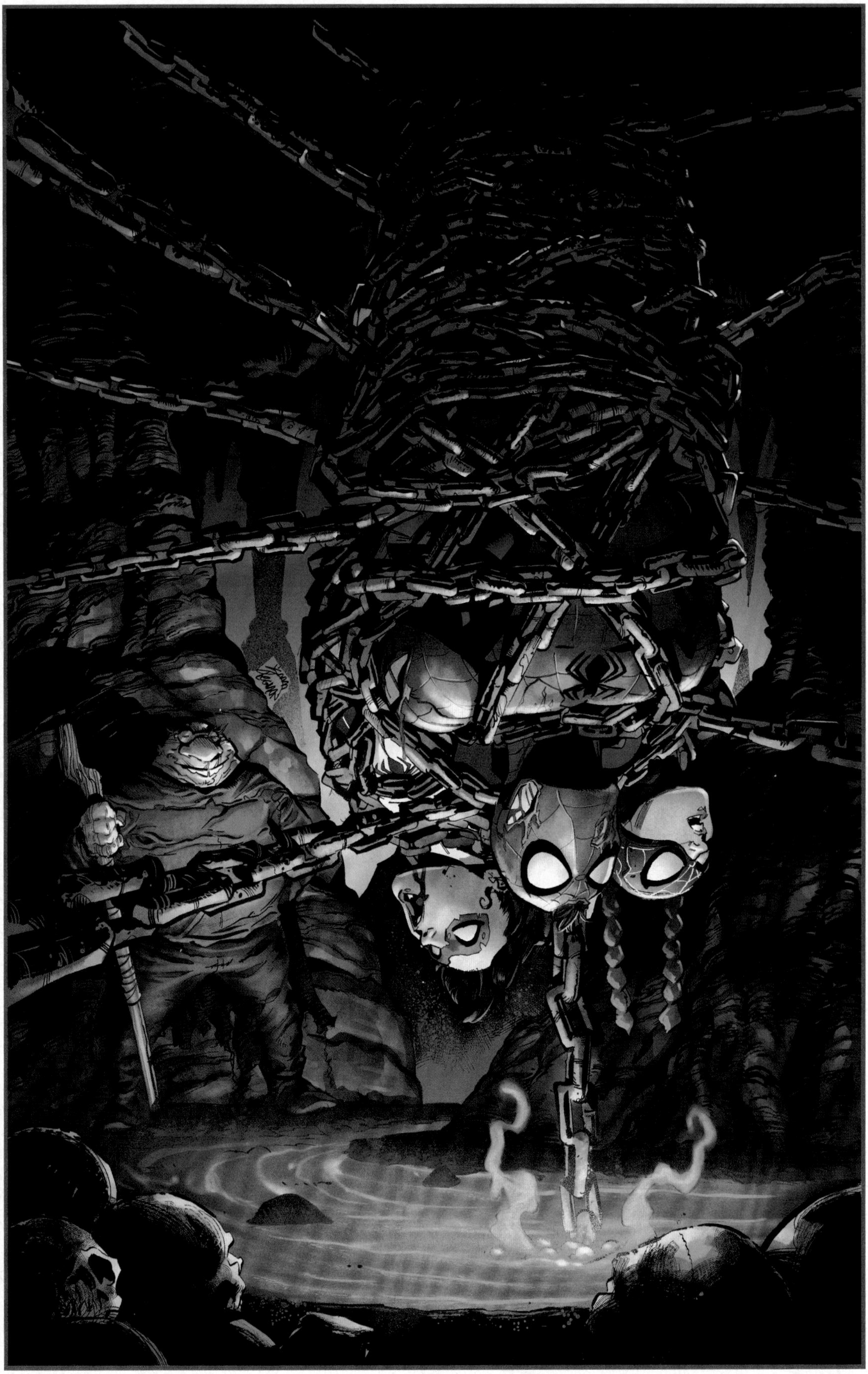

4

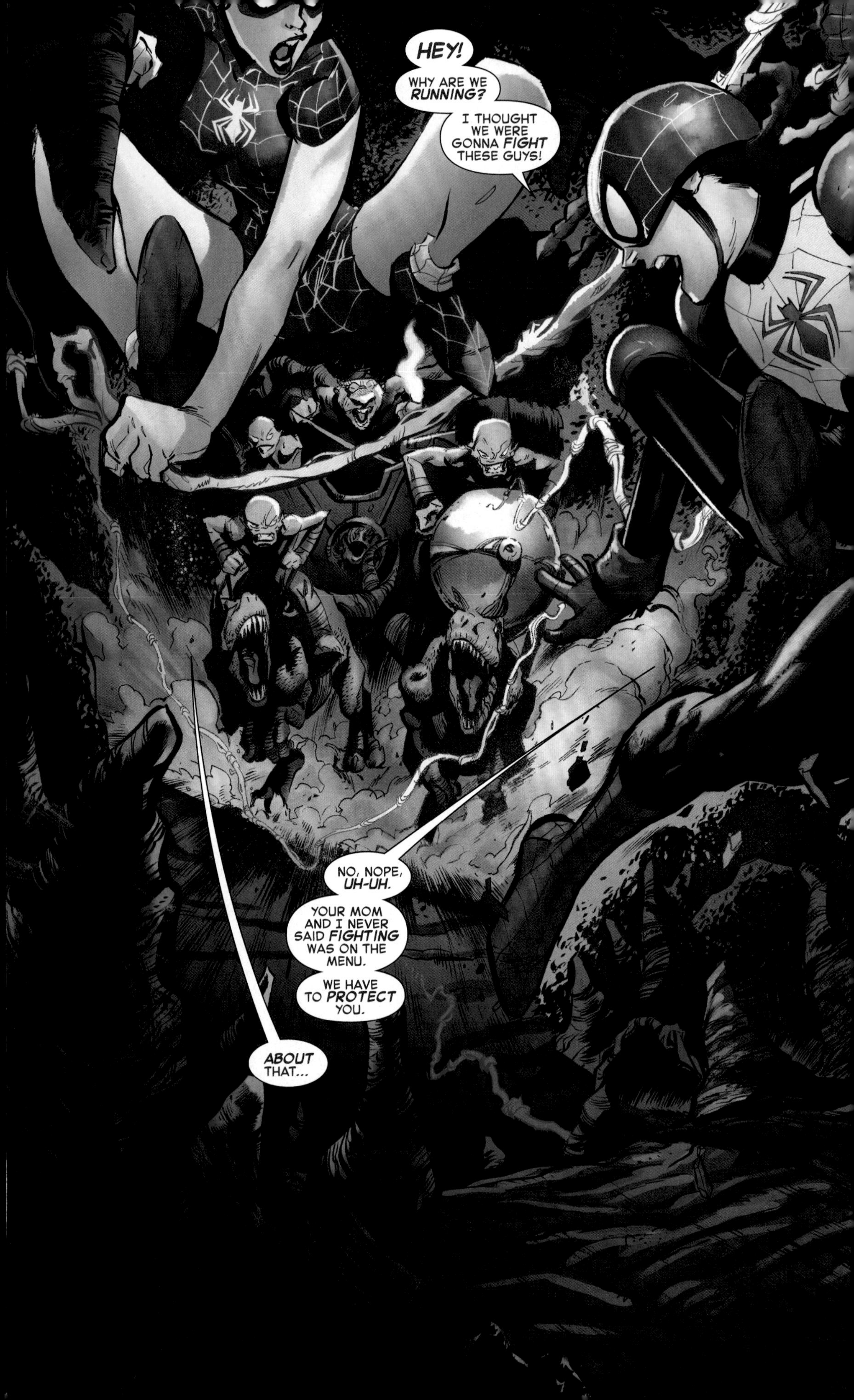
HEY!
WHY ARE WE RUNNING?
I THOUGHT WE WERE GONNA FIGHT THESE GUYS!
NO, NOPE, UH-UH.
YOUR MOM AND I NEVER SAID FIGHTING WAS ON THE MENU.
WE HAVE TO PROTECT YOU.
ABOUT THAT...

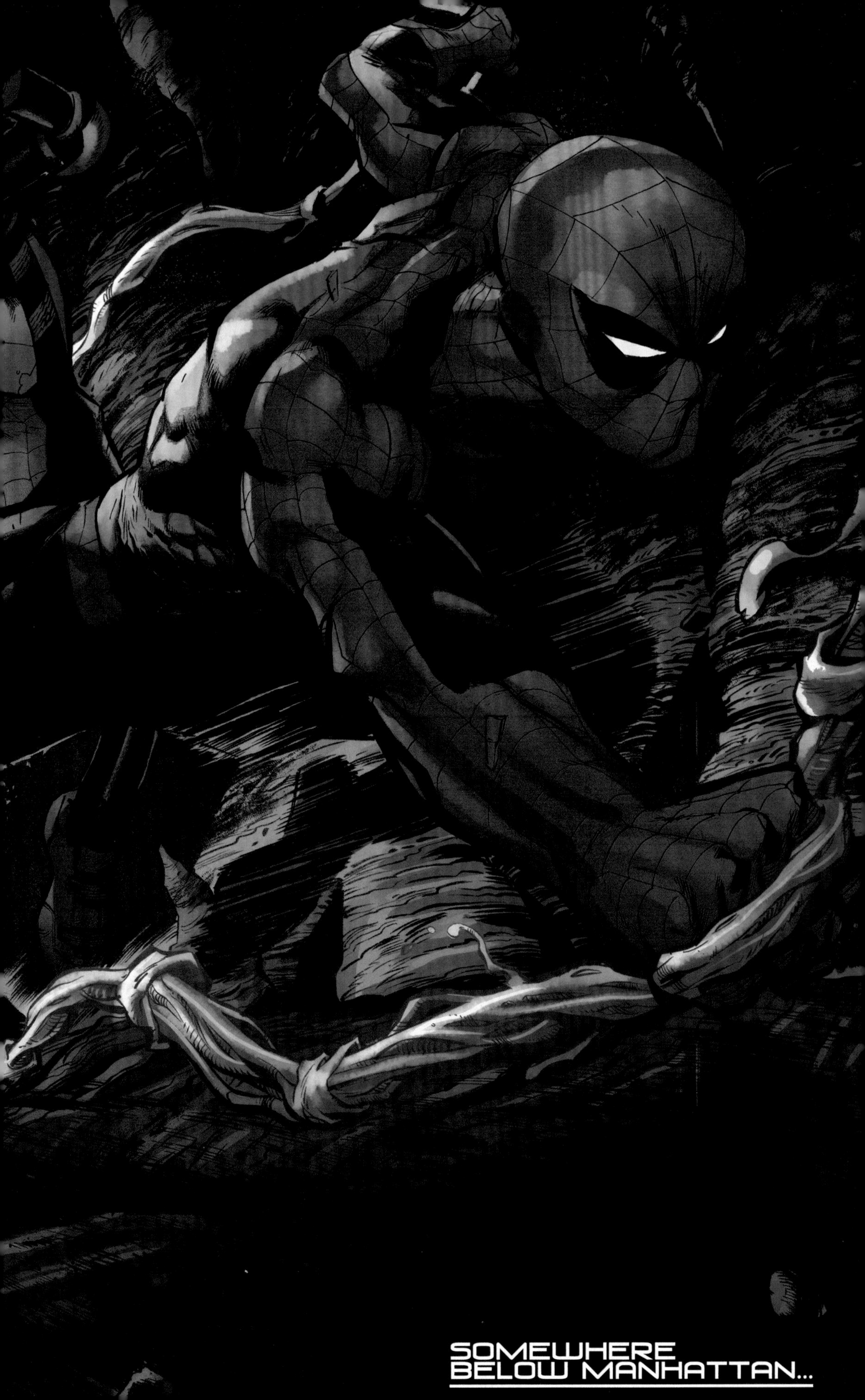
SOMEWHERE
BELOW MANHATTAN...

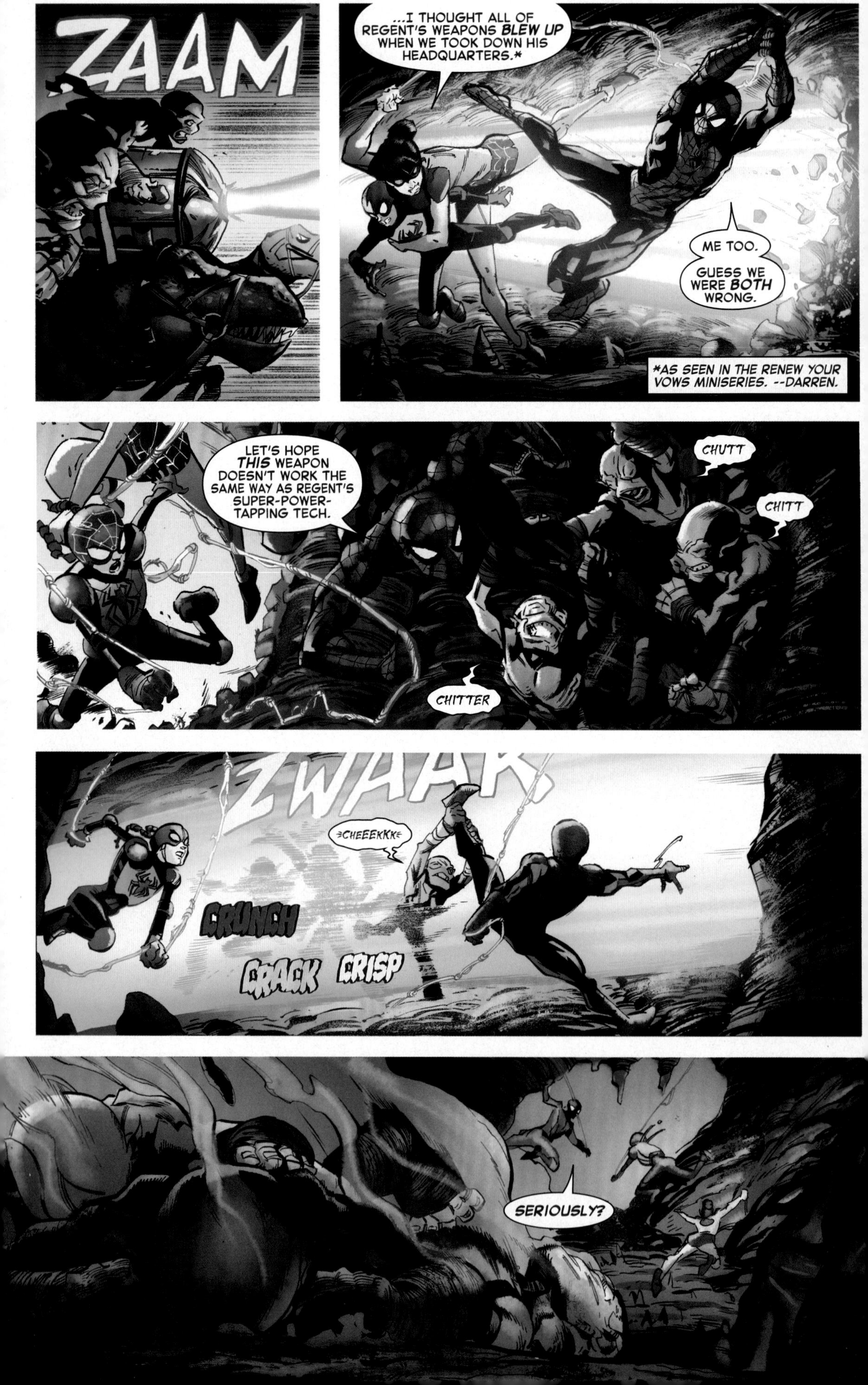
ZAAM
...I THOUGHT ALL OF REGENT'S WEAPONS BLEW UP WHEN WE TOOK DOWN HIS HEADQUARTERS.*
ME TOO.
GUESS WE WERE BOTH WRONG.
*AS SEEN IN THE RENEW YOUR VOWS MINISERIES. --DARREN.
LET'S HOPE THIS WEAPON DOESN'T WORK THE SAME WAY AS REGENT'S SUPER-POWER-TAPPING TECH.
CHUTT
CHITT
CHITTER
ZWAAK
CHEEEKKK
CRUNCH
CRACK
CRISP
SERIOUSLY?

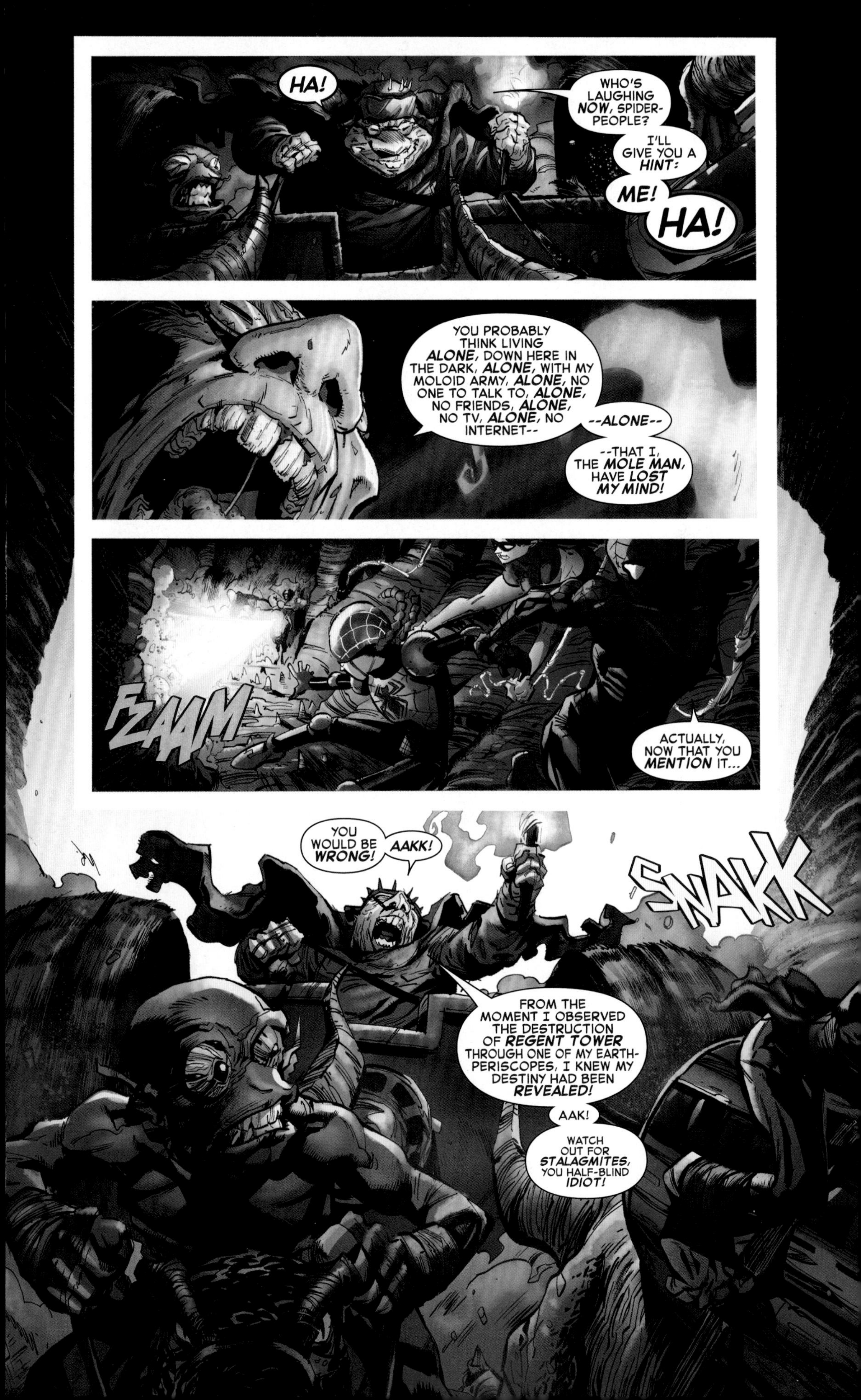
HA!
WHO'S LAUGHING NOW, SPIDER-PEOPLE?
I'LL GIVE YOU A HINT:
ME!
HA!
YOU PROBABLY THINK LIVING ALONE, DOWN HERE IN THE DARK, ALONE, WITH MY MOLOID ARMY, ALONE, NO ONE TO TALK TO, ALONE, NO FRIENDS, ALONE, NO TV, ALONE, NO INTERNET--
--ALONE--
--THAT I, THE MOLE MAN, HAVE LOST MY MIND!
FZAAM
ACTUALLY, NOW THAT YOU MENTION IT...
YOU WOULD BE WRONG!
AAKK!
SNAKK
FROM THE MOMENT I OBSERVED THE DESTRUCTION OF REGENT TOWER THROUGH ONE OF MY EARTH-PERISCOPES, I KNEW MY DESTINY HAD BEEN REVEALED!
AAK!
WATCH OUT FOR STALAGMITES, YOU HALF-BLIND IDIOT!

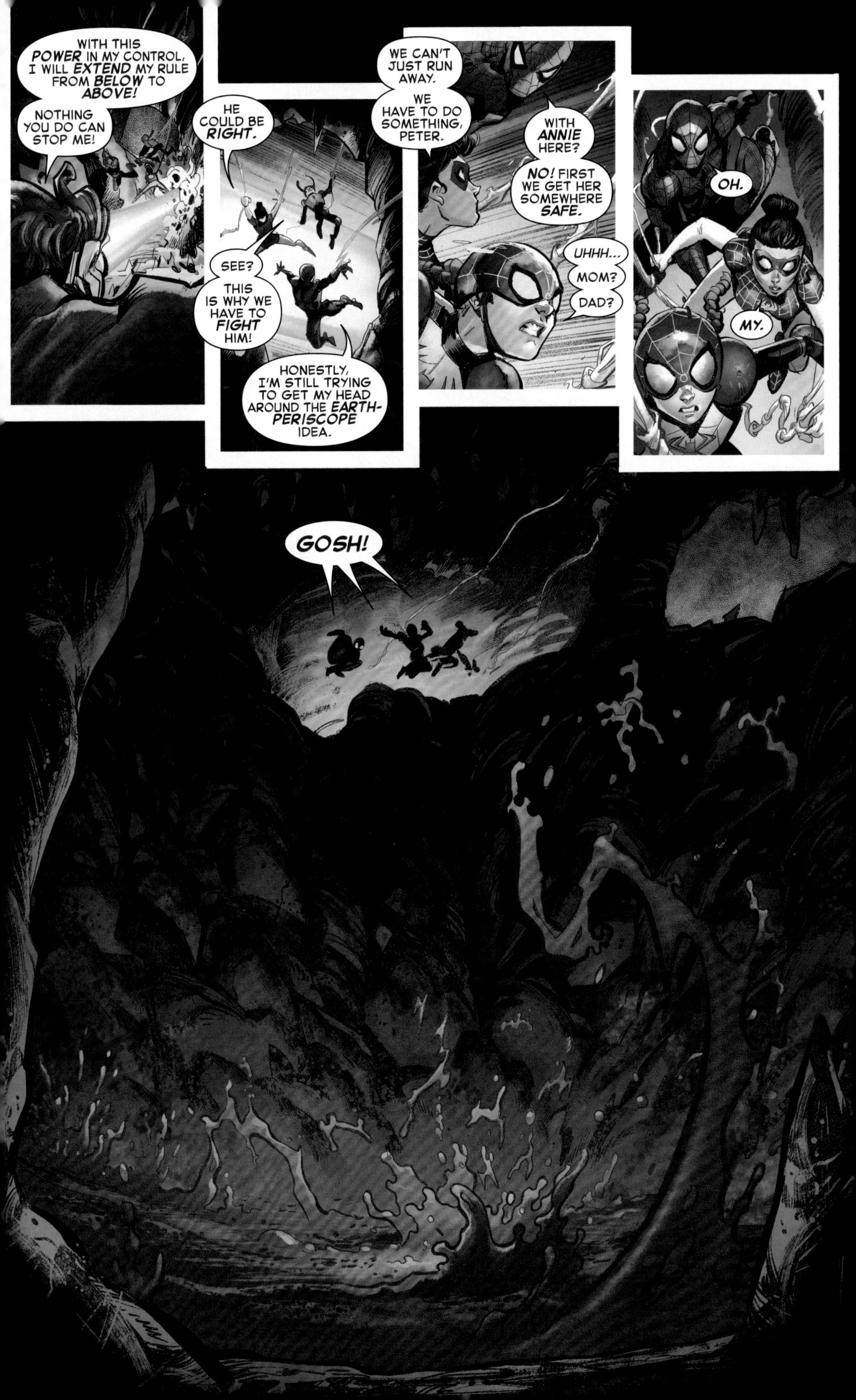

WITH THIS POWER IN MY CONTROL, I WILL EXTEND MY RULE FROM BELOW TO ABOVE!
NOTHING YOU DO CAN STOP ME!
HE COULD BE RIGHT.
SEE?
THIS IS WHY WE HAVE TO FIGHT HIM!
HONESTLY, I'M STILL TRYING TO GET MY HEAD AROUND THE EARTH-PERISCOPE IDEA.
WE CAN'T JUST RUN AWAY.
WE HAVE TO DO SOMETHING, PETER.
WITH ANNIE HERE?
NO! FIRST WE GET HER SOMEWHERE SAFE.
UHHH...
MOM?
DAD?
OH.
MY.
GOSH!

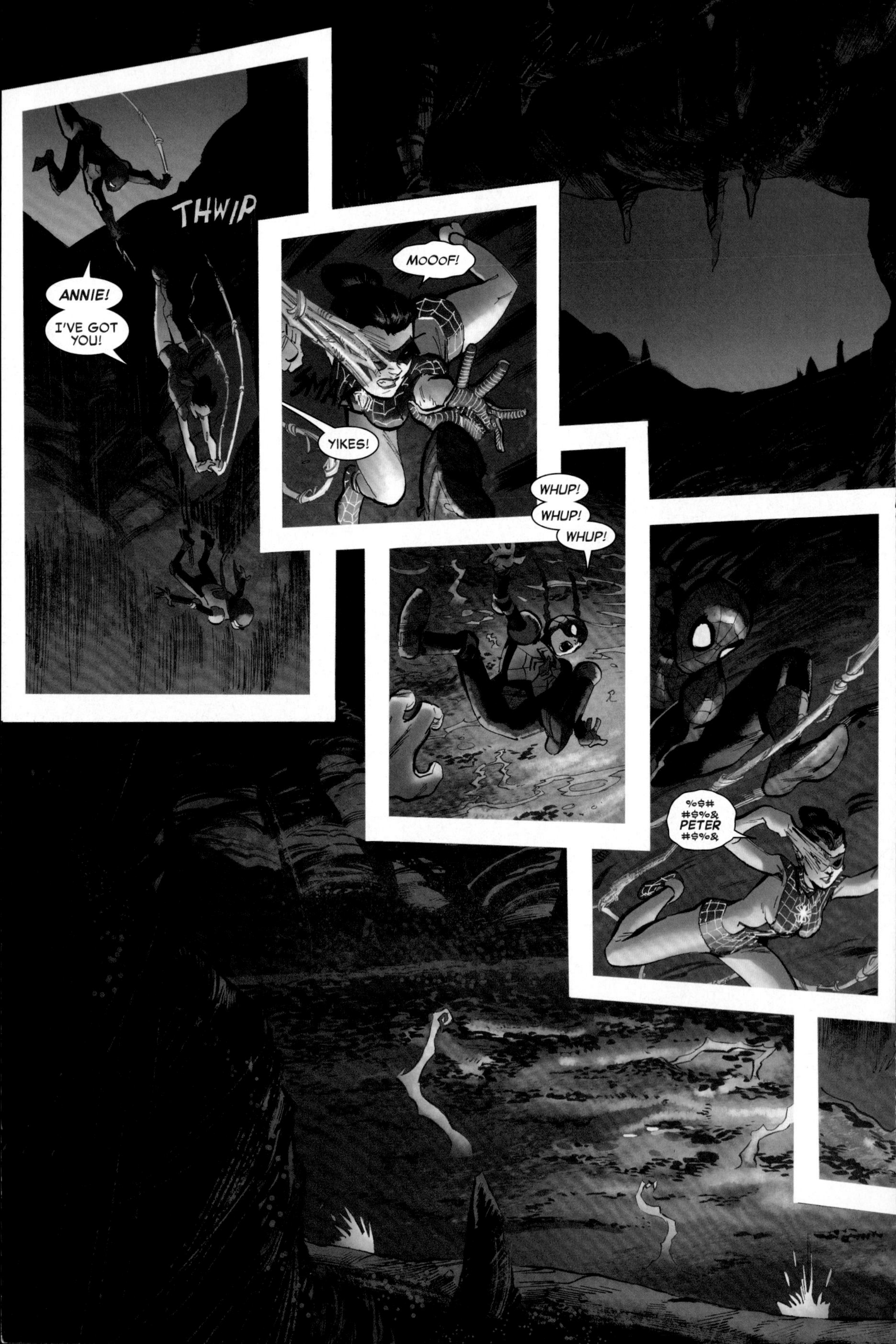
THWIP
ANNIE!
I'VE GOT YOU!
MOOOF!
YIKES!
WHUP!
WHUP!
WHUP!
%$# #$%& PETER #$%&

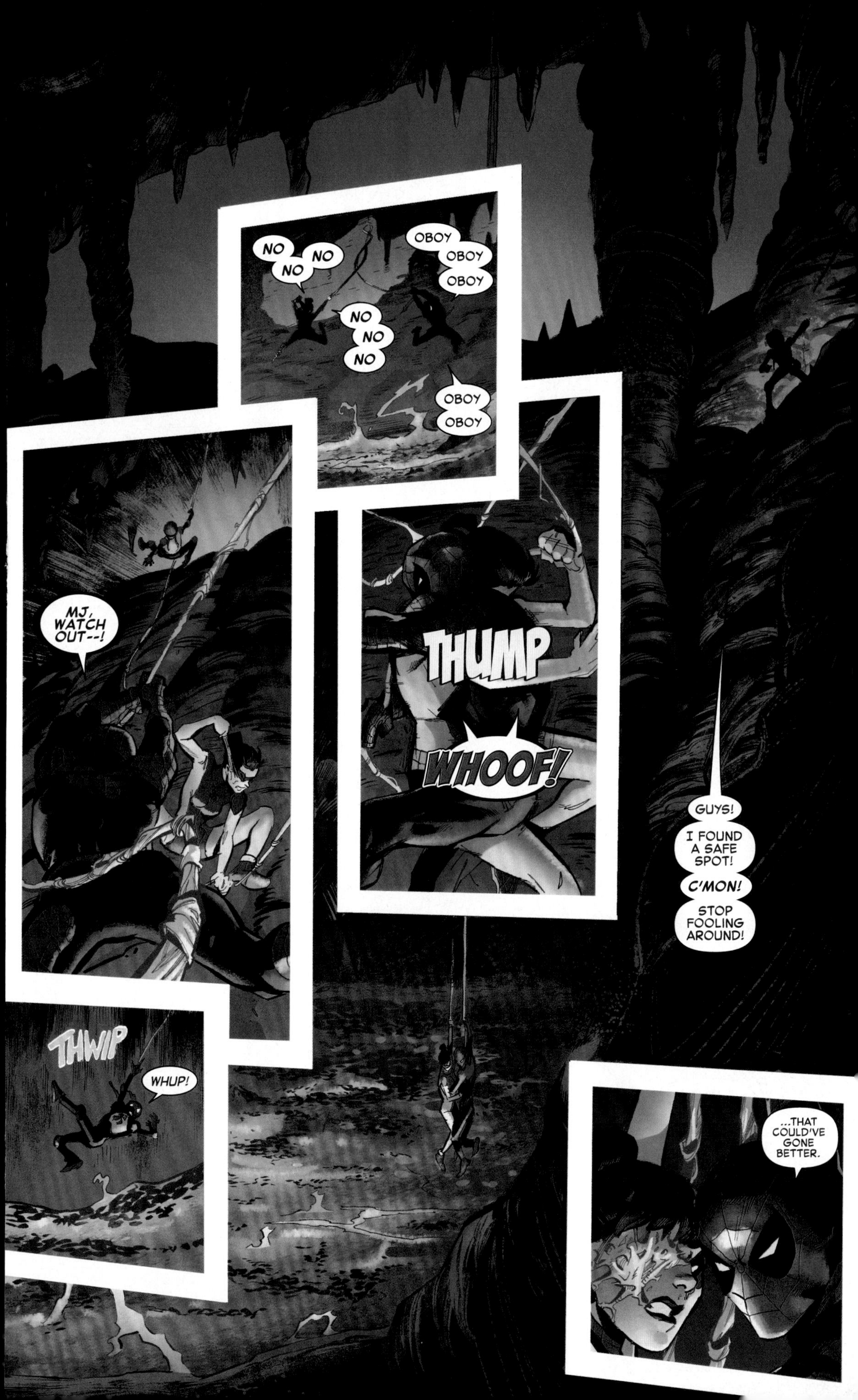
NO
NO
NO
OBOY
OBOY
OBOY
NO
NO
NO
OBOY
OBOY
MJ, WATCH OUT--!
THUMP
WHOOF!
GUYS!
I FOUND A SAFE SPOT!
C'MON!
STOP FOOLING AROUND!
THWIP
WHUP!
...THAT COULD'VE GONE BETTER.

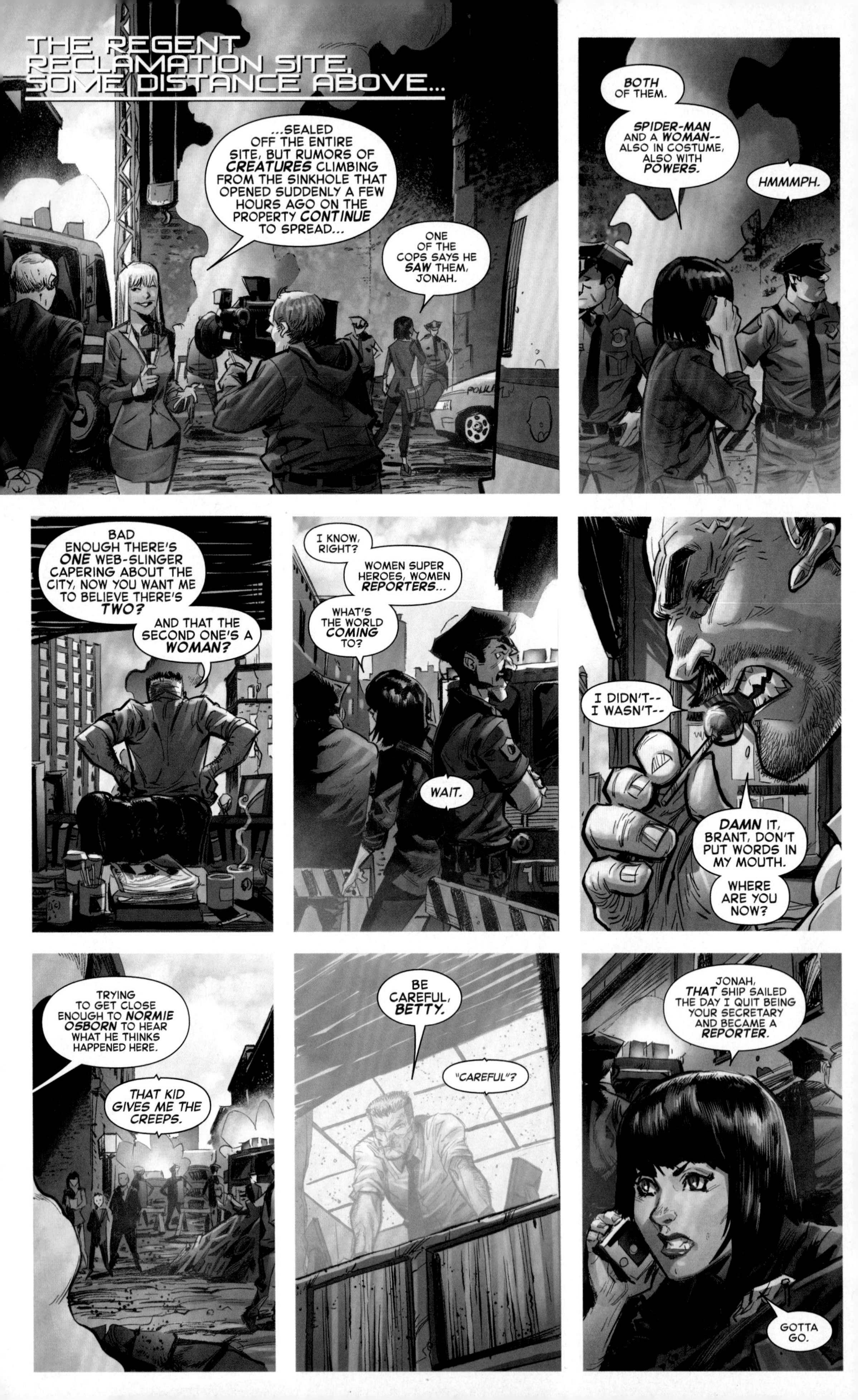
THE REGENT RECLAMATION SITE, SOME DISTANCE ABOVE...
...SEALED OFF THE ENTIRE SITE, BUT RUMORS OF CREATURES CLIMBING FROM THE SINKHOLE THAT OPENED SUDDENLY A FEW HOURS AGO ON THE PROPERTY CONTINUE TO SPREAD...
ONE OF THE COPS SAYS HE SAW THEM, JONAH.
BOTH OF THEM.
SPIDER-MAN AND A WOMAN-- ALSO IN COSTUME, ALSO WITH POWERS.
HMMMPH.
BAD ENOUGH THERE'S ONE WEB-SLINGER CAPERING ABOUT THE CITY, NOW YOU WANT ME TO BELIEVE THERE'S TWO?
AND THAT THE SECOND ONE'S A WOMAN?
I KNOW, RIGHT?
WOMEN SUPER HEROES, WOMEN REPORTERS...
WHAT'S THE WORLD COMING TO?
WAIT.
I DIDN'T-- I WASN'T--
DAMN IT, BRANT, DON'T PUT WORDS IN MY MOUTH.
WHERE ARE YOU NOW?
TRYING TO GET CLOSE ENOUGH TO NORMIE OSBORN TO HEAR WHAT HE THINKS HAPPENED HERE.
THAT KID GIVES ME THE CREEPS.
BE CAREFUL, BETTY.
"CAREFUL"?
JONAH, THAT SHIP SAILED THE DAY I QUIT BEING YOUR SECRETARY AND BECAME A REPORTER.
GOTTA GO.

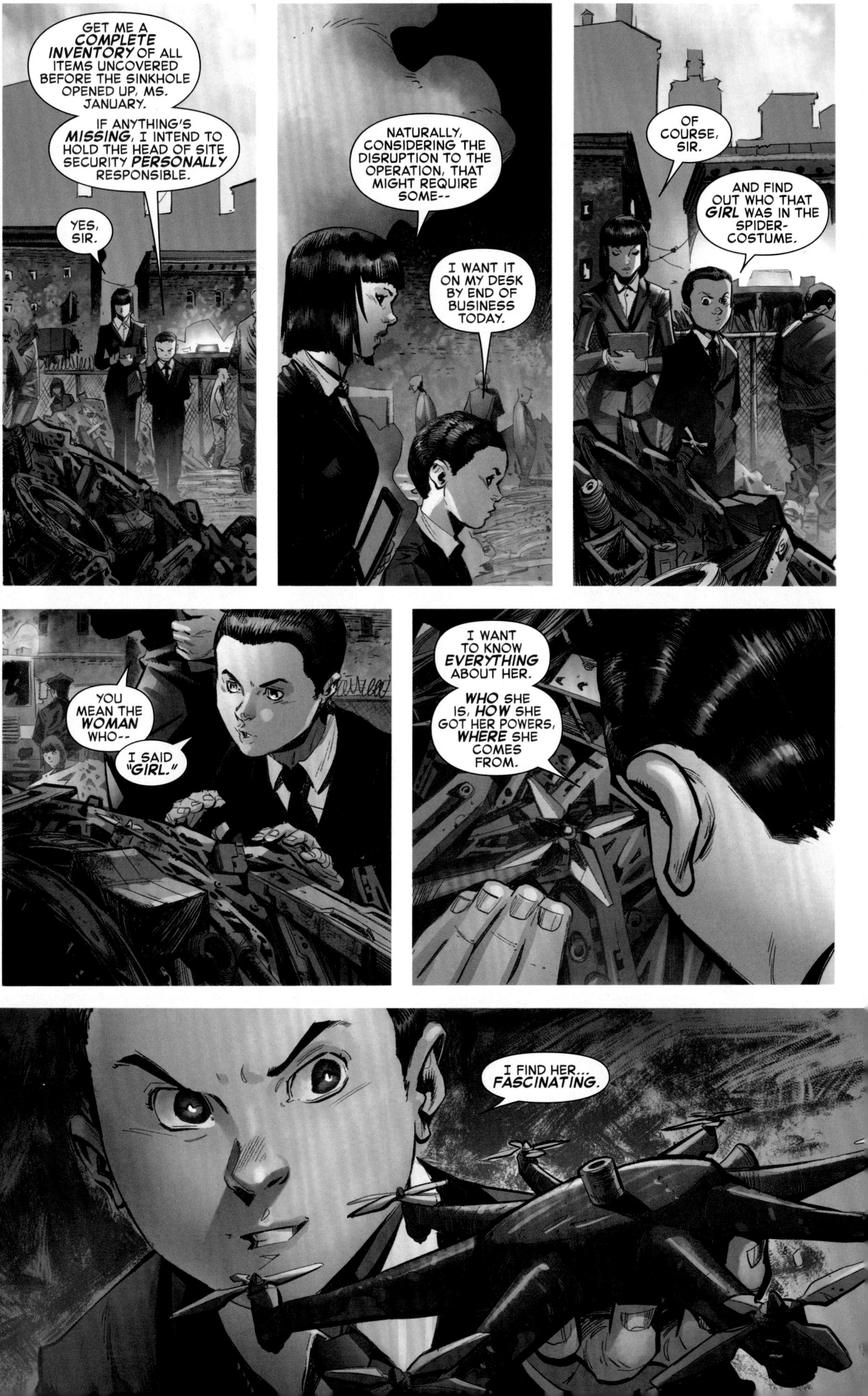
GET ME A *COMPLETE INVENTORY* OF ALL ITEMS UNCOVERED BEFORE THE SINKHOLE OPENED UP, MS. JANUARY.
IF ANYTHING'S *MISSING*, I INTEND TO HOLD THE HEAD OF SITE SECURITY *PERSONALLY* RESPONSIBLE.
YES, SIR.
NATURALLY, CONSIDERING THE DISRUPTION TO THE OPERATION, THAT MIGHT REQUIRE SOME--
I WANT IT ON MY DESK BY END OF BUSINESS TODAY.
OF COURSE, SIR.
AND FIND OUT WHO THAT *GIRL* WAS IN THE SPIDER-COSTUME.
YOU MEAN THE *WOMAN* WHO--
I SAID *"GIRL."*
I WANT TO KNOW *EVERYTHING* ABOUT HER.
*WHO* SHE IS, *HOW* SHE GOT HER POWERS, *WHERE* SHE COMES FROM.
I FIND HER... *FASCINATING*.

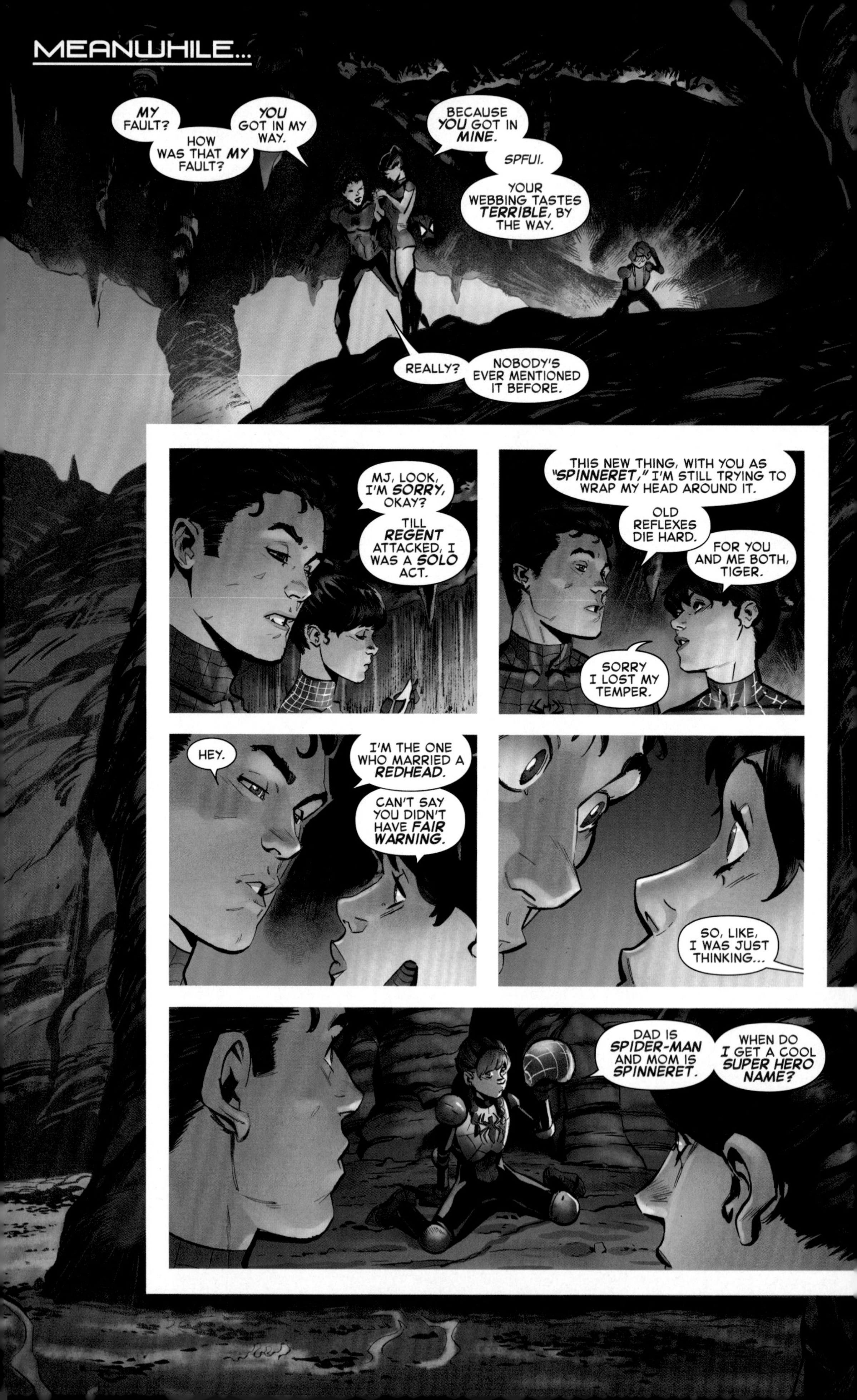
MEANWHILE...
MY FAULT?
HOW WAS THAT MY FAULT?
YOU GOT IN MY WAY.
BECAUSE YOU GOT IN MINE.
SPFUI.
YOUR WEBBING TASTES TERRIBLE, BY THE WAY.
REALLY?
NOBODY'S EVER MENTIONED IT BEFORE.
MJ, LOOK, I'M SORRY, OKAY?
TILL REGENT ATTACKED, I WAS A SOLO ACT.
THIS NEW THING, WITH YOU AS "SPINNERET," I'M STILL TRYING TO WRAP MY HEAD AROUND IT.
OLD REFLEXES DIE HARD.
SORRY I LOST MY TEMPER.
FOR YOU AND ME BOTH, TIGER.
HEY.
I'M THE ONE WHO MARRIED A REDHEAD.
CAN'T SAY YOU DIDN'T HAVE FAIR WARNING.
SO, LIKE, I WAS JUST THINKING...
DAD IS SPIDER-MAN AND MOM IS SPINNERET.
WHEN DO I GET A COOL SUPER HERO NAME?

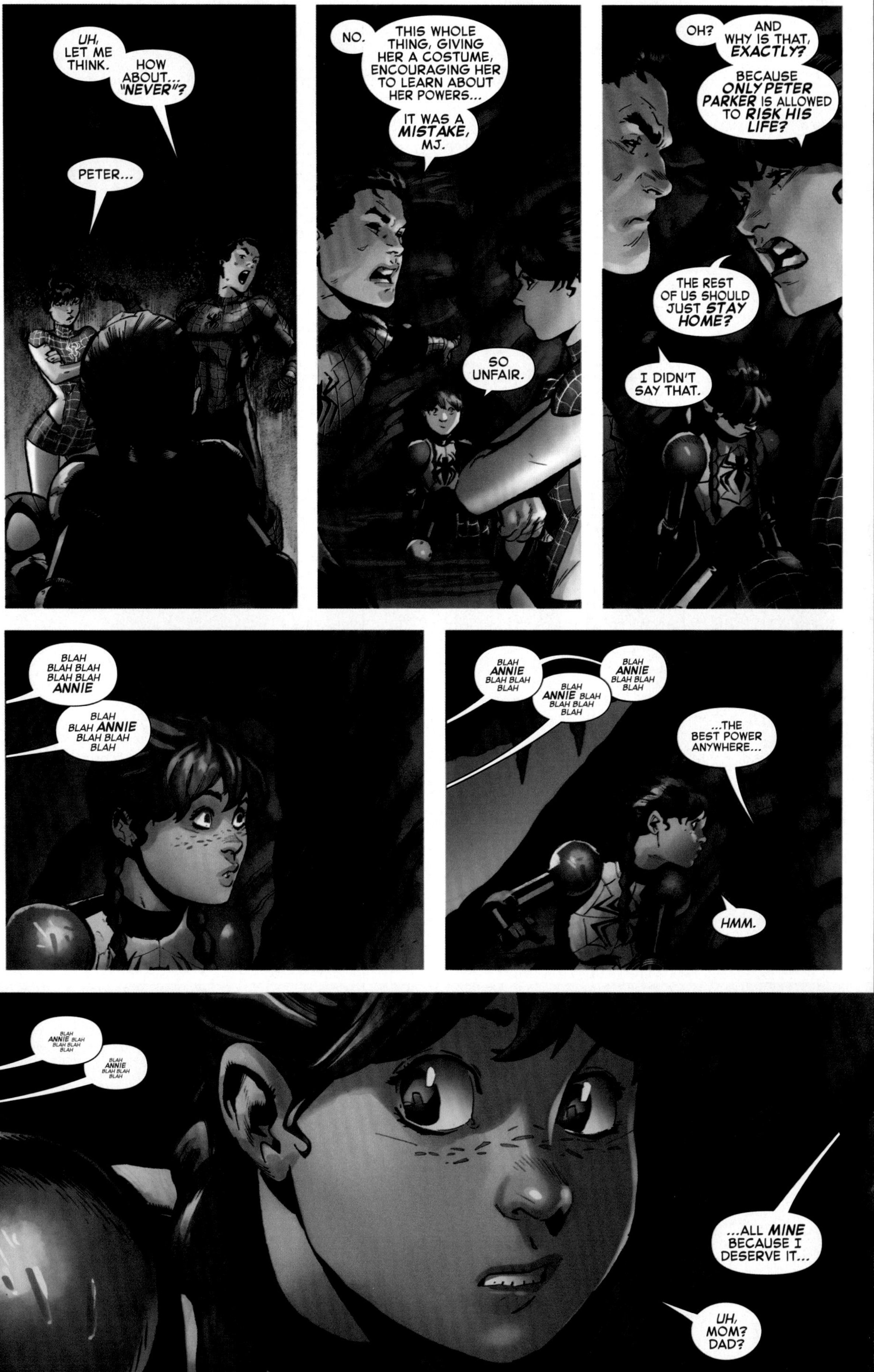
UH, LET ME THINK.
HOW ABOUT... "NEVER"?
PETER...
NO.
THIS WHOLE THING, GIVING HER A COSTUME, ENCOURAGING HER TO LEARN ABOUT HER POWERS...
IT WAS A MISTAKE, MJ.
SO UNFAIR.
OH?
AND WHY IS THAT, EXACTLY?
BECAUSE ONLY PETER PARKER IS ALLOWED TO RISK HIS LIFE?
THE REST OF US SHOULD JUST STAY HOME?
I DIDN'T SAY THAT.
BLAH BLAH BLAH BLAH BLAH ANNIE
BLAH BLAH ANNIE BLAH BLAH BLAH
BLAH ANNIE BLAH BLAH BLAH
BLAH ANNIE BLAH BLAH BLAH BLAH
BLAH ANNIE BLAH BLAH BLAH
...THE BEST POWER ANYWHERE...
HMM.
BLAH ANNIE BLAH BLAH BLAH BLAH
BLAH ANNIE BLAH BLAH BLAH
...ALL MINE BECAUSE I DESERVE IT...
UH, MOM? DAD?

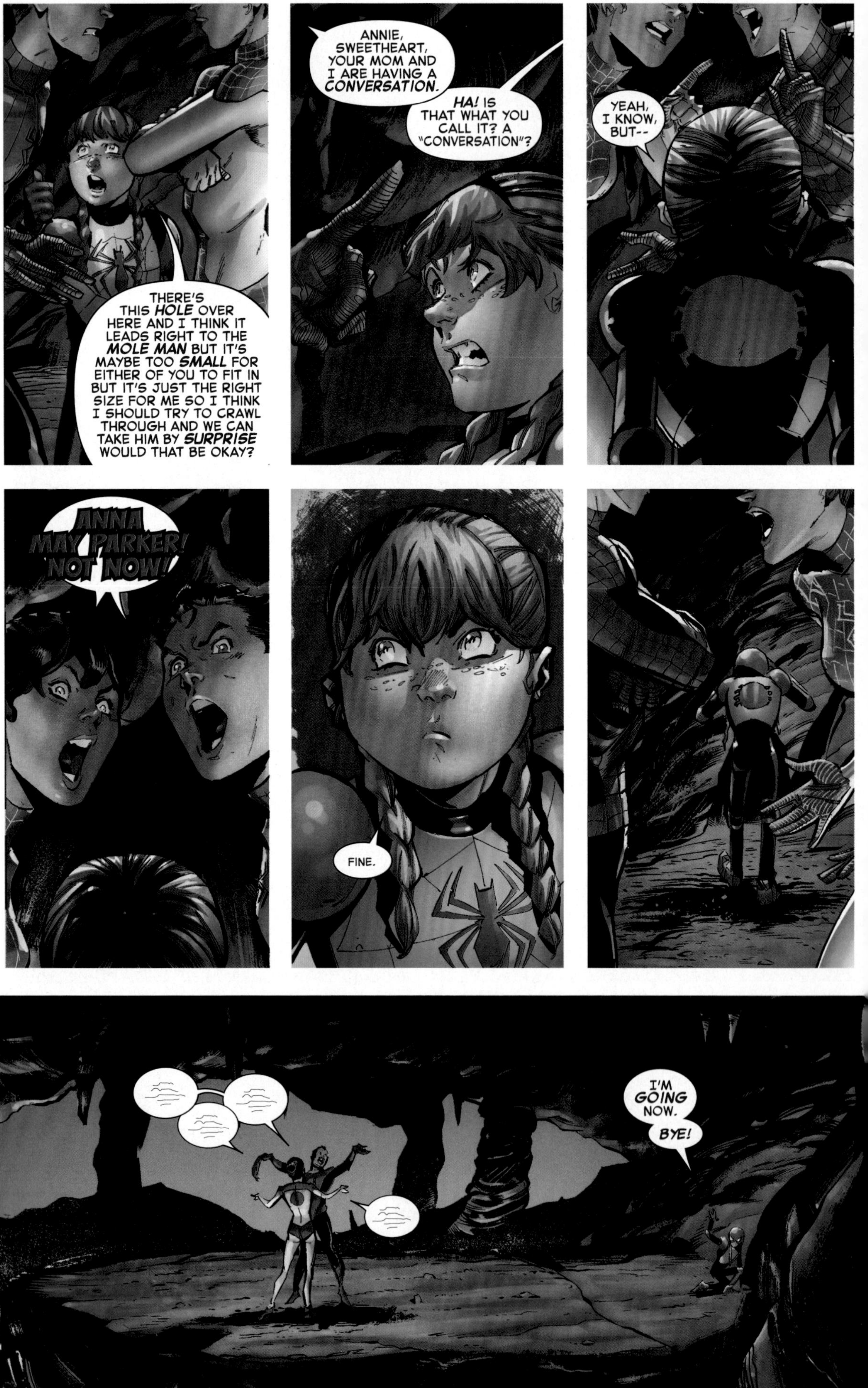
THERE'S THIS HOLE OVER HERE AND I THINK IT LEADS RIGHT TO THE MOLE MAN BUT IT'S MAYBE TOO SMALL FOR EITHER OF YOU TO FIT IN BUT IT'S JUST THE RIGHT SIZE FOR ME SO I THINK I SHOULD TRY TO CRAWL THROUGH AND WE CAN TAKE HIM BY SURPRISE WOULD THAT BE OKAY?
ANNIE, SWEETHEART, YOUR MOM AND I ARE HAVING A CONVERSATION.
HA! IS THAT WHAT YOU CALL IT? A "CONVERSATION"?
YEAH, I KNOW, BUT--
ANNA MAY PARKER! NOT NOW!
FINE.
I'M GOING NOW.
BYE!

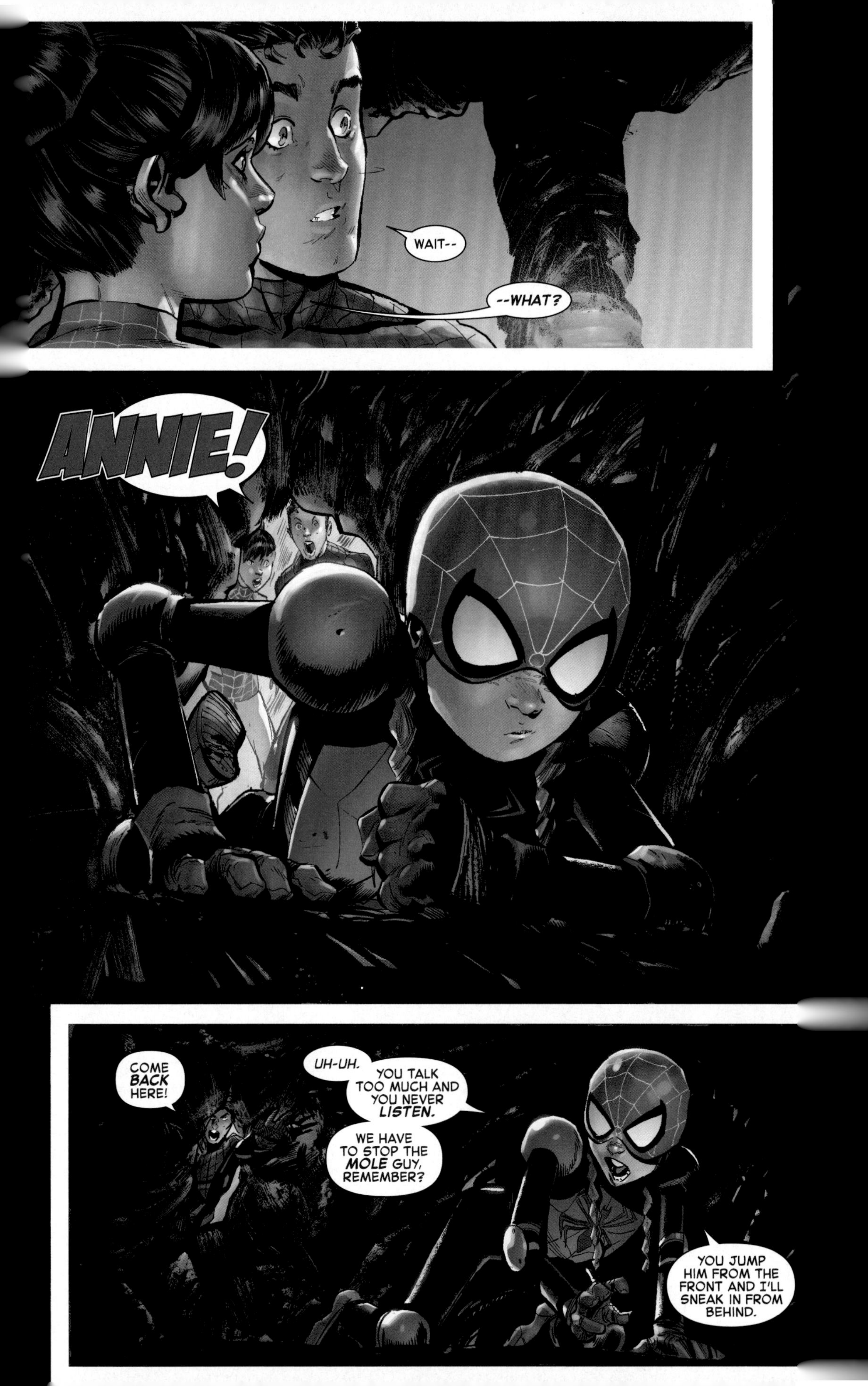
WAIT--
--WHAT?
ANNIE!
COME BACK HERE!
UH-UH.
YOU TALK TOO MUCH AND YOU NEVER LISTEN.
WE HAVE TO STOP THE MOLE GUY, REMEMBER?
YOU JUMP HIM FROM THE FRONT AND I'LL SNEAK IN FROM BEHIND.

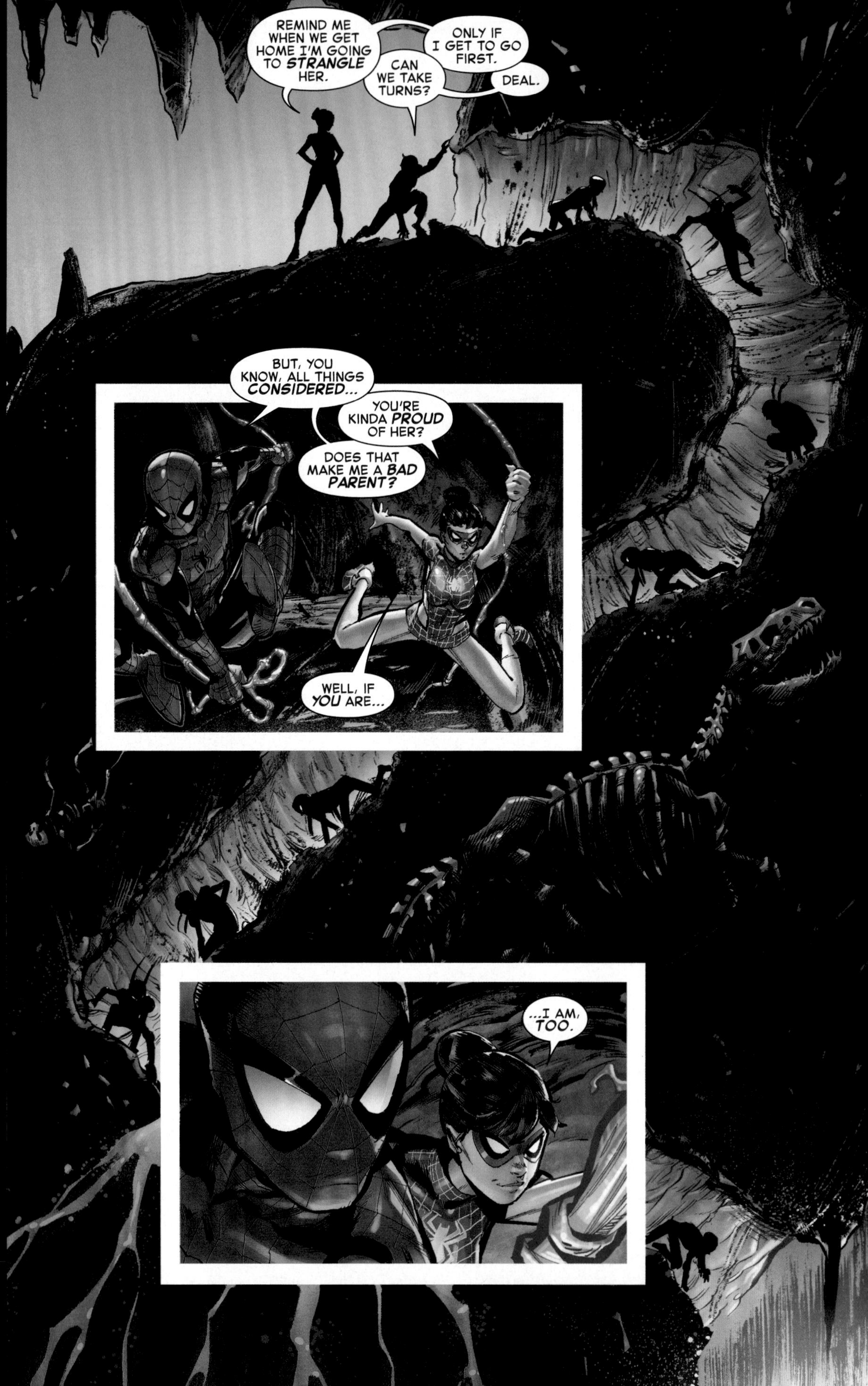
REMIND ME WHEN WE GET HOME I'M GOING TO STRANGLE HER.
ONLY IF I GET TO GO FIRST.
CAN WE TAKE TURNS?
DEAL.
BUT, YOU KNOW, ALL THINGS CONSIDERED...
YOU'RE KINDA PROUD OF HER?
DOES THAT MAKE ME A BAD PARENT?
WELL, IF YOU ARE...
...I AM, TOO.

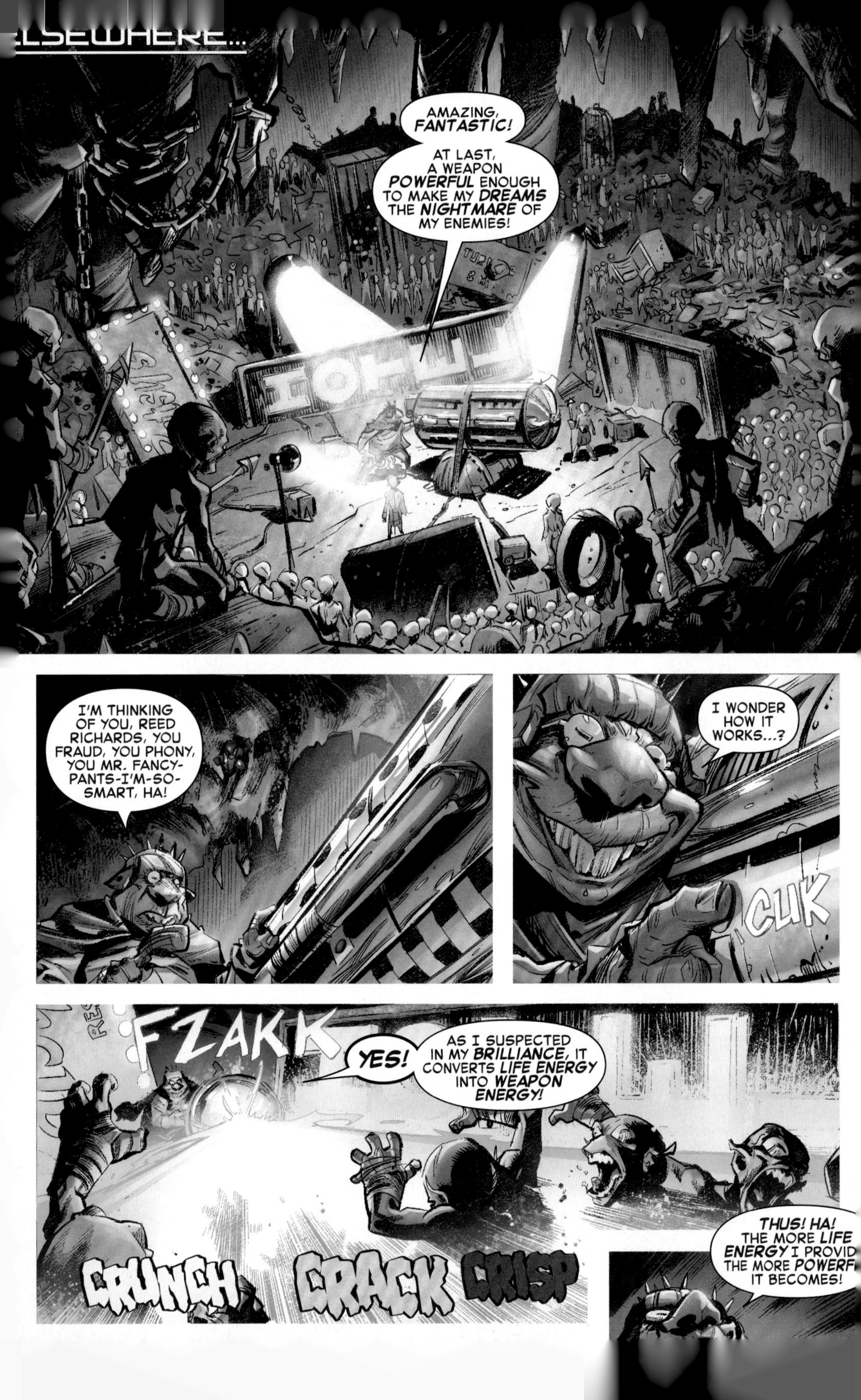
ELSEWHERE...
AMAZING, FANTASTIC!
AT LAST, A WEAPON POWERFUL ENOUGH TO MAKE MY DREAMS THE NIGHTMARE OF MY ENEMIES!
I'M THINKING OF YOU, REED RICHARDS, YOU FRAUD, YOU PHONY, YOU MR. FANCY-PANTS-I'M-SO-SMART, HA!
I WONDER HOW IT WORKS...?
CLIK
FZAKK
YES!
AS I SUSPECTED IN MY BRILLIANCE, IT CONVERTS LIFE ENERGY INTO WEAPON ENERGY!
CRUNCH
CRACK
CRISP
THUS! HA! THE MORE LIFE ENERGY I PROVID THE MORE POWERF IT BECOMES!

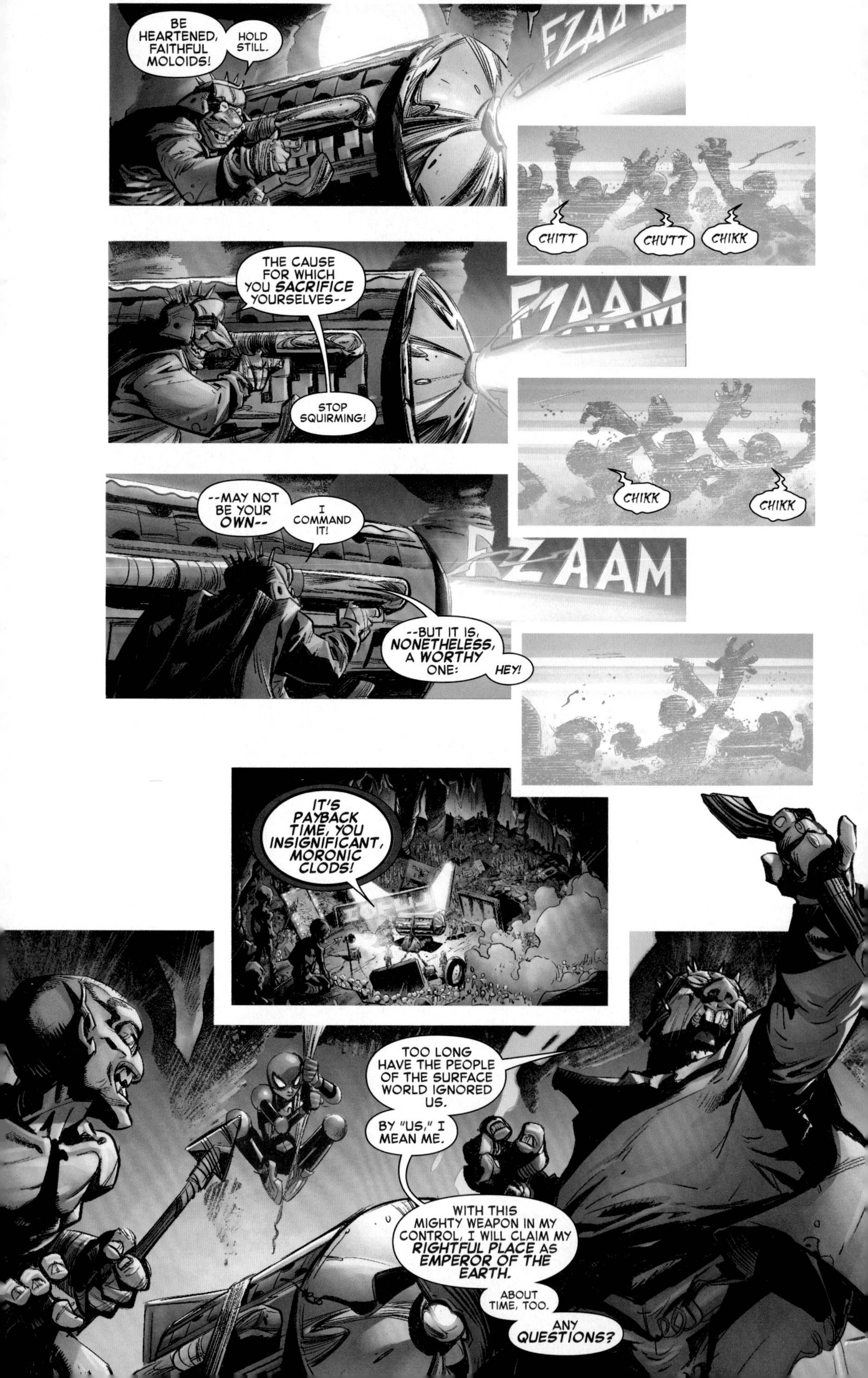
BE HEARTENED, FAITHFUL MOLOIDS!
HOLD STILL.
FZAAM
CHITT
CHUTT
CHIKK
THE CAUSE FOR WHICH YOU SACRIFICE YOURSELVES--
STOP SQUIRMING!
FZAAM
CHIKK
CHIKK
--MAY NOT BE YOUR OWN--
I COMMAND IT!
FZAAM
--BUT IT IS, NONETHELESS, A WORTHY ONE:
HEY!
IT'S PAYBACK TIME, YOU INSIGNIFICANT, MORONIC CLODS!
TOO LONG HAVE THE PEOPLE OF THE SURFACE WORLD IGNORED US.
BY "US," I MEAN ME.
WITH THIS MIGHTY WEAPON IN MY CONTROL, I WILL CLAIM MY RIGHTFUL PLACE AS EMPEROR OF THE EARTH.
ABOUT TIME, TOO.
ANY QUESTIONS?

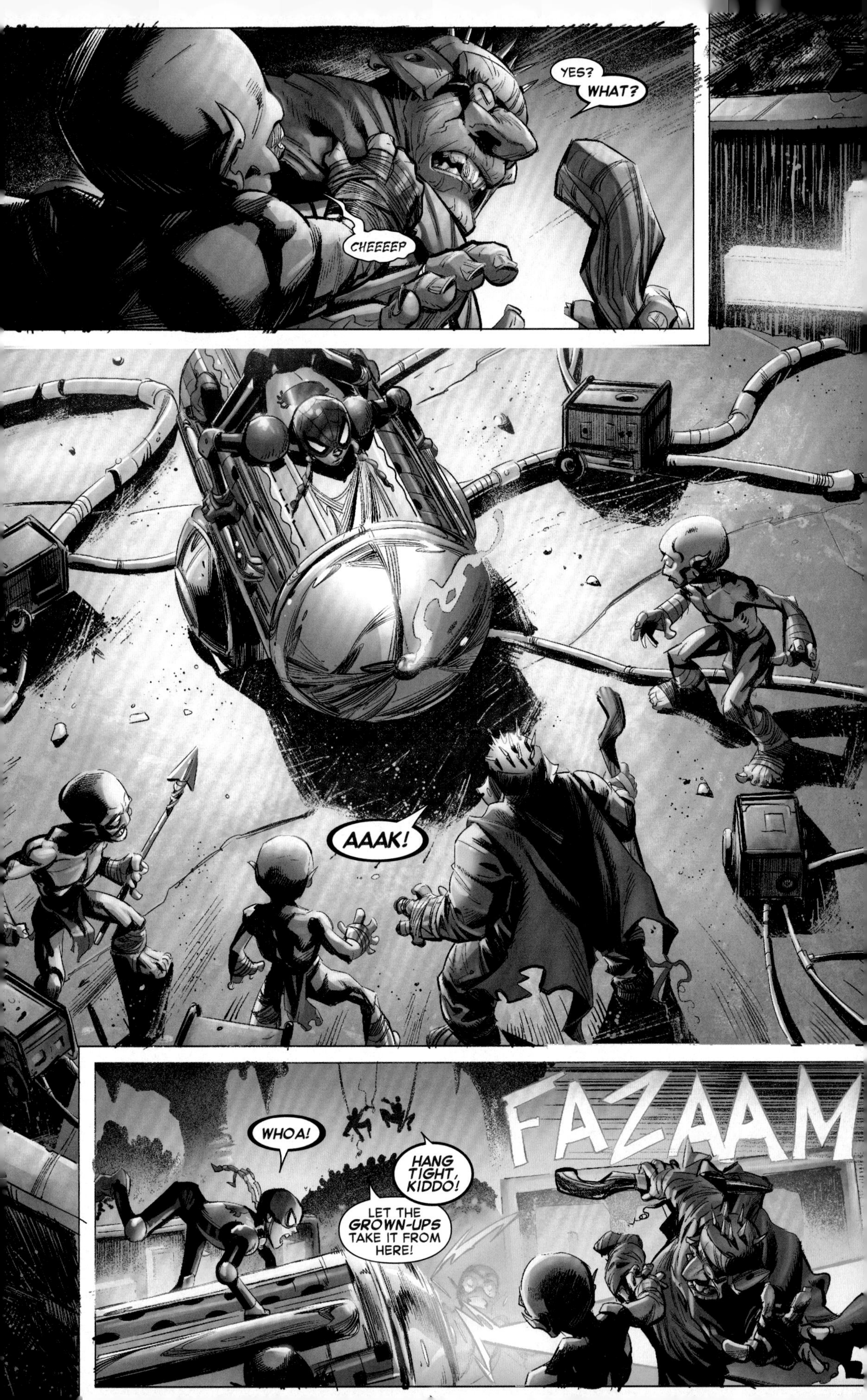
YES? WHAT?
CHEEEEP
AAAK!
FAZAAM
WHOA!
HANG TIGHT, KIDDO!
LET THE GROWN-UPS TAKE IT FROM HERE!

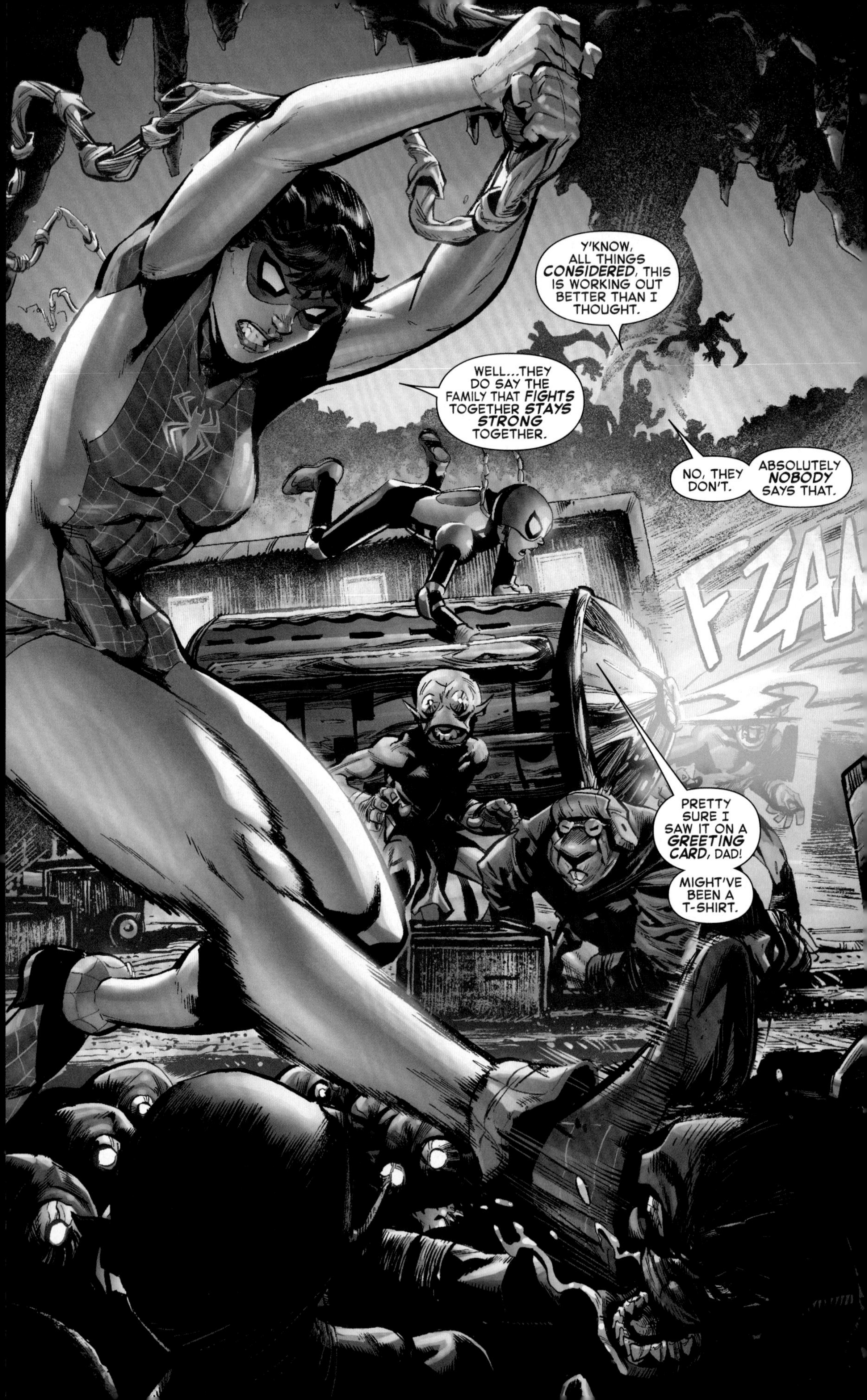
Y'KNOW, ALL THINGS CONSIDERED, THIS IS WORKING OUT BETTER THAN I THOUGHT.
WELL...THEY DO SAY THE FAMILY THAT FIGHTS TOGETHER STAYS STRONG TOGETHER.
NO, THEY DON'T.
ABSOLUTELY NOBODY SAYS THAT.
FZAM
PRETTY SURE I SAW IT ON A GREETING CARD, DAD!
MIGHT'VE BEEN A T-SHIRT.

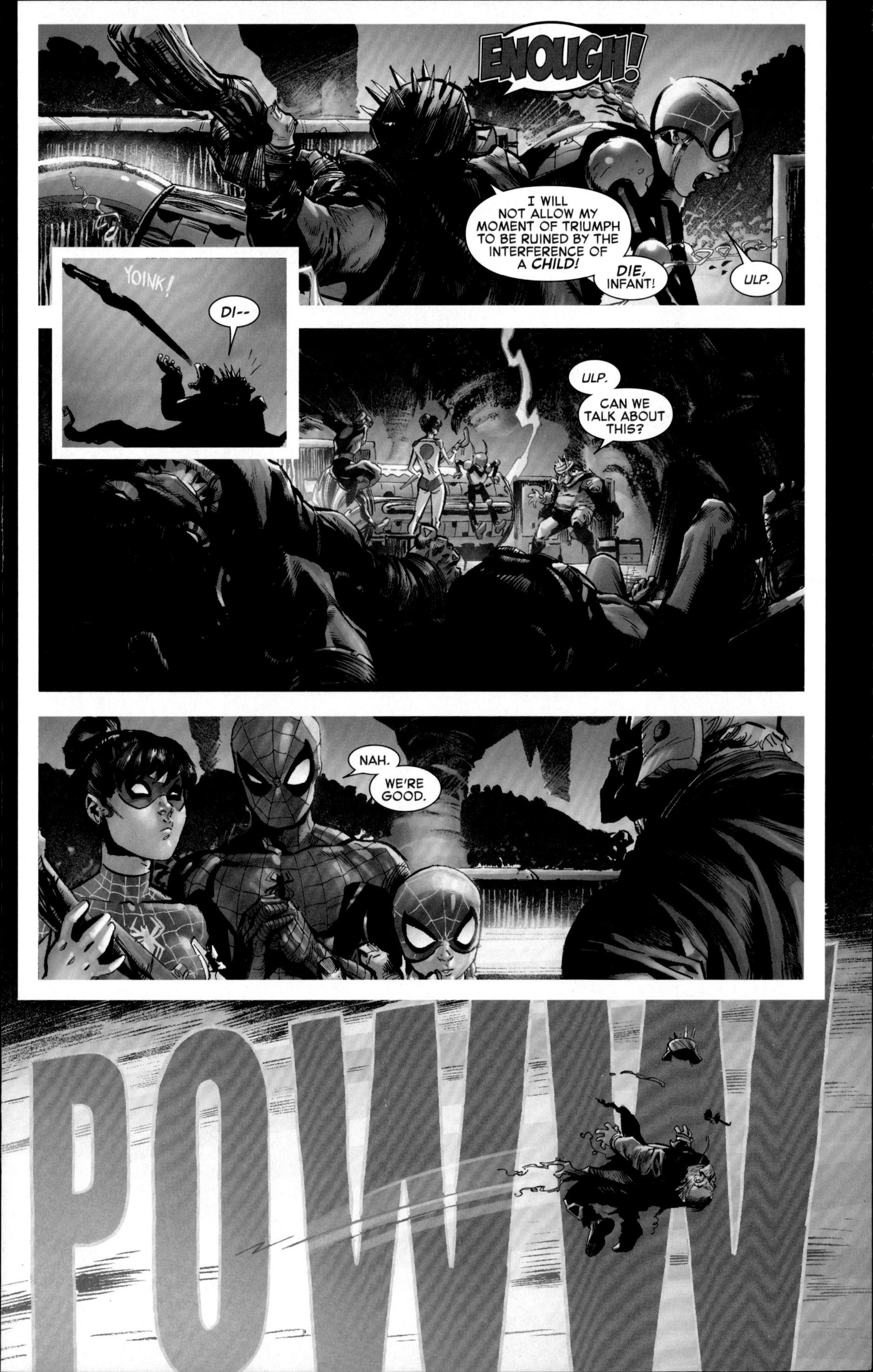
ENOUGH!
I WILL NOT ALLOW MY MOMENT OF TRIUMPH TO BE RUINED BY THE INTERFERENCE OF A *CHILD*!
*DIE*, INFANT!
*ULP.*
YOINK!
*DI--*
*ULP.*
CAN WE TALK ABOUT THIS?
NAH.
WE'RE GOOD.
POWW

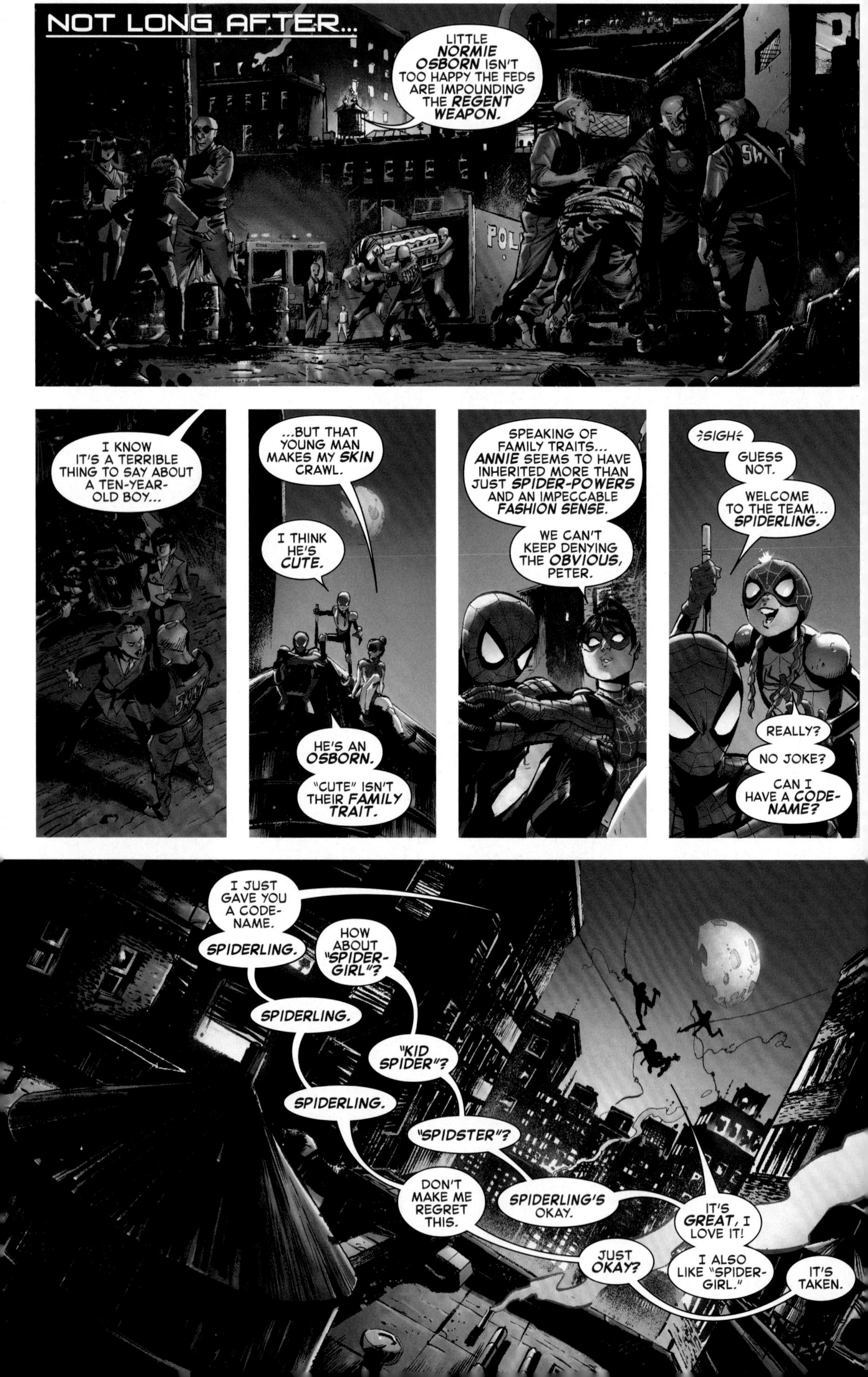
NOT LONG AFTER...
LITTLE NORMIE OSBORN ISN'T TOO HAPPY THE FEDS ARE IMPOUNDING THE REGENT WEAPON.
I KNOW IT'S A TERRIBLE THING TO SAY ABOUT A TEN-YEAR-OLD BOY...
...BUT THAT YOUNG MAN MAKES MY SKIN CRAWL.
I THINK HE'S CUTE.
HE'S AN OSBORN.
"CUTE" ISN'T THEIR FAMILY TRAIT.
SPEAKING OF FAMILY TRAITS... ANNIE SEEMS TO HAVE INHERITED MORE THAN JUST SPIDER-POWERS AND AN IMPECCABLE FASHION SENSE.
WE CAN'T KEEP DENYING THE OBVIOUS, PETER.
SIGH
GUESS NOT.
WELCOME TO THE TEAM... SPIDERLING.
REALLY?
NO JOKE?
CAN I HAVE A CODE-NAME?
I JUST GAVE YOU A CODE-NAME.
SPIDERLING.
HOW ABOUT "SPIDER-GIRL"?
SPIDERLING.
"KID SPIDER"?
SPIDERLING.
"SPIDSTER"?
DON'T MAKE ME REGRET THIS.
SPIDERLING'S OKAY.
IT'S GREAT, I LOVE IT!
JUST OKAY?
I ALSO LIKE "SPIDER-GIRL."
IT'S TAKEN.

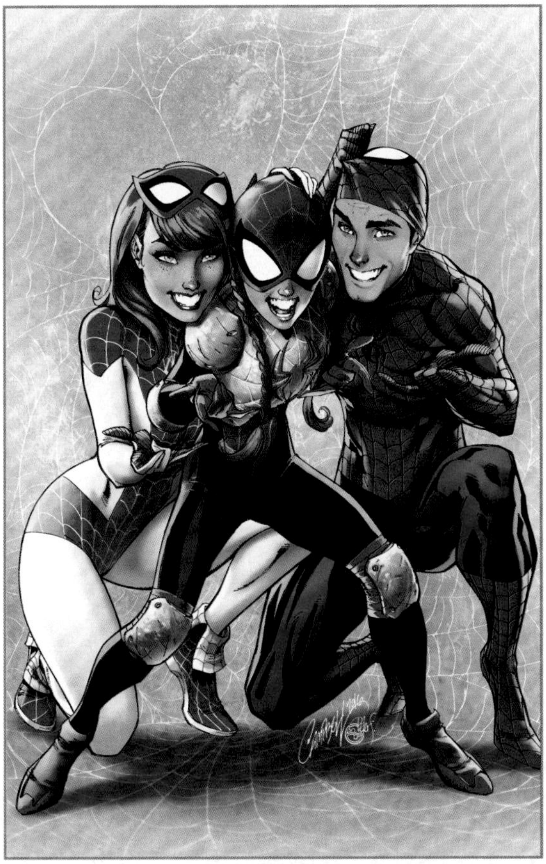

2 variant by **J. SCOTT CAMPBELL** & **PETER STEIGERWALD**

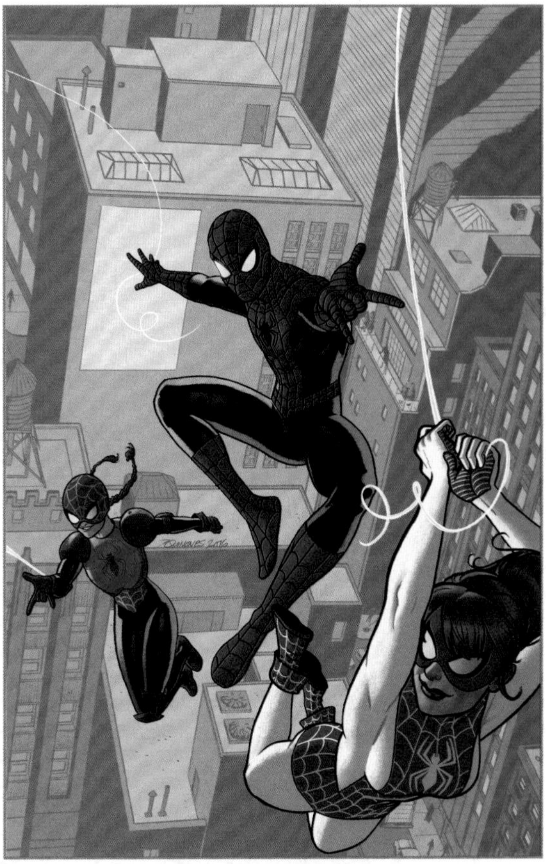

3 variant by **JOE QUINONES**

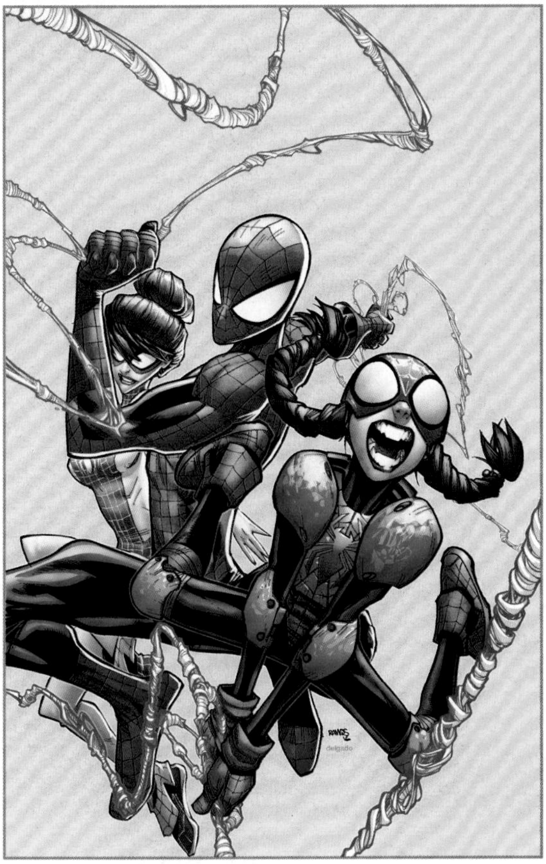

4 variant by **HUMBERTO RAMOS** & **EDGAR DELGADO**

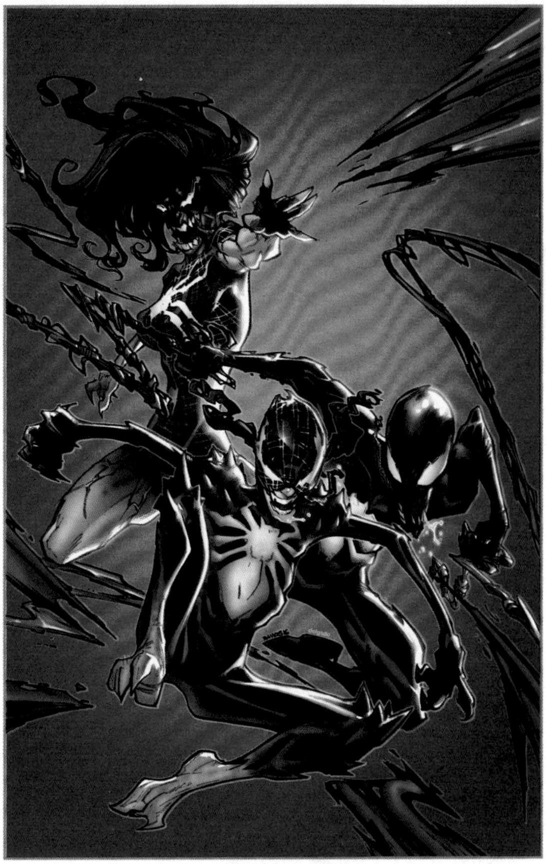

5 venomized variant by **HUMBERTO RAMOS** & **EDGAR DELGADO**

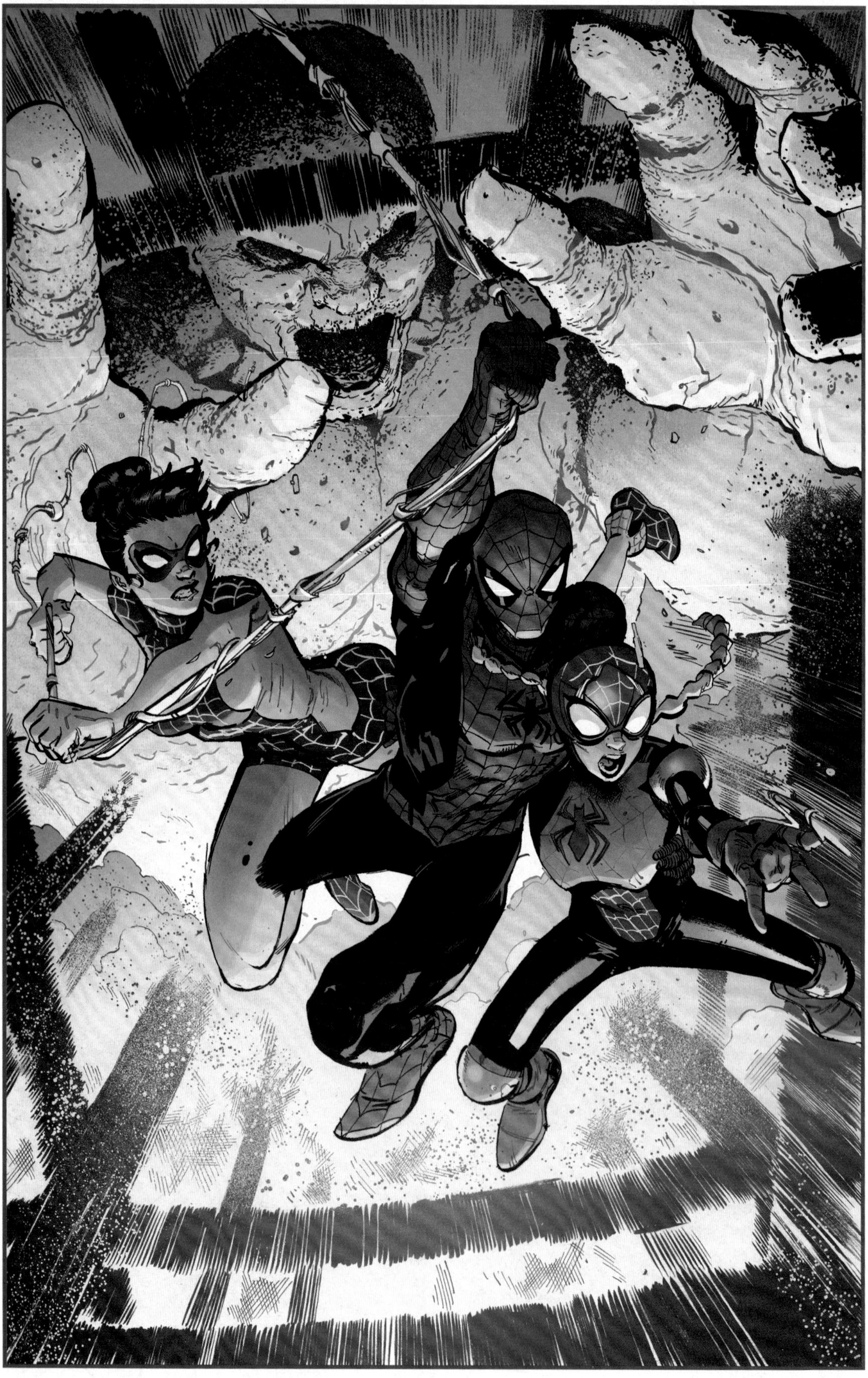

5

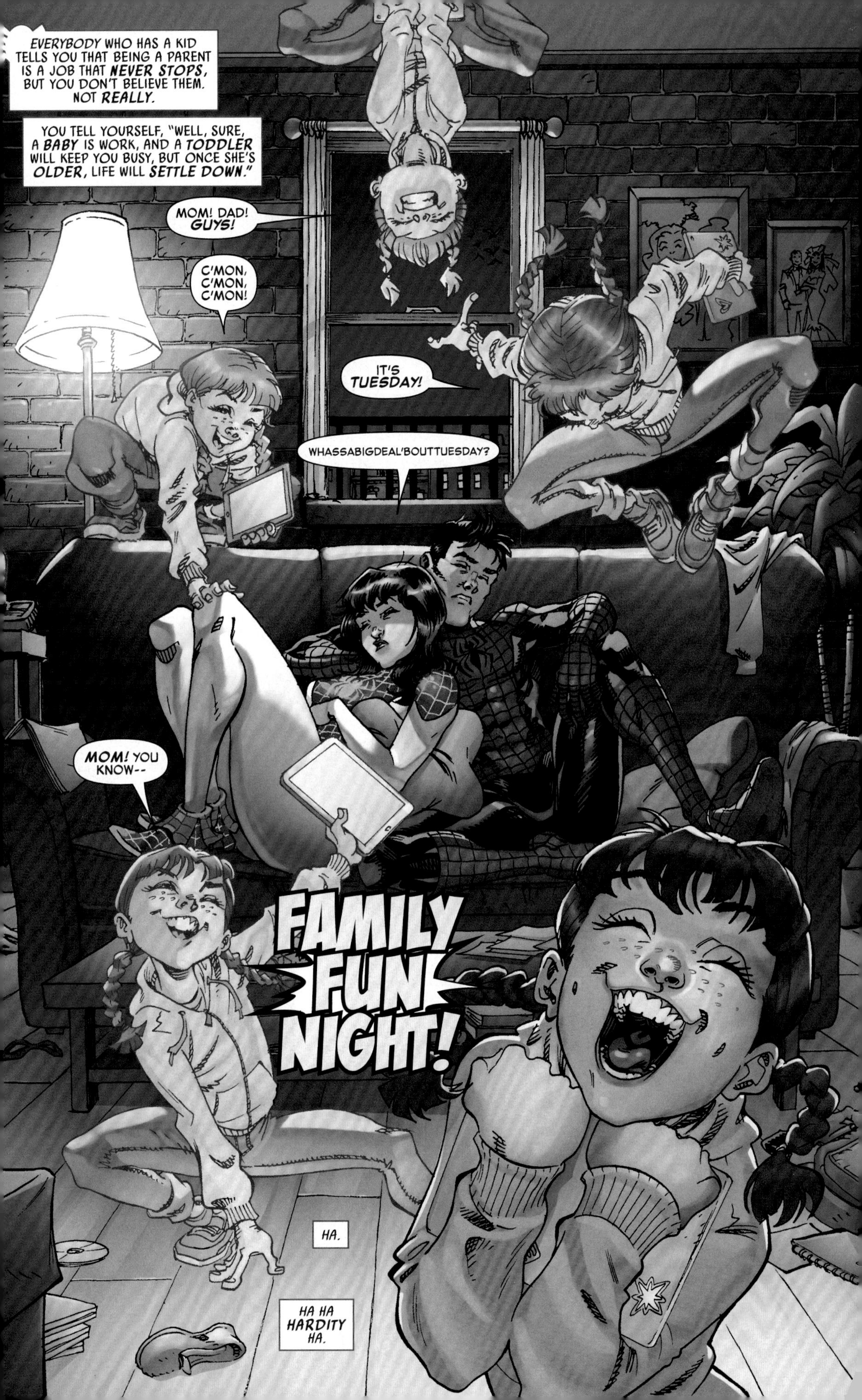
EVERYBODY WHO HAS A KID TELLS YOU THAT BEING A PARENT IS A JOB THAT NEVER STOPS, BUT YOU DON'T BELIEVE THEM. NOT REALLY.
YOU TELL YOURSELF, "WELL, SURE, A BABY IS WORK, AND A TODDLER WILL KEEP YOU BUSY, BUT ONCE SHE'S OLDER, LIFE WILL SETTLE DOWN."
MOM! DAD! GUYS!
C'MON, C'MON, C'MON!
IT'S TUESDAY!
WHASSABIGDEAL'BOUTTUESDAY?
MOM! YOU KNOW--
FAMILY FUN NIGHT!
HA.
HA HA HARDITY HA.

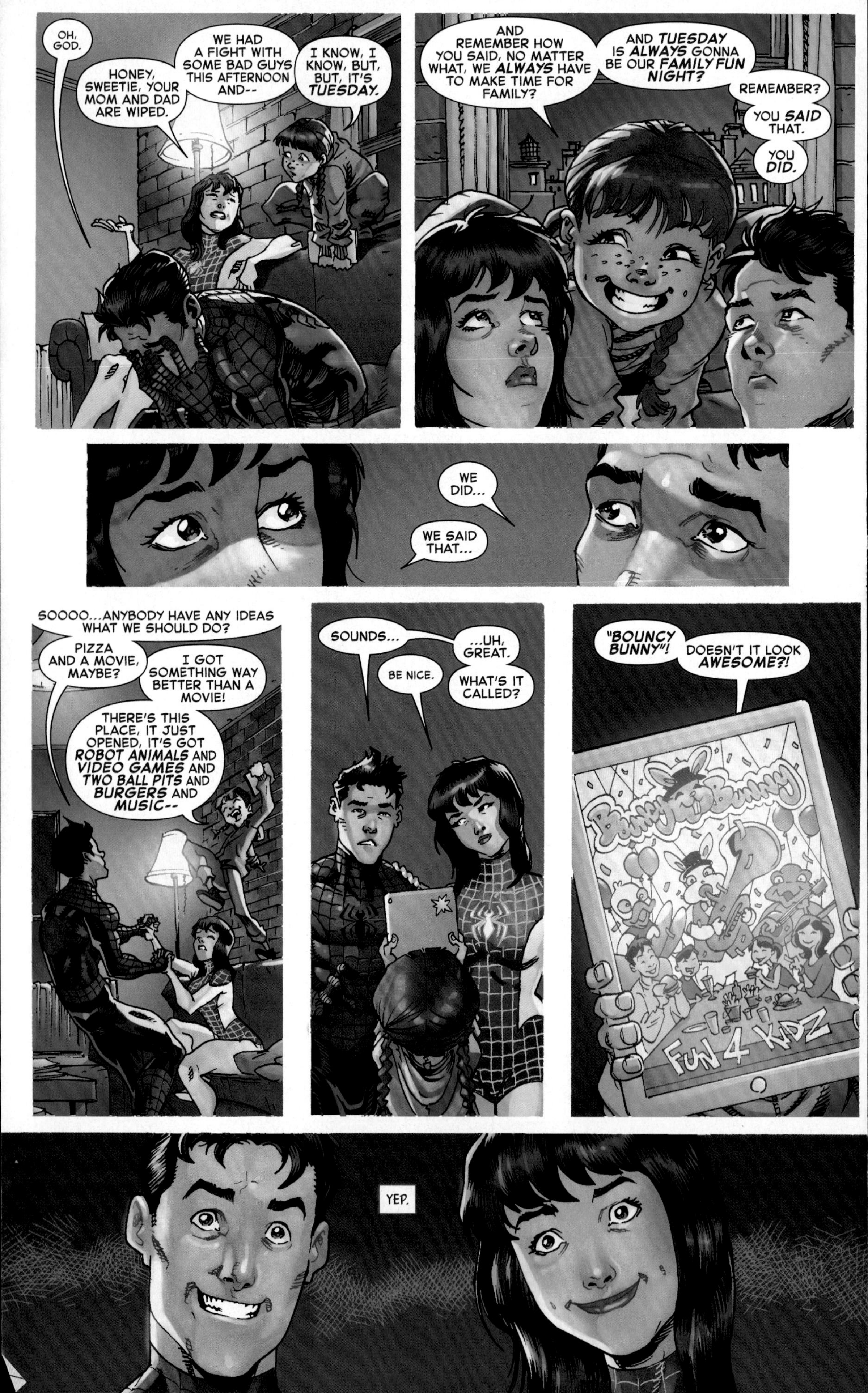

OH, GOD.
HONEY, SWEETIE, YOUR MOM AND DAD ARE WIPED.
WE HAD A FIGHT WITH SOME BAD GUYS THIS AFTERNOON AND--
I KNOW, I KNOW, BUT, BUT, IT'S TUESDAY.
AND REMEMBER HOW YOU SAID, NO MATTER WHAT, WE ALWAYS HAVE TO MAKE TIME FOR FAMILY?
AND TUESDAY IS ALWAYS GONNA BE OUR FAMILY FUN NIGHT?
REMEMBER?
YOU SAID THAT.
YOU DID.
WE DID...
WE SAID THAT...
SOOOO...ANYBODY HAVE ANY IDEAS WHAT WE SHOULD DO?
PIZZA AND A MOVIE, MAYBE?
I GOT SOMETHING WAY BETTER THAN A MOVIE!
THERE'S THIS PLACE, IT JUST OPENED, IT'S GOT ROBOT ANIMALS AND VIDEO GAMES AND TWO BALL PITS AND BURGERS AND MUSIC--
SOUNDS...
...UH, GREAT.
BE NICE.
WHAT'S IT CALLED?
"BOUNCY BUNNY"!
DOESN'T IT LOOK AWESOME?!
FUN 4 KIDZ
YEP.

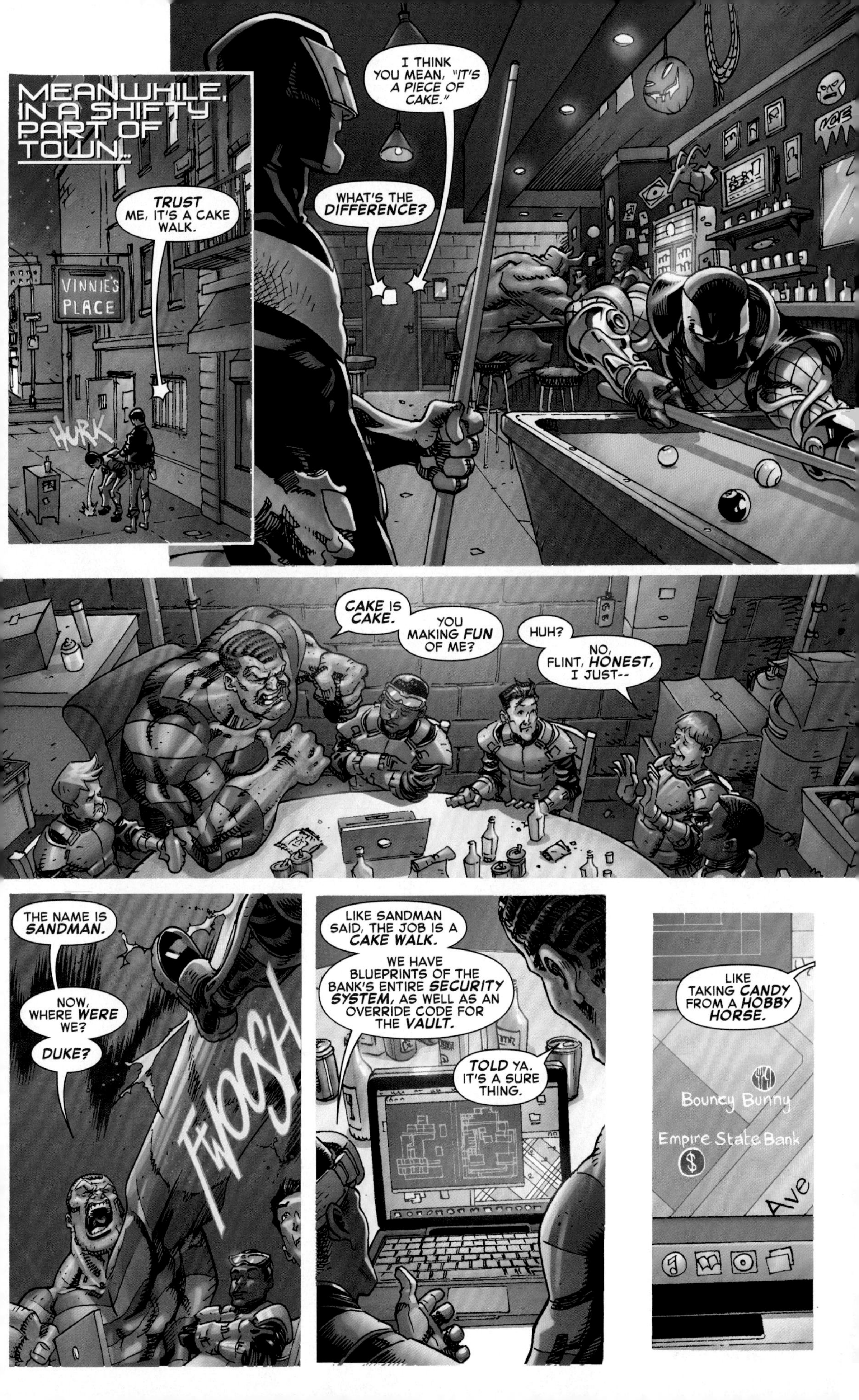
MEANWHILE, IN A SHIFTY PART OF TOWN...
VINNIE'S PLACE
TRUST ME, IT'S A CAKE WALK.
HURK
WHAT'S THE DIFFERENCE?
I THINK YOU MEAN, "IT'S A PIECE OF CAKE."
CAKE IS CAKE.
YOU MAKING FUN OF ME?
HUH?
NO, FLINT, HONEST, I JUST--
THE NAME IS SANDMAN.
NOW, WHERE WERE WE?
DUKE?
FWOOSH
LIKE SANDMAN SAID, THE JOB IS A CAKE WALK.
WE HAVE BLUEPRINTS OF THE BANK'S ENTIRE SECURITY SYSTEM, AS WELL AS AN OVERRIDE CODE FOR THE VAULT.
TOLD YA. IT'S A SURE THING.
LIKE TAKING CANDY FROM A HOBBY HORSE.
Bouncy Bunny
Empire State Bank
Ave

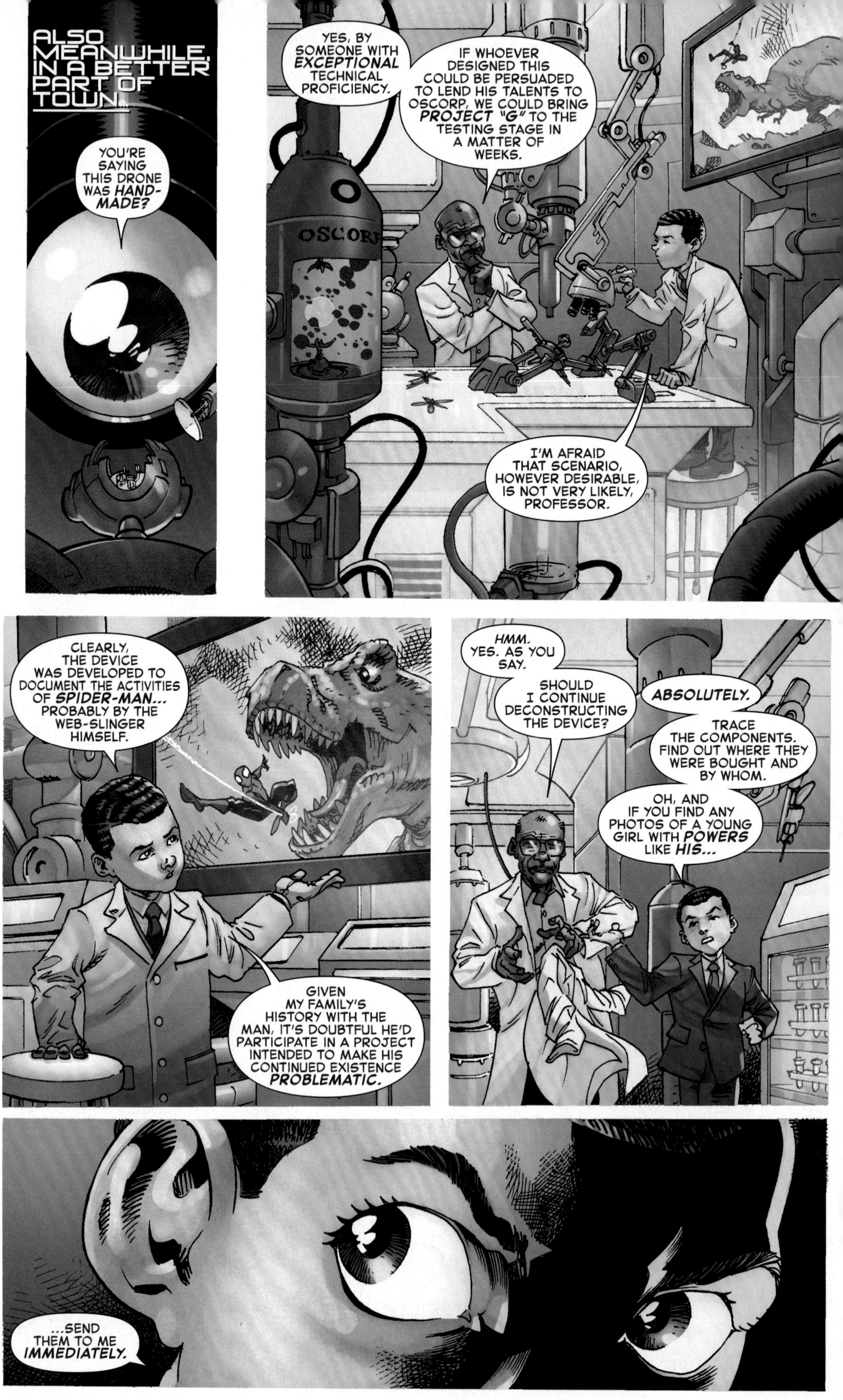
ALSO MEANWHILE, IN A BETTER PART OF TOWN...
YOU'RE SAYING THIS DRONE WAS HAND-MADE?
YES, BY SOMEONE WITH EXCEPTIONAL TECHNICAL PROFICIENCY.
IF WHOEVER DESIGNED THIS COULD BE PERSUADED TO LEND HIS TALENTS TO OSCORP, WE COULD BRING PROJECT "G" TO THE TESTING STAGE IN A MATTER OF WEEKS.
OSCORP
I'M AFRAID THAT SCENARIO, HOWEVER DESIRABLE, IS NOT VERY LIKELY, PROFESSOR.
CLEARLY, THE DEVICE WAS DEVELOPED TO DOCUMENT THE ACTIVITIES OF SPIDER-MAN... PROBABLY BY THE WEB-SLINGER HIMSELF.
GIVEN MY FAMILY'S HISTORY WITH THE MAN, IT'S DOUBTFUL HE'D PARTICIPATE IN A PROJECT INTENDED TO MAKE HIS CONTINUED EXISTENCE PROBLEMATIC.
HMM. YES. AS YOU SAY.
SHOULD I CONTINUE DECONSTRUCTING THE DEVICE?
ABSOLUTELY.
TRACE THE COMPONENTS. FIND OUT WHERE THEY WERE BOUGHT AND BY WHOM.
OH, AND IF YOU FIND ANY PHOTOS OF A YOUNG GIRL WITH POWERS LIKE HIS...
...SEND THEM TO ME IMMEDIATELY.

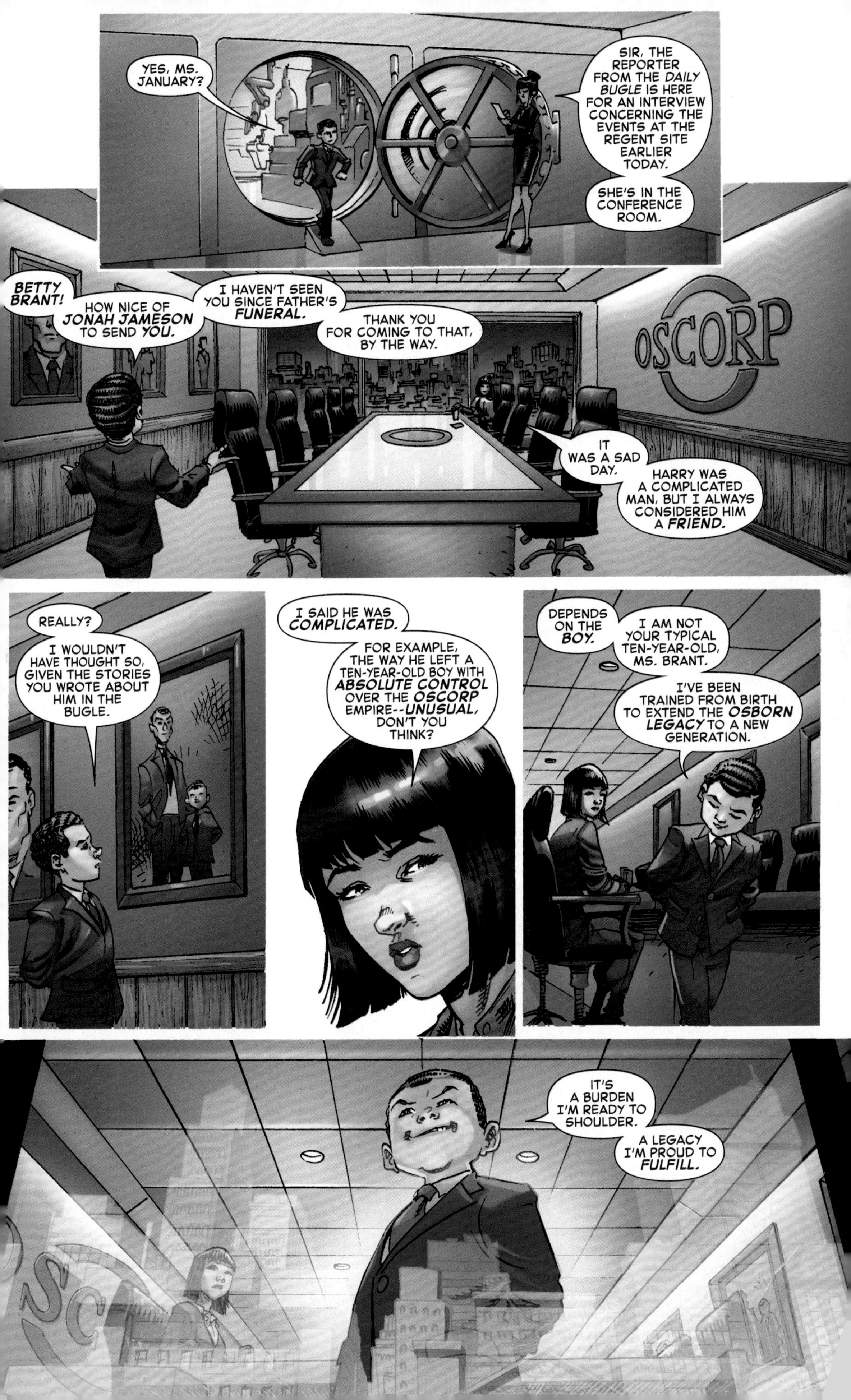
YES, MS. JANUARY?
SIR, THE REPORTER FROM THE DAILY BUGLE IS HERE FOR AN INTERVIEW CONCERNING THE EVENTS AT THE REGENT SITE EARLIER TODAY.
SHE'S IN THE CONFERENCE ROOM.
BETTY BRANT!
HOW NICE OF JONAH JAMESON TO SEND YOU.
I HAVEN'T SEEN YOU SINCE FATHER'S FUNERAL.
THANK YOU FOR COMING TO THAT, BY THE WAY.
OSCORP
IT WAS A SAD DAY.
HARRY WAS A COMPLICATED MAN, BUT I ALWAYS CONSIDERED HIM A FRIEND.
REALLY?
I WOULDN'T HAVE THOUGHT SO, GIVEN THE STORIES YOU WROTE ABOUT HIM IN THE BUGLE.
I SAID HE WAS COMPLICATED.
FOR EXAMPLE, THE WAY HE LEFT A TEN-YEAR-OLD BOY WITH ABSOLUTE CONTROL OVER THE OSCORP EMPIRE--UNUSUAL, DON'T YOU THINK?
DEPENDS ON THE BOY.
I AM NOT YOUR TYPICAL TEN-YEAR-OLD, MS. BRANT.
I'VE BEEN TRAINED FROM BIRTH TO EXTEND THE OSBORN LEGACY TO A NEW GENERATION.
IT'S A BURDEN I'M READY TO SHOULDER.
A LEGACY I'M PROUD TO FULFILL.

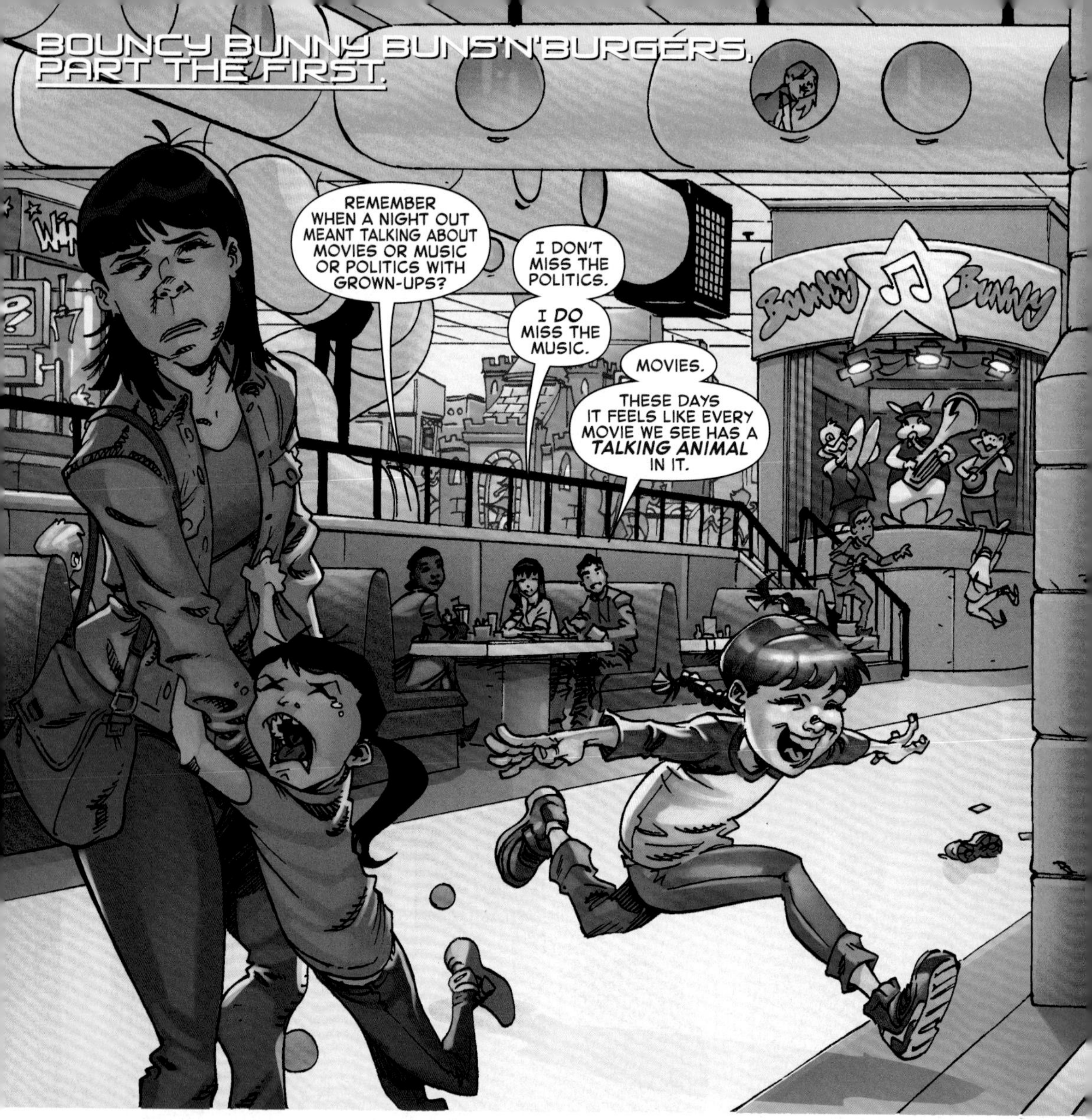
BOUNCY BUNNY BUNS'N'BURGERS, PART THE FIRST.
REMEMBER WHEN A NIGHT OUT MEANT TALKING ABOUT MOVIES OR MUSIC OR POLITICS WITH GROWN-UPS?
I DON'T MISS THE POLITICS.
I *DO* MISS THE MUSIC.
MOVIES.
THESE DAYS IT FEELS LIKE EVERY MOVIE WE SEE HAS A ***TALKING ANIMAL*** IN IT.
Bouncy Bunny

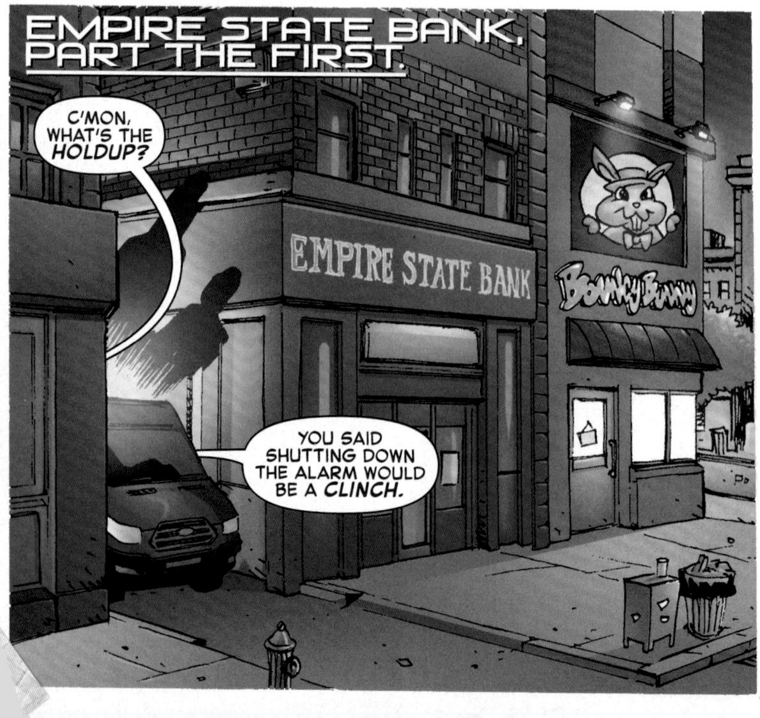
EMPIRE STATE BANK, PART THE FIRST.
C'MON, WHAT'S THE ***HOLDUP?***
EMPIRE STATE BANK
Bouncy Bunny
YOU SAID SHUTTING DOWN THE ALARM WOULD BE A ***CLINCH.***

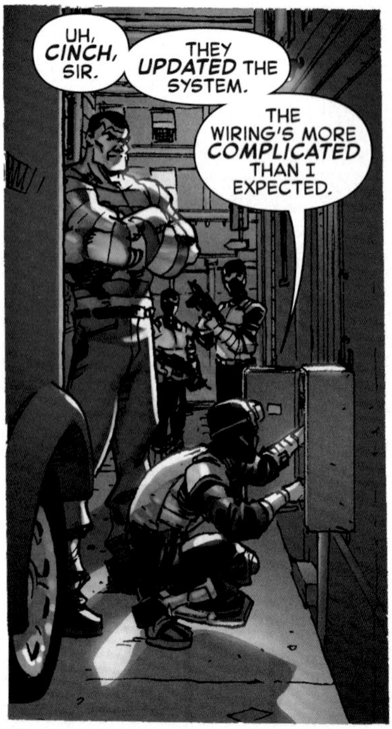
UH, ***CINCH,*** SIR.
THEY ***UPDATED*** THE SYSTEM.
THE WIRING'S MORE ***COMPLICATED*** THAN I EXPECTED.

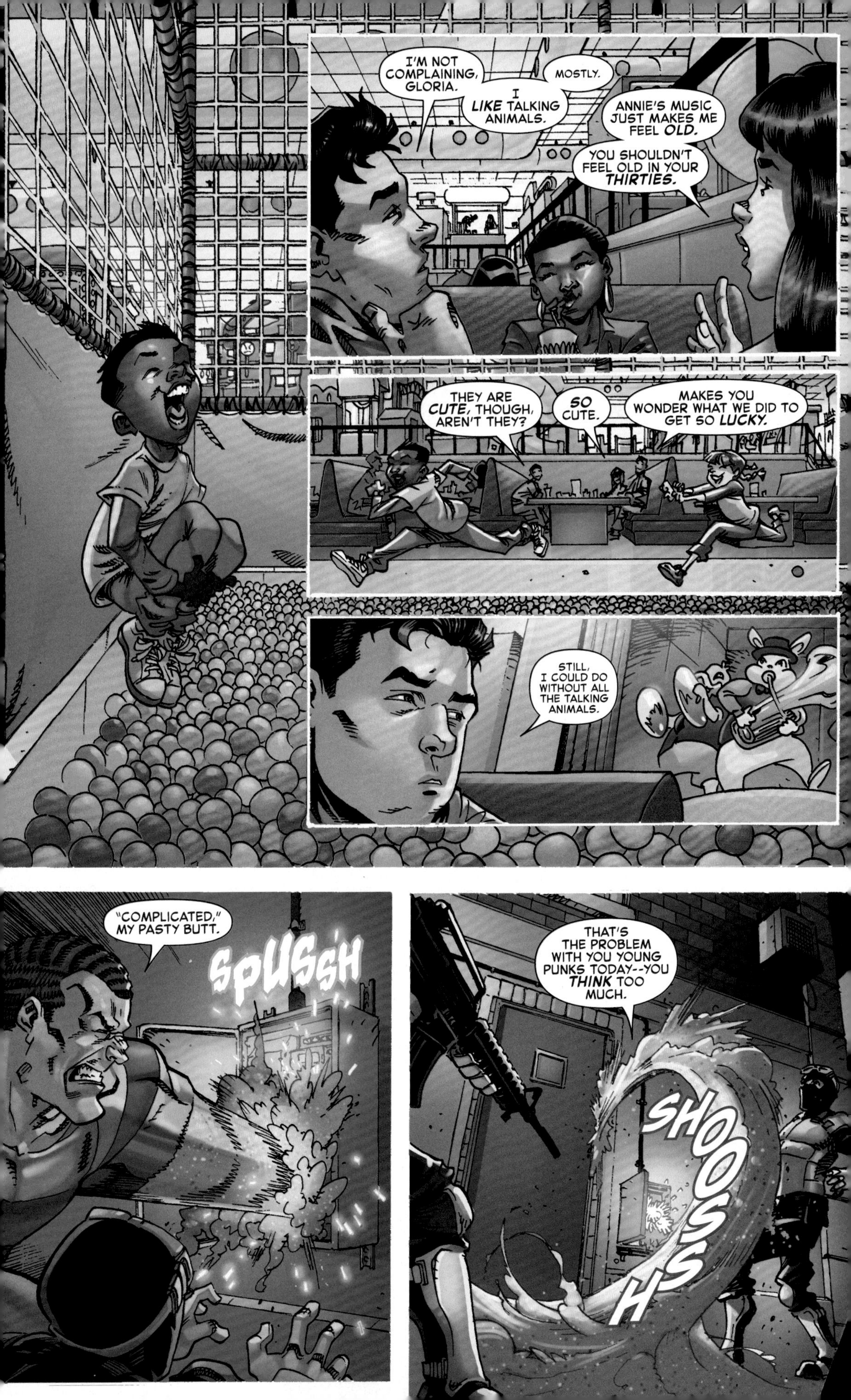
I'M NOT COMPLAINING, GLORIA.
MOSTLY.
I LIKE TALKING ANIMALS.
ANNIE'S MUSIC JUST MAKES ME FEEL OLD.
YOU SHOULDN'T FEEL OLD IN YOUR THIRTIES.
THEY ARE CUTE, THOUGH, AREN'T THEY?
SO CUTE.
MAKES YOU WONDER WHAT WE DID TO GET SO LUCKY.
STILL, I COULD DO WITHOUT ALL THE TALKING ANIMALS.
"COMPLICATED," MY PASTY BUTT.
SPUSSH
THAT'S THE PROBLEM WITH YOU YOUNG PUNKS TODAY--YOU THINK TOO MUCH.
SHOOSSH

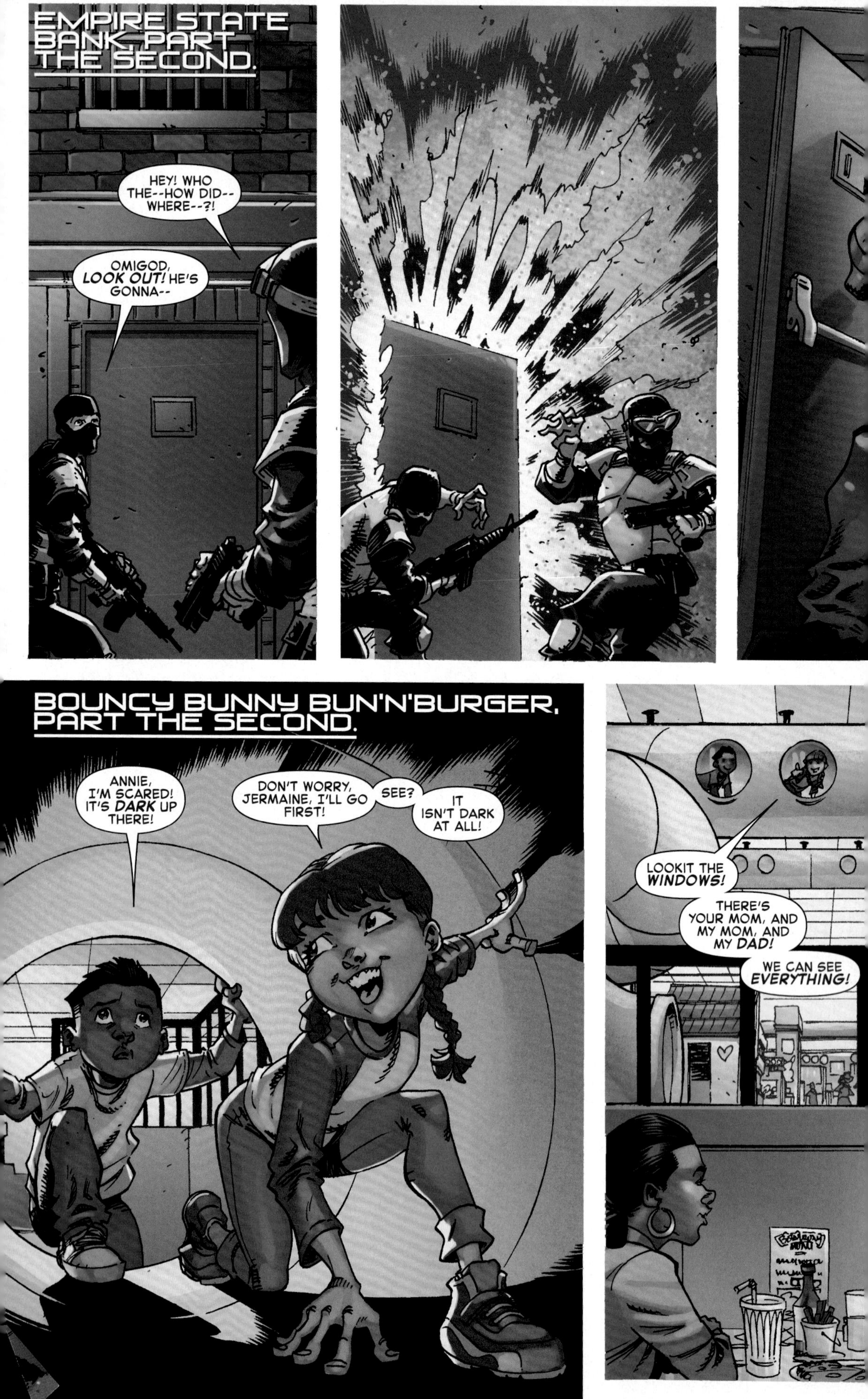

EMPIRE STATE BANK, PART THE SECOND.
HEY! WHO THE--HOW DID--WHERE--?!
OMIGOD, LOOK OUT! HE'S GONNA--
BOUNCY BUNNY BUN'N'BURGER, PART THE SECOND.
ANNIE, I'M SCARED! IT'S DARK UP THERE!
DON'T WORRY, JERMAINE, I'LL GO FIRST!
SEE?
IT ISN'T DARK AT ALL!
LOOKIT THE WINDOWS!
THERE'S YOUR MOM, AND MY MOM, AND MY DAD!
WE CAN SEE EVERYTHING!

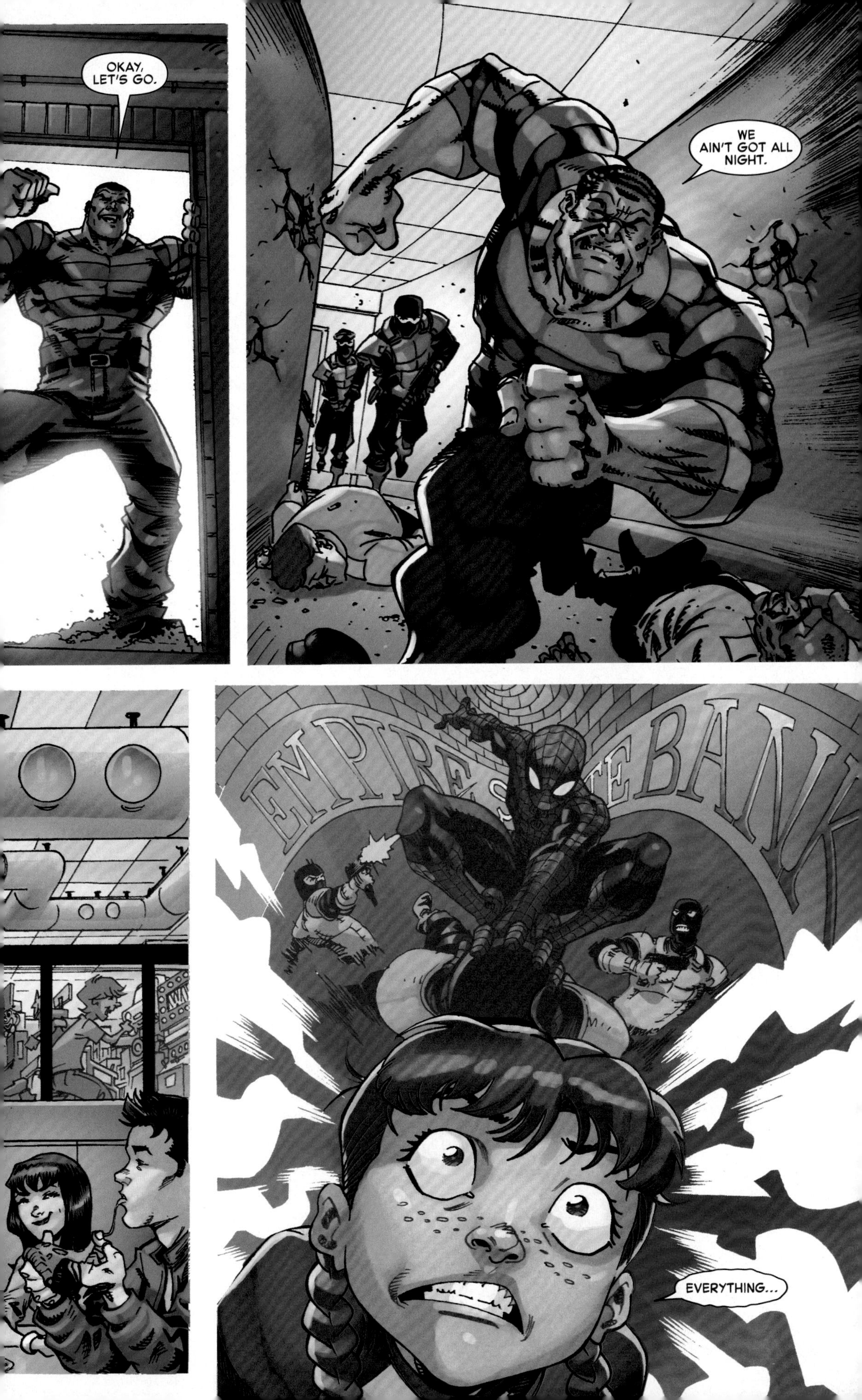
OKAY, LET'S GO.
WE AIN'T GOT ALL NIGHT.
EMPIRE STATE BANK
EVERYTHING...

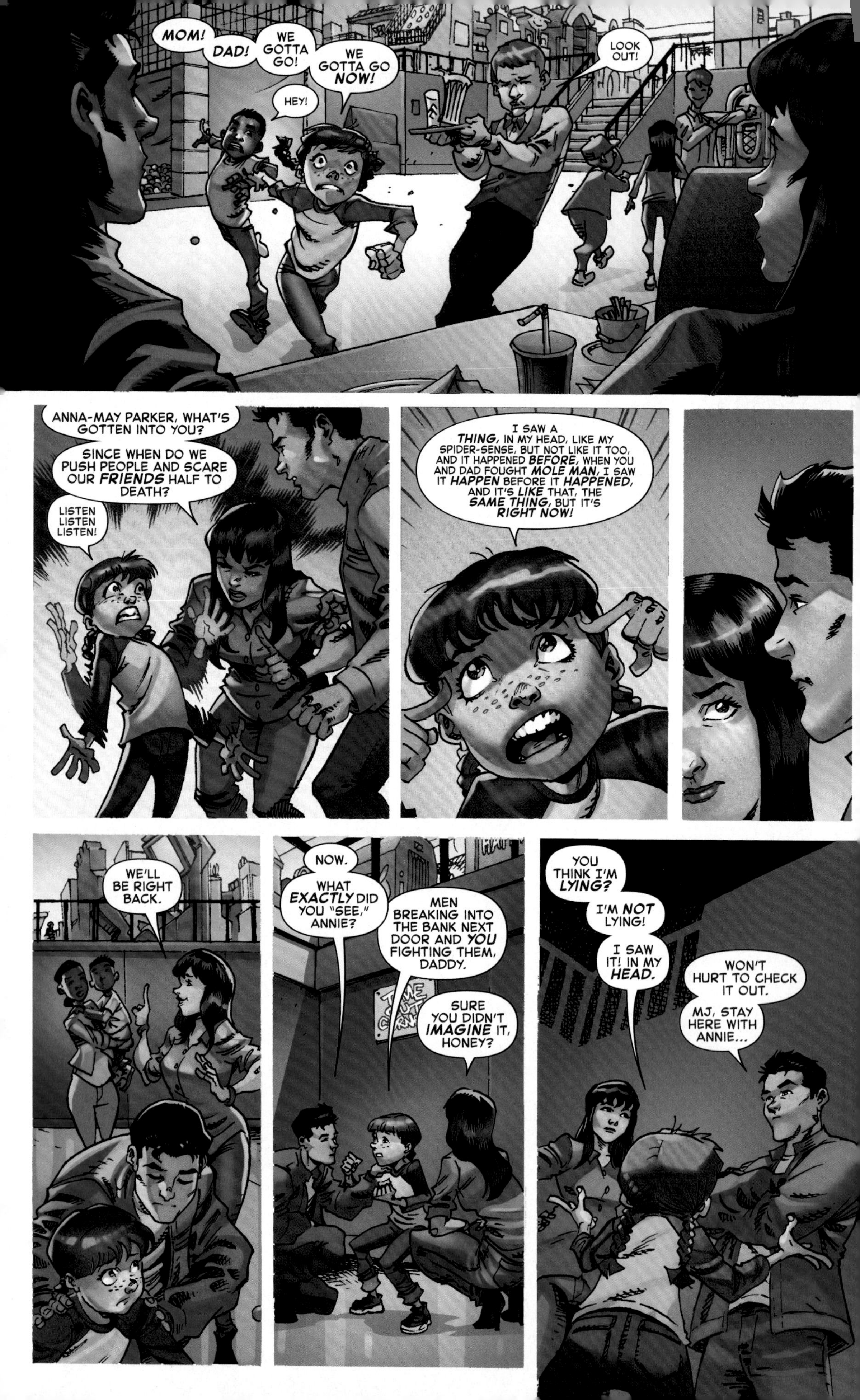
MOM!
DAD!
WE GOTTA GO!
WE GOTTA GO NOW!
HEY!
LOOK OUT!
ANNA-MAY PARKER, WHAT'S GOTTEN INTO YOU?
SINCE WHEN DO WE PUSH PEOPLE AND SCARE OUR FRIENDS HALF TO DEATH?
LISTEN LISTEN LISTEN!
I SAW A THING, IN MY HEAD, LIKE MY SPIDER-SENSE, BUT NOT LIKE IT TOO, AND IT HAPPENED BEFORE, WHEN YOU AND DAD FOUGHT MOLE MAN, I SAW IT HAPPEN BEFORE IT HAPPENED, AND IT'S LIKE THAT, THE SAME THING, BUT IT'S RIGHT NOW!
WE'LL BE RIGHT BACK.
NOW.
WHAT EXACTLY DID YOU "SEE," ANNIE?
MEN BREAKING INTO THE BANK NEXT DOOR AND YOU FIGHTING THEM, DADDY.
SURE YOU DIDN'T IMAGINE IT, HONEY?
YOU THINK I'M LYING?
I'M NOT LYING!
I SAW IT! IN MY HEAD.
WON'T HURT TO CHECK IT OUT.
MJ, STAY HERE WITH ANNIE...

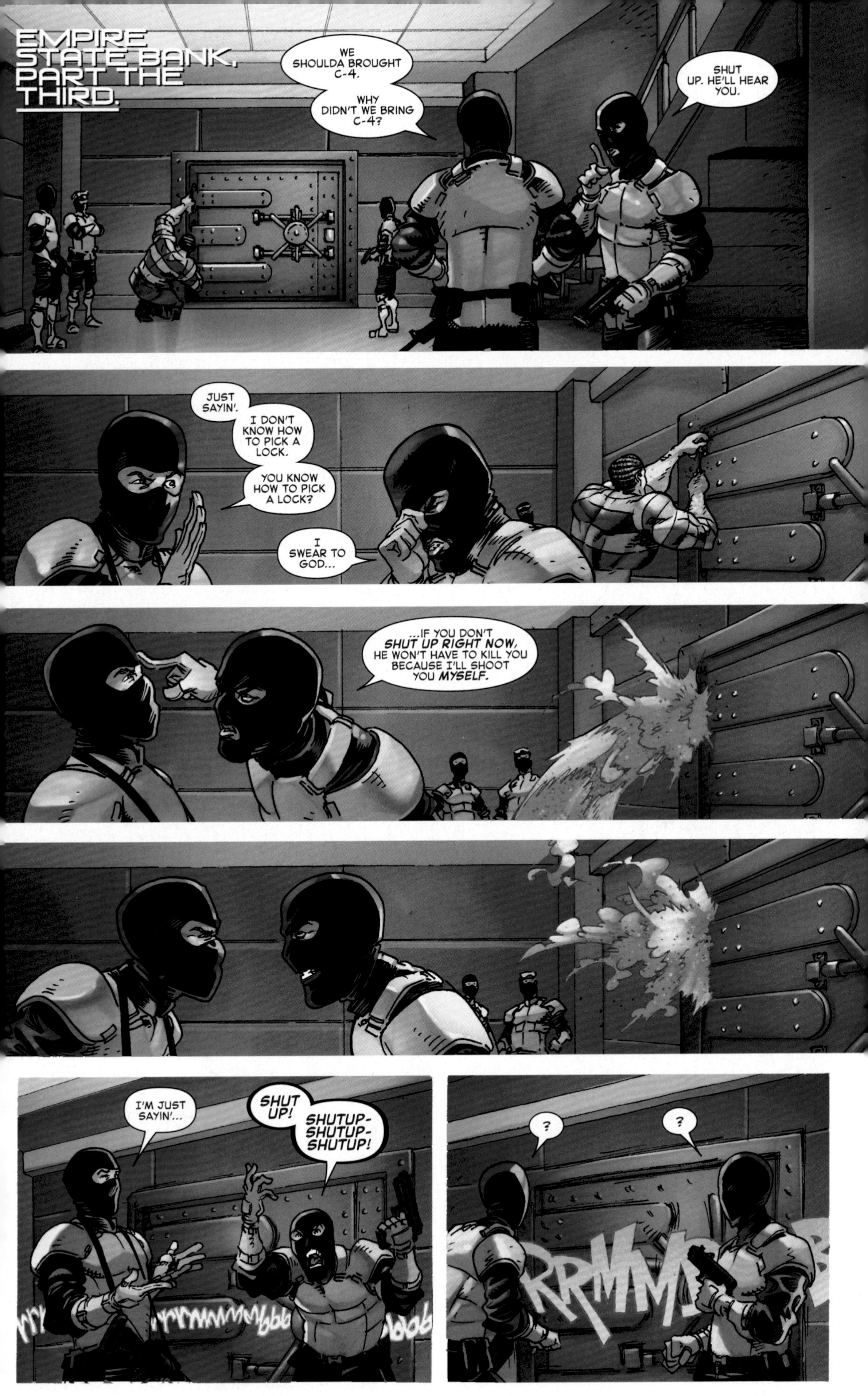
EMPIRE STATE BANK, PART THE THIRD.
WE SHOULDA BROUGHT C-4.
WHY DIDN'T WE BRING C-4?
SHUT UP. HE'LL HEAR YOU.
JUST SAYIN'.
I DON'T KNOW HOW TO PICK A LOCK.
YOU KNOW HOW TO PICK A LOCK?
I SWEAR TO GOD...
...IF YOU DON'T SHUT UP RIGHT NOW, HE WON'T HAVE TO KILL YOU BECAUSE I'LL SHOOT YOU MYSELF.
I'M JUST SAYIN'...
SHUT UP!
SHUTUP-SHUTUP-SHUTUP!
?
?

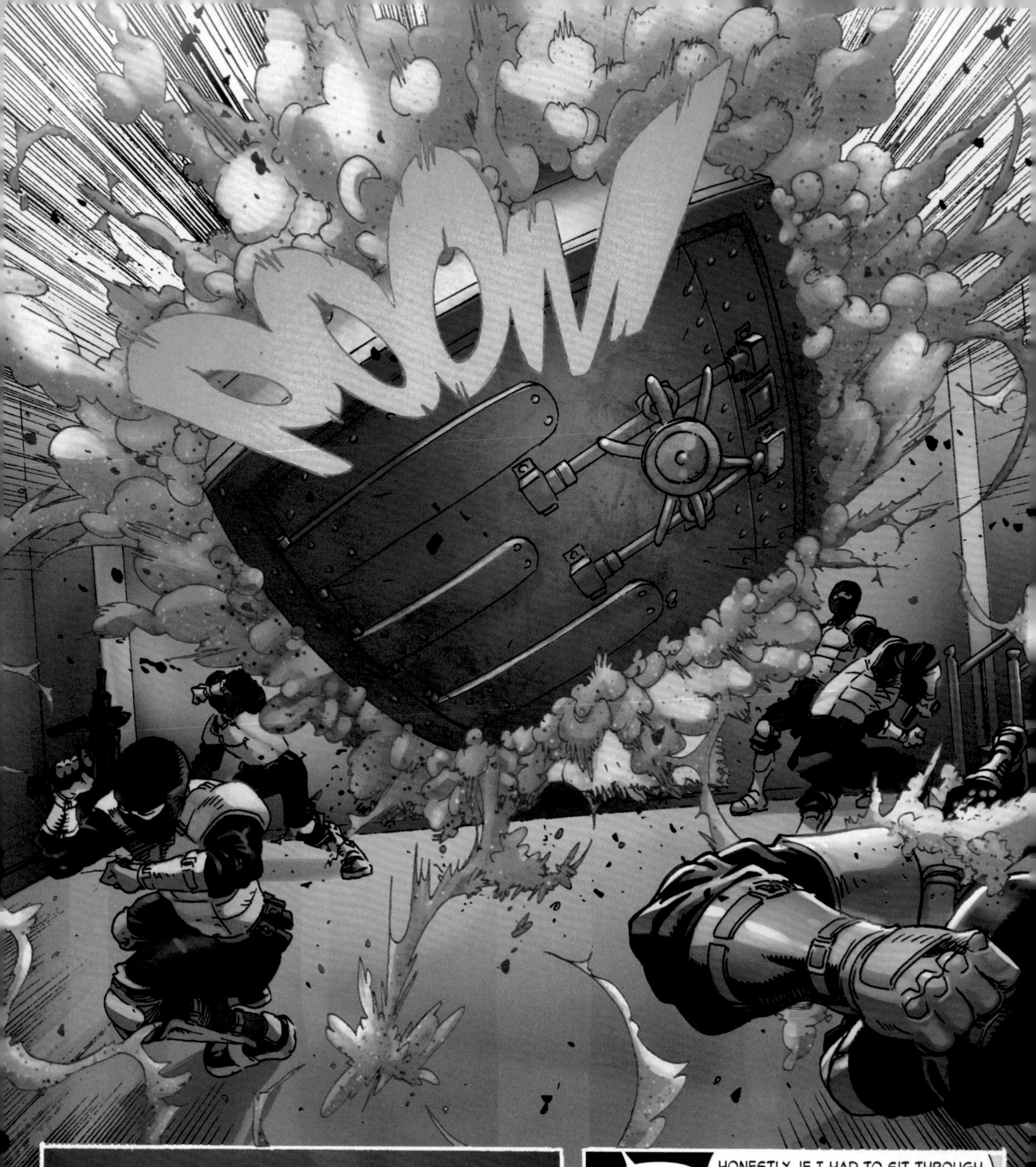
BOOM!

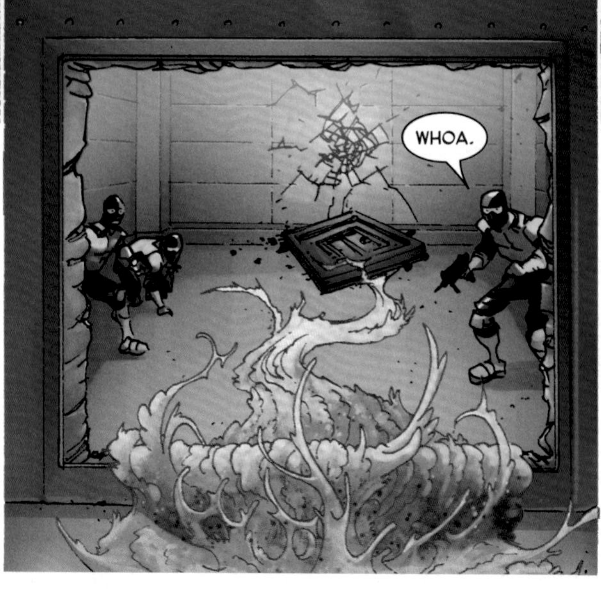
WHOA.

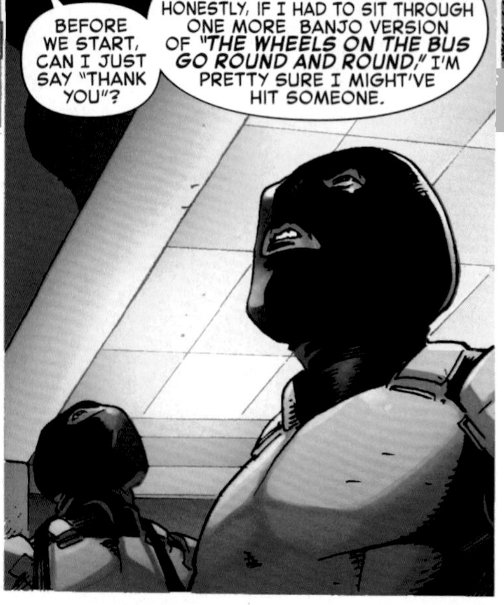
BEFORE WE START, CAN I JUST SAY "THANK YOU"?
HONESTLY, IF I HAD TO SIT THROUGH ONE MORE BANJO VERSION OF "THE WHEELS ON THE BUS GO ROUND AND ROUND," I'M PRETTY SURE I MIGHT'VE HIT SOMEONE.

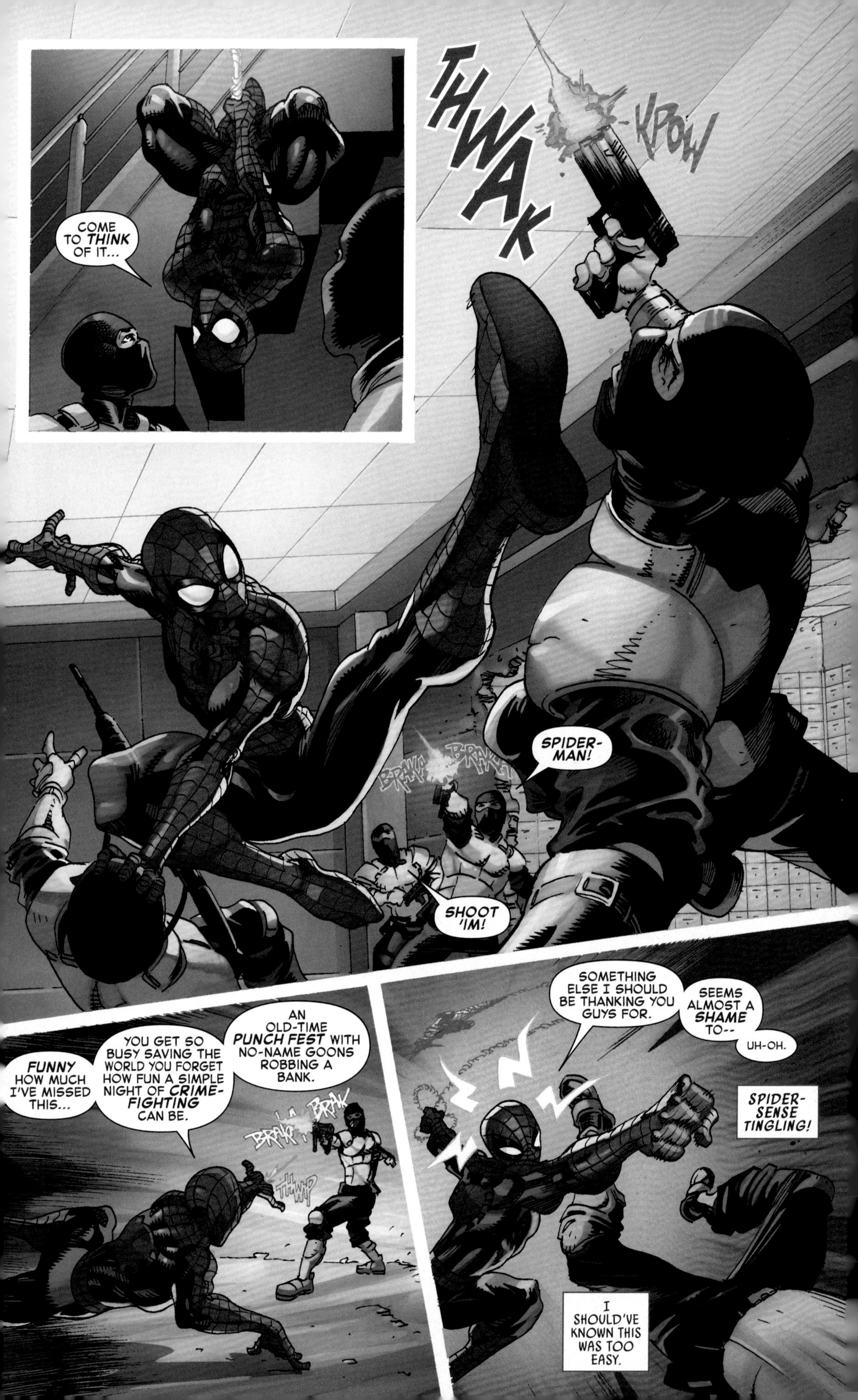
COME TO THINK OF IT...
THWAK
KPOW
SPIDER-MAN!
BRAK BRAKT
SHOOT 'IM!
FUNNY HOW MUCH I'VE MISSED THIS...
YOU GET SO BUSY SAVING THE WORLD YOU FORGET HOW FUN A SIMPLE NIGHT OF CRIME-FIGHTING CAN BE.
AN OLD-TIME PUNCH FEST WITH NO-NAME GOONS ROBBING A BANK.
BRAK
BRAK
THWIP
SOMETHING ELSE I SHOULD BE THANKING YOU GUYS FOR.
SEEMS ALMOST A SHAME TO--
UH-OH.
SPIDER-SENSE TINGLING!
I SHOULD'VE KNOWN THIS WAS TOO EASY.

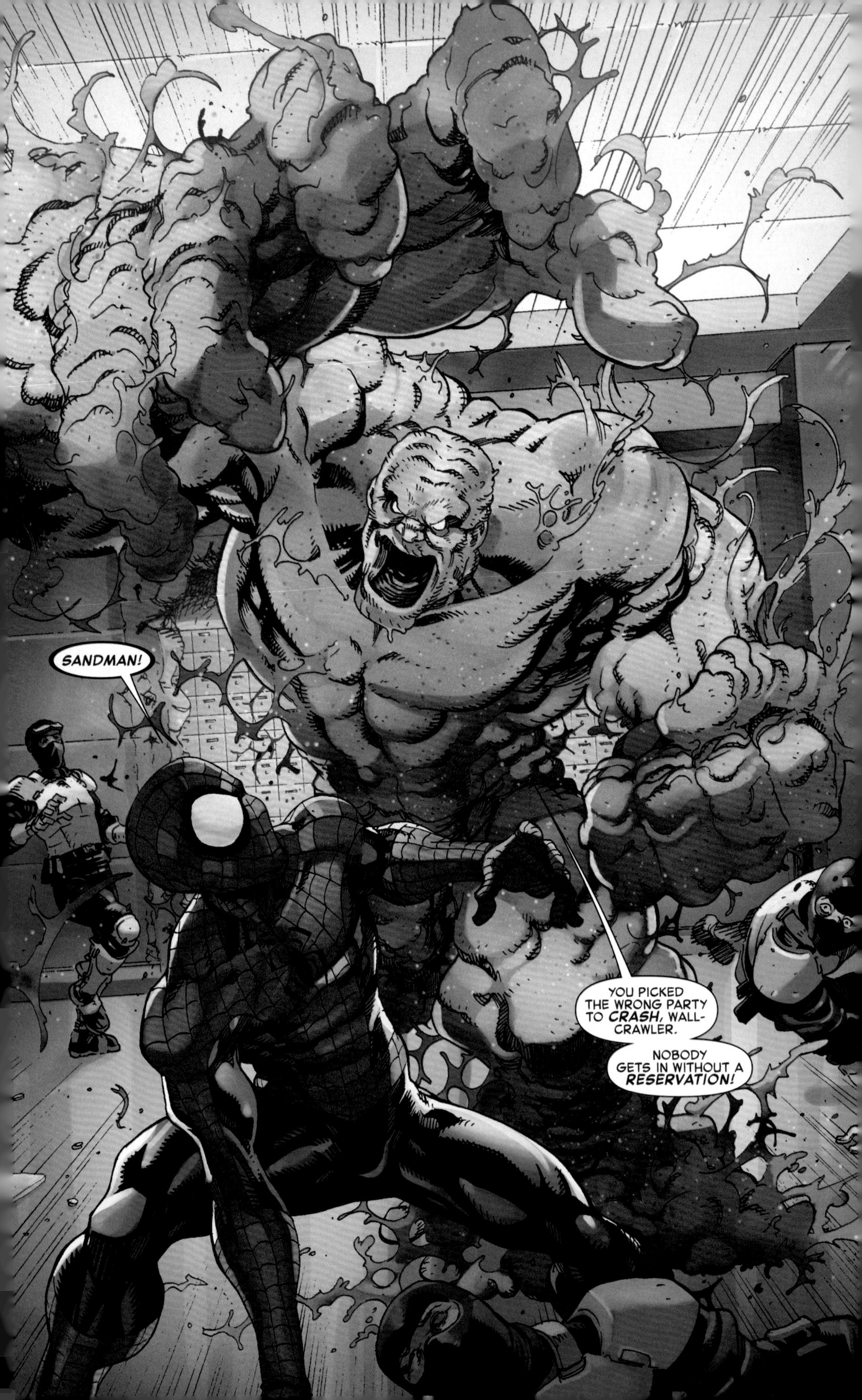
SANDMAN!
YOU PICKED THE WRONG PARTY TO CRASH, WALL-CRAWLER.
NOBODY GETS IN WITHOUT A RESERVATION!

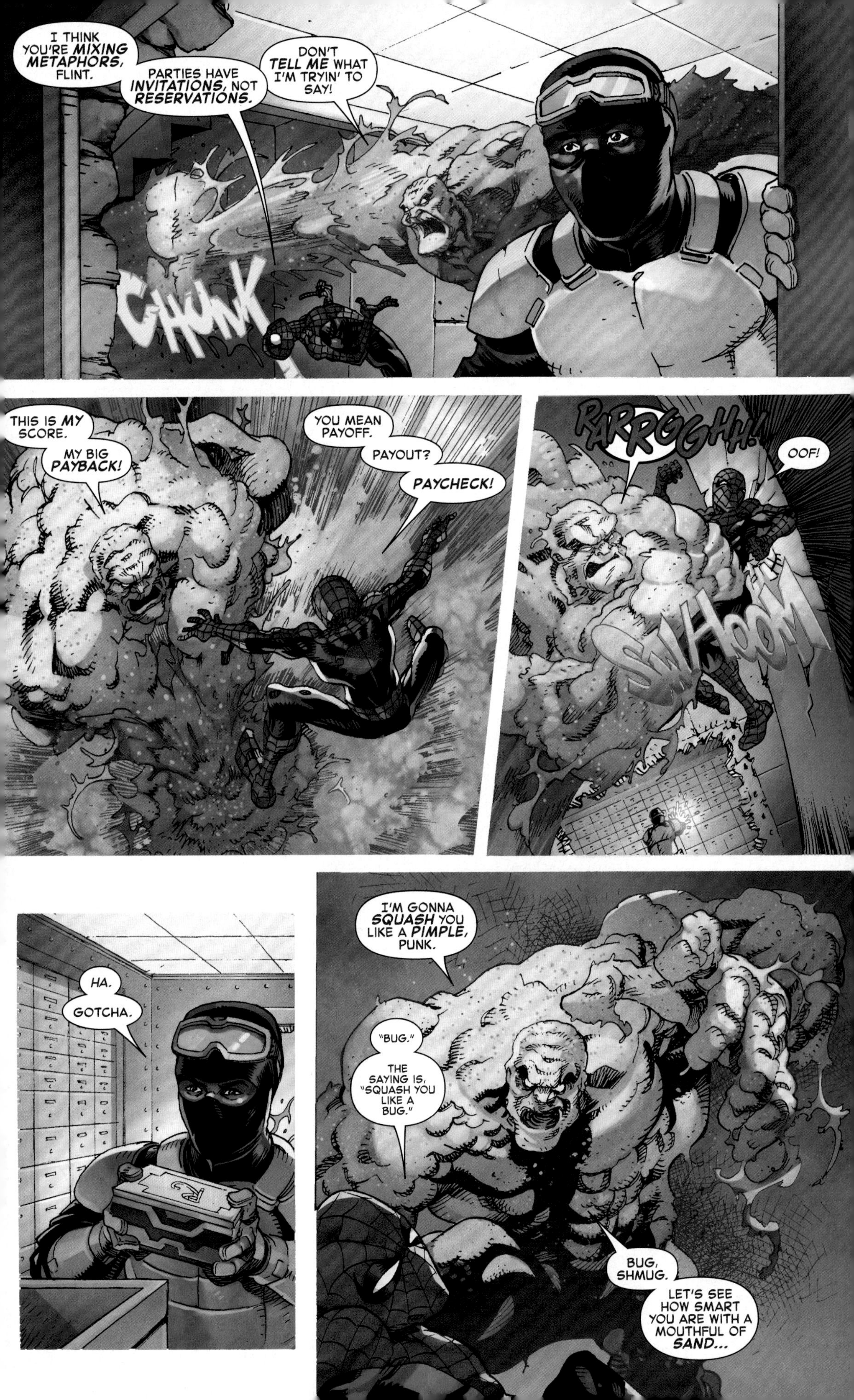

I THINK YOU'RE MIXING METAPHORS, FLINT.
PARTIES HAVE INVITATIONS, NOT RESERVATIONS.
DON'T TELL ME WHAT I'M TRYIN' TO SAY!
CHUNK
THIS IS MY SCORE.
MY BIG PAYBACK!
YOU MEAN PAYOFF.
PAYOUT?
PAYCHECK!
RARRGGHH!!
OOF!
SWHOOM
HA.
GOTCHA.
I'M GONNA SQUASH YOU LIKE A PIMPLE, PUNK.
"BUG."
THE SAYING IS, "SQUASH YOU LIKE A BUG."
BUG, SHMUG.
LET'S SEE HOW SMART YOU ARE WITH A MOUTHFUL OF SAND...

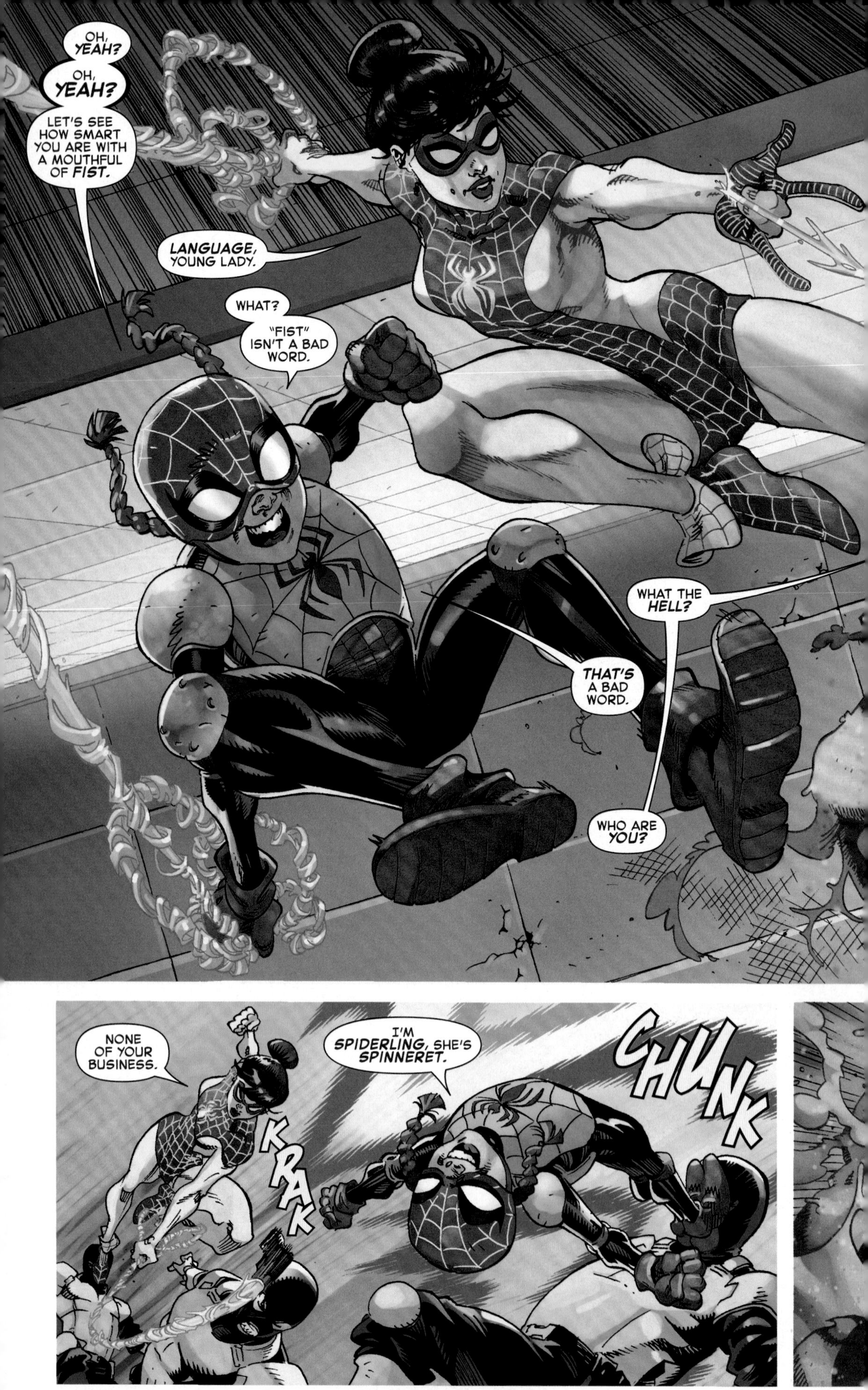

OH, YEAH?
OH, YEAH?
LET'S SEE HOW SMART YOU ARE WITH A MOUTHFUL OF FIST.
LANGUAGE, YOUNG LADY.
WHAT?
"FIST" ISN'T A BAD WORD.
WHAT THE HELL?
THAT'S A BAD WORD.
WHO ARE YOU?
NONE OF YOUR BUSINESS.
KRAK
I'M SPIDERLING, SHE'S SPINNERET.
CHUNK

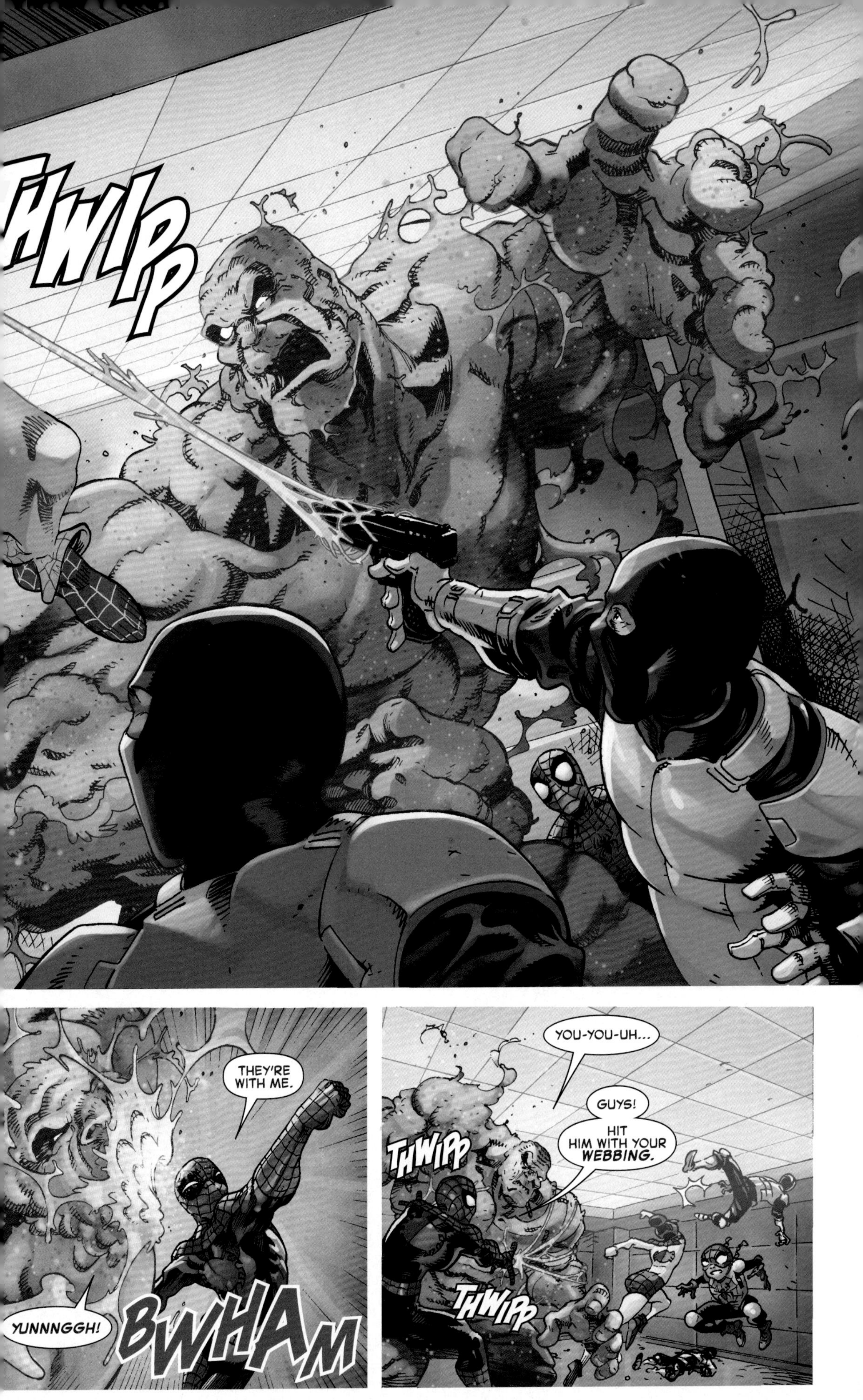
THWIPP
THEY'RE WITH ME.
YUNNNGGH!
BWHAM
YOU-YOU-UH...
GUYS!
HIT HIM WITH YOUR WEBBING.
THWIPP
THWIPP

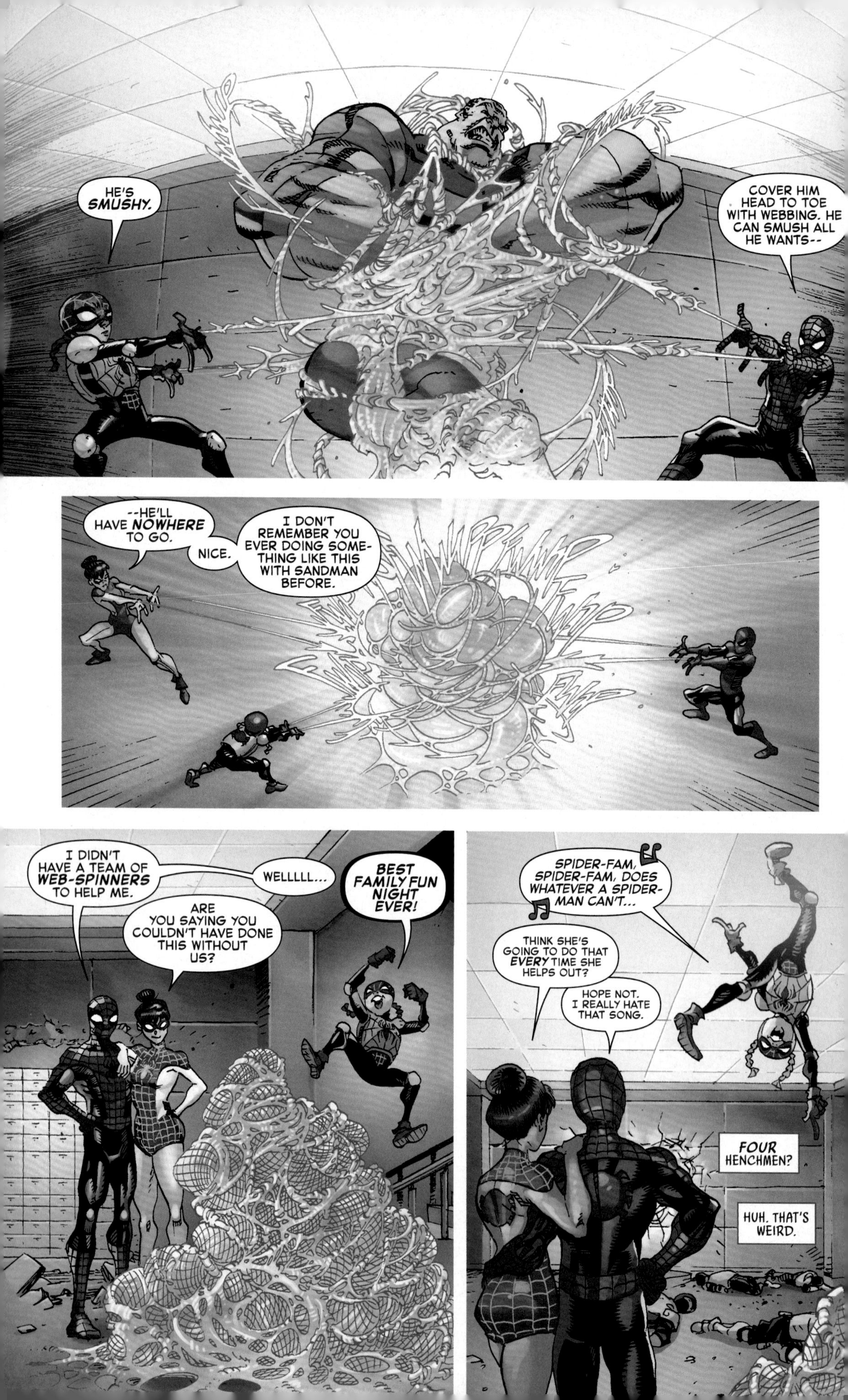
HE'S SMUSHY.
COVER HIM HEAD TO TOE WITH WEBBING. HE CAN SMUSH ALL HE WANTS--
--HE'LL HAVE NOWHERE TO GO.
NICE.
I DON'T REMEMBER YOU EVER DOING SOMETHING LIKE THIS WITH SANDMAN BEFORE.
I DIDN'T HAVE A TEAM OF WEB-SPINNERS TO HELP ME.
WELLLLL...
ARE YOU SAYING YOU COULDN'T HAVE DONE THIS WITHOUT US?
BEST FAMILY FUN NIGHT EVER!
SPIDER-FAM, SPIDER-FAM, DOES WHATEVER A SPIDER-MAN CAN'T...
THINK SHE'S GOING TO DO THAT EVERY TIME SHE HELPS OUT?
HOPE NOT. I REALLY HATE THAT SONG.
FOUR HENCHMEN?
HUH. THAT'S WEIRD.

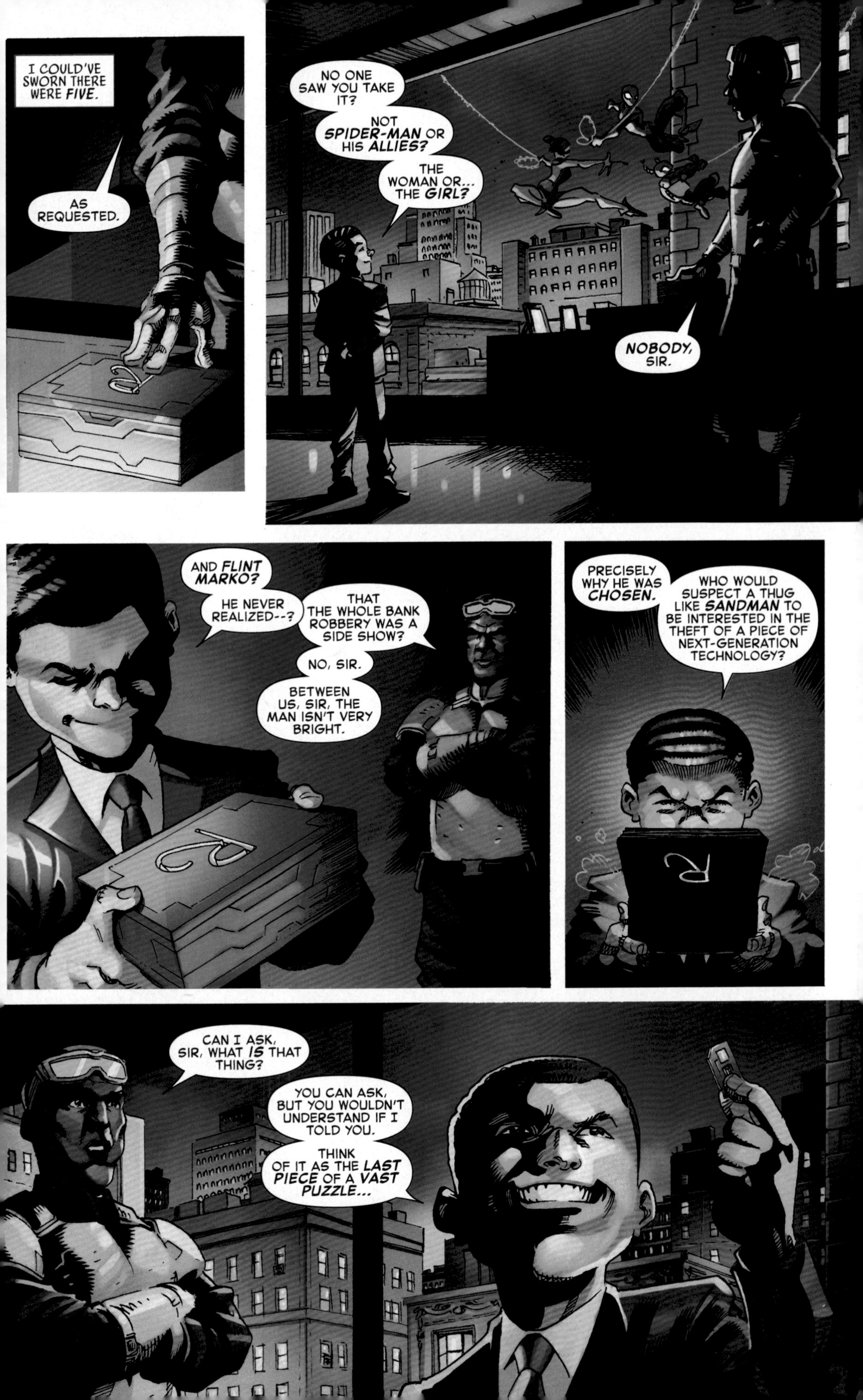
I COULD'VE SWORN THERE WERE FIVE.
AS REQUESTED.
NO ONE SAW YOU TAKE IT?
NOT SPIDER-MAN OR HIS ALLIES?
THE WOMAN OR... THE GIRL?
NOBODY, SIR.
AND FLINT MARKO?
HE NEVER REALIZED--?
THAT THE WHOLE BANK ROBBERY WAS A SIDE SHOW?
NO, SIR.
BETWEEN US, SIR, THE MAN ISN'T VERY BRIGHT.
PRECISELY WHY HE WAS CHOSEN.
WHO WOULD SUSPECT A THUG LIKE SANDMAN TO BE INTERESTED IN THE THEFT OF A PIECE OF NEXT-GENERATION TECHNOLOGY?
CAN I ASK, SIR, WHAT IS THAT THING?
YOU CAN ASK, BUT YOU WOULDN'T UNDERSTAND IF I TOLD YOU.
THINK OF IT AS THE LAST PIECE OF A VAST PUZZLE...

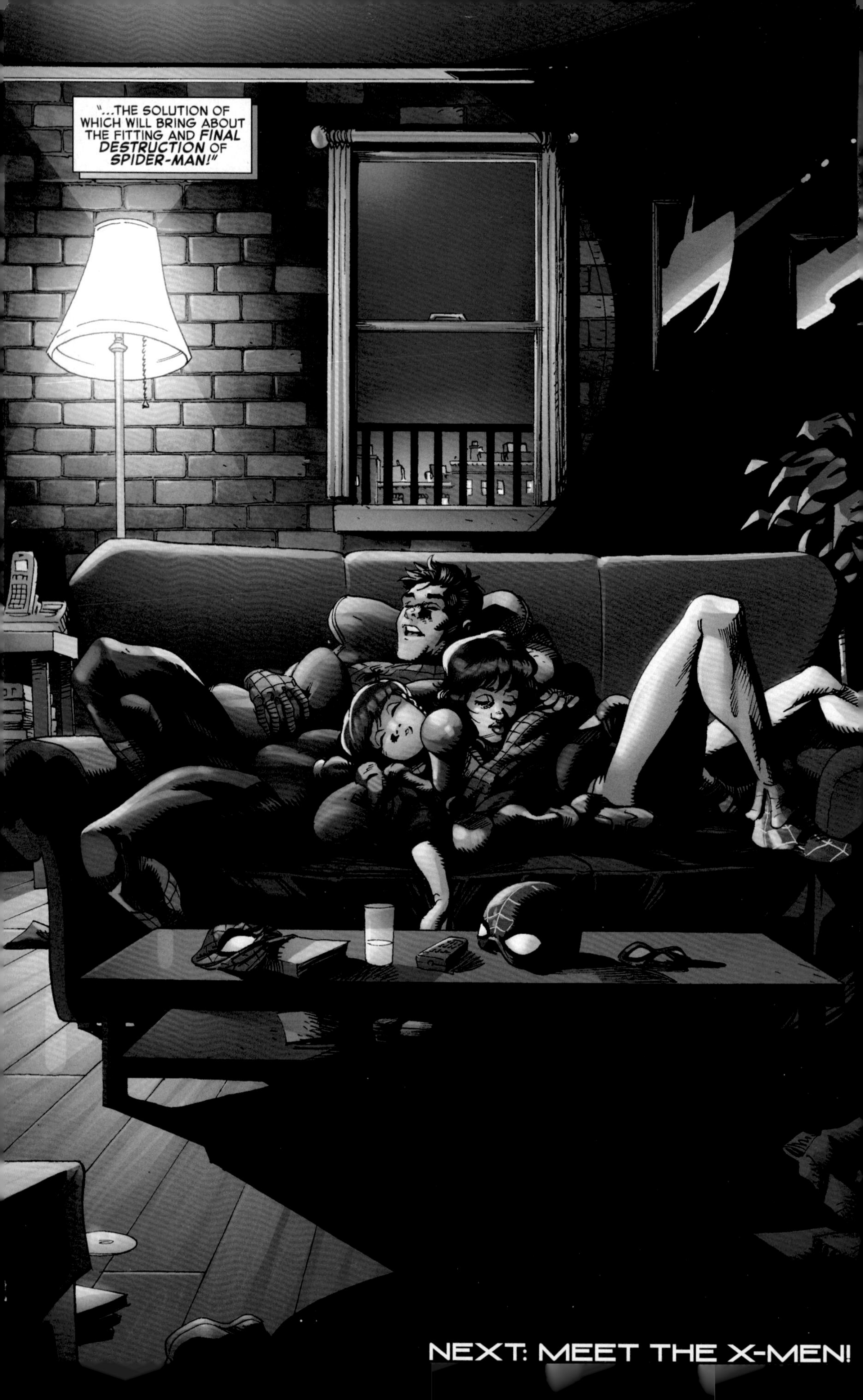
"...THE SOLUTION OF WHICH WILL BRING ABOUT THE FITTING AND FINAL DESTRUCTION OF SPIDER-MAN!"
NEXT: MEET THE X-MEN!